Sherrin's Year

Sherrin's Year

Ned Sherrin

Virgin

First published in Great Britain in 1996 by
Virgin Publishing Ltd
332 Ladbroke Grove
London W10 5AH

Reprinted 1996

ISBN 1 85227 542 1

Type design by Roger Kohn Designs, London
Phototypeset by Intype London Ltd
Printed and bound in Great Britain by
Mackays of Chatham PLC, Chatham, Kent

Sherrin's Year

January

Sunday 1st January

I TRY NEVER to leave home on New Year's Eve. In *The Loved One* Evelyn Waugh described Hogmanay as 'people being sick on the pavements of Glasgow'. Growing up on a farm in Somerset, I did not acquire the habit of staying up to see in the New Year – milking came around too soon.

Caryl Brahms, with whom I collaborated for nearly 30 years until she died in 1982, and I used to go to the Ritz for dinner. When I rang to book they always said apologetically, 'I'm afraid there are no festivities, sir,' which was all right because that is what we were trying to avoid.

So now I stay home and cook for whoever signifies that they have nowhere better to go. It is also a night for moderate drinking. It is no good pretending it's fine if you have a hangover on New Year's Day. Thank God I wasn't born a Tibetan. For them New Year's Eve started in February and the eating and drinking and dancing went on for the best part of a month. The festival gave magistrates and tax-gatherers a chance to amass a sizeable fortune, fining revellers for disorderly conduct.

Smoked salmon (a Christmas present from my old *Loose Ends* producer Ian Gardhouse), duck and two Marks and Spencer's bread puddings bound together with extra custard was the menu.

The three guests left around 12.30 a.m. Desmond O'Donovan, with whom I was at Oxford; Barry Ayres, who helped decorate this flat when I moved in, and Gary Pollard, with whom he lives. Gary is the surviving Pollard twin: the other, Gavin, died back in their home country, Australia, a few years ago. An early AIDS victim. Identical brothers, they were ballet dancers. They both joined Festival Ballet,

1

as it was then, in the seventies, and were promptly and confusingly cast as rivals Montague and Capulet in Festival's *Romeo and Juliet*. Then the artistic director Beryl Grey had a brilliant idea. One of the identicals should change his name to spare the audience's confusion. Judgement of a female Solomon open to question. Gary is not well, again AIDS-related, but it was good to see him. Barry, who looks after a gallery in Hampstead, is devoted in support. Desmond is unhappy. He was a promising Royal Court and National Theatre director, now he divides his time between home and hospital.

Is it unusual to regret the passing of the year? When we were doing *That Was The Week That Was* back in 1963 I always used to characterise it as a mini-New Year's Eve. Shake off the frustrations and disappointments of the last week – 'It's over, let it go!' – and look forward to a brighter one next week.

After they had gone I finished off the Perrier-Jouet and reflected that I was sad to say goodbye to 1994. Right up to the end, the year tried to be helpful. There was a happy 400th 'Birthday' of *Loose Ends* celebrated in my flat. A jolly visit to Singapore as a guest of the fledgling Singapore Stephen Sondheim Society. *Ned Sherrin in his Anecdotage* is selling in paperback and so is a talking book of *Theatrical Anecdotes*. *A Passionate Woman* strides on confidently in the West End. As *Variety* might have said, 'She has legs'. And the novel which has been bugging me for two years – *Scratch an Actor* – looks as if it might get itself finished on time by the first day in February. And I look forward to wresting the rights in *Jules et Jim* from the dilatory, difficult-to-get-off-the-pot Truffaut Estate in Paris so that I can turn it into a chamber musical with Glen Roven's score.

Glen is a small American genius. Short on height, not on talent. At sixteen he took over the musical direction of a raunchy off-Broadway revue *Let My People Come*. At nineteen he was the original conductor for *Sugar Babies*, a splashy Broadway show starring Mickey Rooney and Ann Miller – and lots of old vaudevillians and young chorus girls – a demanding assignment for a teenager.

I met him in New York when we were doing *Side By Side By Sondheim* – he was irritated not to have been cast as one of the two on-stage pianists. Since then he has written a couple of musicals, one of which looks like reaching Broadway next year; and he played piano or conducted for an incredible roster of stars – Liza Minnelli, Julie

Andrews, Ethel Merman, Placido Domingo, Whitney Houston, Diana Ross, Kathleen Battle; conducted Bernstein concerts all over Europe and innumerable recording sessions, often for Disney. His demonstration CD for his latest show is recorded with an orchestra of nearly fifty. Somehow he saved the time at other recording sessions so that he put down his own tracks in the few minutes left over. He also co-MD'd the Clinton Presidential Inaugural Concert on Capitol Hill with Quincy Jones. It was an open-air daytime do and I was amused to see him on TV conducting away in the neat little grey suit he ordered from my Savile Row tailor. Apart from tuxedos it's his only suit. He is an invaluable gossip and loves to tell the story of being flown in Liza's private jet to one of her concerts and phoning all his friends from the plane and opening, 'Hi, this is homo heaven . . .'

He is finding it easier to write in England and enjoys the stimulus of British theatre which he attends assiduously. I started work on *Jules et Jim* before Caryl died. It's now called *Jules and Jim and Caroline*. It's devised as a narrative for the three principals with a backing group of five who also play small parts. A chamber work. I wanted to prove to myself that I could write it all the way through before acquiring the rights or involving a composer. When I had finished I talked first to Andrew Lloyd Webber who flirted with the idea for a couple of years; but then decided it was too near to *Aspects of Love* – shifting relationships. Also, I don't think the scale of a chamber work appealed to the old elephantine! Glen has written a ravishing opening waltz, 'Another Paris Song' and we shall now have to deconstruct the rest of my libretto as he adds his music – but not until I have acquired the rights. Paris is proving infuriatingly elusive.

Anyway, that and the other projects feel like enough to be going on with.

It would be churlish to complain about my year. I chuckled instead and recalled the last anecdote of 1994. At a Christmas party of Charles Moore's, Peter Ackroyd saw and took a fancy to Peter Lilley, Secretary of State of Social Security. Crossing the room to introduce himself Ackroyd opened with: 'And what do you do?' 'Social Security,' said Lilley.

'You poor boy,' Ackroyd sympathised, "Come home with me and we'll see what we can do about it.

NEW YEAR'S HONOURS

Not a very exciting list. How many people refuse? Somerset Maugham was the most honest. He later explained that at literary gatherings he would have to hear the announcement; 'Mr Bernard Shaw, Mr H.G. Wells, Mr John Galsworthy, Mr Rudyard Kipling,' and then, to his embarrassment, 'Sir Somerset Maugham.'

Kipling turned down the job of Poet Laureate three times and refused all gongs, from the KCB (in 1898 when Lord Salisbury was PM) to the OM (from George V in 1921). Without his consent he was appointed Companion of Honour in 1917. He wrote a furious letter to the future Prime Minister, Bonar Law, ending 'How would you like it if you woke up and found yourself Archbishop of Canterbury?'

In entertainment, Bob Stephens got a knighthood, for his Falstaff and Lear, and for services to the Prince of Wales. They collaborated on a Shakespeare Speeches album. I suppose. He's not in good health so it's a generous and timely gesture. Apart from his physically showy Atahualpa in *The Royal Hunt of the Sun* he never quite made the first division. Joss Ackland's RSC Falstaff was better, and of modern Lears (we have to exclude Wolfit from competition if there is to be any sort of contest) Robert is splendid – but he still comes after John Wood and Paul Scofield.

David Puttnam gets one – for services to exports, I imagine. Felicity Kendal's CBE suggests a damehood ten years hence. Delia Smith's OBE may be as far as she'll go – but David Frost wisely accepted an 'O' after he'd been struck off Lady Falkender's Lavender List and was later rewarded with a knighthood for his patience. There's a prodigious list of unknowns honoured for 'pol. services'; but it was a delight to see that Jane Bown, the unpretentious, magical photographer of the *Observer* got a 'C'. It won't worry or impress her.

12.30 p.m.

To Brentford Dock for a warm family New Year's lunch with the Nathans – David and Norma. Lifted there by Herbert Kretzmer and Sybil. David wrote for *That Was The Week That Was* and now is a busy freelance and dramatic critic for the *Jewish Chronicle*. Kretzmer was also on *TW3*: a biting lyricist. *Les Miserables* has made him millions.

Herbie had a good story on the way back. Just after he and Sybil were married, he had brought her back to England and they visited Rye. Having taken in the Henry James/E.F. Benson shrine, Lamb House, they had lunch at the Mermaid. They were waited on by a fresh-faced youth. Herbie studied the menu and was attracted to the 'sea food platter'. However, he hates leathery calamari rings. (When Caryl Brahms was in San Francisco the proud inhabitants were forever trying to pass abalone on her – 'like eating kid gloves' she used to say.) Herbie was anxious to establish that there were no calamari rings among the sea food.

'What's in the sea-food platter?' he asked.

The pink-cheeked waiter considered the request for some considerable time and then, placing his finger firmly in his pink dimple the better to concentrate, finally came up with the answer: 'I think it's beef.'

The Sunday papers continued to rake over the death of dear old John Osborne and the temporary stage fright of John Sessions in *My Night With Reg* at the Criterion.

John Junor in *The Mail on Sunday* is predictably spiteful about John O. However, he shows some solidarity for his fellow Scot. Stage fright is an odd phenomenon, and often due more to pressure off-stage than on. After all, why should a supremely talented performer like Sessions suddenly confess to it in the middle of a wonderful play in which he profoundly believes, and in which he relishes his ebullient, extrovert, life-of-the-party role as much as does his audience?

It is no good asking me. Or, at least, it's no good asking me from personal experience. Happy amateurs like me are not privy to the traumas of a proper performing artist attacked by this pernicious problem. When I speak, as long as I have worked out roughly what I am going to say and the writers have supplied me with some good lines, I am happy to show off.

That is not an actor's discipline. Severe stage fright hits actors in times of success just as often as in nights of failure. It has to be distinguished from 'nerves' and from faulty memory. Stage fright is a severe emotional crisis which immobilises the actor on the stage. It doesn't just cause him the odd uncomfortable moment.

The classic case of temporary memory loss is the excellent actor, Paul Greenwood, who dried so many times in an RSC first night of

The Happiest Days of Your Life that the curtain was dropped and they started again. Unfortunately, on resuming no one had replaced the essential props on which the cues depended. For the rest of the performance Paul's nightmare was re-doubled. However, he made a complete recovery and went on quickly to play even bigger parts with the same company.

Judy Garland suffered an intense and complicated stage fright which sometimes meant she kept audiences waiting for an hour or so.

Two magnificent musical warhorses, Ethel Merman and Marlene Dietrich were surely fired by nerves, despite denials. However, neither allowed stage fright to interfere with a performance. You could only identify their nerves by the attack with which they swept their audiences along. An American friend, the actress and stylish cabaret singer Marti Stevens, once told me about those two steel maidens. Marti had her own 'perhaps' stage fright in the States when she was young and in a show with Hermione Gingold. She was cured by somebody pushing her stage-wards and saying without sympathy, 'Get on with it.'

Ditto a chorus boy due to enter opposite the formidable Lauren Bacall:

Stage Manager: 'Get on, it's your cue!'
Chorus Boy: 'I'm not going out there until they feed her.'

Dietrich had no sympathy with a nervous Van Johnson: 'So what, if you're frightened, be a housewife.'

Ethel Merman was the queen of the ice-cool. Another chorus boy, on the first night of *Annie Get Your Gun*, asked her in the wings if she was nervous, to which Merman replied, 'Why should I be? I know my lines.' She had just refused some new ones with the immortal reply, 'Call me Miss Birds Eye – the show is frozen.' When she first opened in London at the Talk of the Town she said with very little conviction, 'I'm so excited. I'm so overawed, I'm so nervous,' and then swept into 'I Got Rhythm'. Marti Stevens asked her if she had noticed that the band was more than a beat behind her. Had it not worried her? 'No,' she said. 'Why should I worry? They don't pay any attention to me. Why should I pay any attention to them?' Her stock reply to enquiries if she was nervous was the Olympian 'If they can do it better than me then let 'em get up and try' – but the determination to prove they couldn't drove her performance.

So what is stage fright?

There have been two classic cases among great actors in recent years. One of the most public was Ian Holm's withdrawal from O'Neill's *The Iceman Cometh*. Ian hardly approached the stage for years afterwards: but now he has finally (and happily for us) brought himself back with an award-winning performance in a difficult Pinter piece and in a second play by the same author. Who knows how the demons were exorcised?

The other famous case is Laurence Olivier. Victor Spinetti once recalled Olivier telling him that in his well-documented period of stage panic while he was running the National Theatre and playing Othello, 'All I could see, my baby, were the exit signs; and all I wanted to do was to run off the stage each night towards them.'

Five years later, in 1970, Jonathan Miller directed Olivier's Shylock. Miller is quoted by Olivier's flashy biographer, Donald Spoto.

> Almost paralysed with stage fright, the perspiration flowed heavily, his breathing irregular. His eyes went blank and there was a dreadful silence backstage for it seemed that Olivier might not continue. But he did, and from the second performance on, he obtained a generous prescription for the tranquiliser Valium.

Olivier refused to yield to the attack. Until it was time to retreat into films and television, he overcame it.

The *Concise Oxford Dictionary* defines 'stage fright' as 'Nervousness on facing an audience – especially for the first time.' Experience does not entirely bear this out. Often it is those who have worked longest and borne most who find it harder to face the footlights and not only on first nights – John Sessions was in the middle of a successful run. No one, I think, has tried scientifically to assess the actor's predicament in approaching the audience in these circumstances. Perhaps Dr Jonathan should return to the laboratory.

The only time I sat in dressing-rooms backstage alongside actors was in *Side By Side By Sondheim*. They had their different ways of concealing nerves and stoking up energy. David Kernan fussed over his clothes. Julia McKenzie busily arranged flowers. Millicent Martin shouted at her dresser, who took it in her stride and, apparently, had done so for years. She certainly knew why it was happening.

I love to watch actors prepare. Dame Judi Dench during the run of *Mr & Mrs Nobody* kept the company manager, Brian Kirk, playing a game of 'who's in tonight?' in the wings right up until the very moment before she stepped on stage and straight into character. When they celebrated Peggy Ashcroft's eightieth birthday at the Vic Judi stood in the stalls behind a pillar enjoying her peers (if they exist) until the last *possible* moment. Then she slid unobtrusively through the pass door to make her entrance upstage and on cue and came down to deliver a deeply felt Shakespearean monologue.

Is that how she wards off this curious, compelling, irresistible stage fright? Or is it just how she calms her thoroughbred nerves? Which actor has not wondered when fright may knock on the dressing-room door or invade the stage in mid-performance?

Monday 2nd January

Growing older is usually associated with watching policemen, taxi-drivers, then MPs, then cabinet ministers look progressively younger. John Thaw's début in the new ITV series *Kavanagh* suggests a new intimation of mortality. I have seen him go from ex-drama student sharing digs with Tom Courtenay to violent Action Cop in *The Sweeney*, to Intellectual Cop in *Morse*, to Investigative QC in his new show. What next? High Court Judge as crime buster?

It will be time to go when Dennis Waterman limps onto the screen as a Lord of Appeal.

Fanny Cradock, the TV cook, is dead. Her voice was once described as 'a circular saw going through a sheet of gin-soaked cardboard'.

Tuesday 3rd January

Keith Waterhouse sent me Peter Nichols's appreciation of John Osborne from the *Guardian* – with footnotes. Nichols and Osborne first met in the mid-fifties acting in *Ten Little Niggers* and *See How They Run* at Frinton-on-Sea. The friendship survived repertory and their joint fame as playwrights, though barely their period as neighbours in Shropshire: ' . . . we were wonderful neighbours as long as we never met more than once a week. The moment we did, we fell out,' Peter wrote.

Osborne characterised his fifth wife Helen, and Peter's wife Thelma, as a playwright's essential partner – 'A Washed Out Wife'. It yielded the acronym WOW. The WOW responded by forming a luncheon club for Playwrights' Pitiable Spouses. PPS. They co-opted the Mesdames Hampton (Christopher), Wood (Charles) and Mortimer (John). The wives of Pinter, Rosenthal and Stoppard were held to be too famous in their own right to qualify.

Nichols lists Osborne's describing his children as 'pests' as one cause of their breach. Inside information suggests that the great invectivist employed a far more vivid description: 'Your children walk about on all fours and are covered in hair'; and later, 'Your children still walk about on all fours.' It recalls Tennessee Williams's label for Brick's nieces in *Cat on a Hot Tin Roof* – 'the no-neck monsters', a phrase which he nicked from the late Lady St Just, his literary executor. Now that she is dead, Maria has just been cruelly traduced in an 'impartial' article by John Lahr in the *New Yorker*. I thought of writing to reply but argued that it would only keep a sordid and misleading controversy alive. Maria made the mistake of dismissing him from his job of editing her letters to Tennessee. Unwise.

DICKENS TWICE

Ever since 1982 when I started to stay at Hickstead Place, Douglas Bunn's home, for Xmas, I have taken the family to a Christmas play. (Douglas created the All-England Show Jumping arena more than thirty years ago. A unique contribution to sport. God knows why *he* hasn't been given a knighthood.) Sadly Douglas and his third wife, Lorna, have now parted. The only benefit is that I now get two Christmas treats – or, if I'm feeling in a Scrooge mood, I have to *pay* for two outings. This time I took Lorna and the children to John Mortimer's adaptation of *A Christmas Carol* at the Barbican. It is quite spectacular; but the Nickleby-esque group narration doesn't work as well on the broad, often empty stage, and it didn't take off until Scrooge's reformed caperings at the end of the evening. Clive Francis became a delightful, reclaimed sinner. Lorna reproved me for giving Charlie, my godson, Arnold Schwarzenegger's *Last Action Hero* video for Christmas – I thought it must be harmless as it involved a child. How wrong can one be?

Charlie, who is coming up to eight, absolved me over my other misjudged present. 'It doesn't matter,' he had said graciously on Christmas Day, 'but you did give me the *Children's Illustrated Bible* last year as well.'

Charlie is becoming an over-sophisticated theatre-goer, 'Ned', he said, as we settled into our very comfortable eight seats in row 1 in the stalls, 'couldn't you get a box?' David Land who owns the Theatre Royal in Brighton had put him and the family into a box for *Aladdin* on Christmas Eve.

Oliver! has not lifted since the first night in December – elephantine and pedestrian. Jonathan Pryce is still nearer Mr Mantalini in his fetching dressing-gown. His ridiculous politically correct non-Jewish Fagin makes a nonsense of Dickens and of Lionel Bart's vaudeville character so inventively played by Ron Moody and Roy Hudd. Sadly Sally Dexter looks like Georgia Brown but her loud voice is unappealing and has none of Georgia's depths of emotion. I can still hear Georgia in my mind's ear. The same boys whom I saw on the first night were playing Oliver and the Dodger. The Oliver is dull. The Dodger is very good; but I wanted to see the alternative, so splendid in the recent television *Martin Chuzzlewit*. The second Oliver sang outstandingly in the National Youth Music Theatre's production. I don't think I could sit through the Palladium version again – not even for ready money.

Saturday 7ᵗʰ January

Loose Ends. I always flick through the papers in case there is something about a guest on the show. Nothing today; but an enchanting story from Antonia Fraser Pinter in a review of the volume of poetry edited to provide a *Poem for the Day* in the *Daily Mail*. Her reminiscence is plainly a favourite family story about the courtship of her parents, Frank and Elizabeth Longford.

> In the thirties my father, then a young don at Oxford, was
> courting my mother. He took her out to dinner, wine flowed,
> lamps were low. Finally, late in the meal, my father leant
> forward over the table. He, too, began to quote 'Now sleeps
> the crimson petal . . .'
> Furthermore, he was able to do the whole poem by heart,

concluding in a low and thrilling voice: 'So fold thyself, my dearest, thou, and slip/ Into my bosom and be lost in me.'

There was a dramatic pause. In the course of it, my mother, who had always loved Tennyson and was, as a matter of fact, currently giving some lectures on nineteenth-century literature, had time to think how pleasing it was to find that they both shared the same taste in poetry.

Then my father spoke. 'I wrote that,' he said simply.

My mother had to take a quick decision. I suppose you could say that my entire future (and that of seven brothers and sisters, 27 grandchildren, five great-grandchildren) trembled in the balance at that moment. Then she decided to go for it.

'How wonderful you are!' said my mother. 'I think it's simply beautiful.'

When we got to do *Loose Ends* the writers of the monologue were Andrew Nickolds and Richard Stoneman. Barbara Windsor's first husband Ronnie Knight's prison sentence for receiving stolen goods gave them a couple of good jokes in a week of prison escapes. 'The former fugitive received seven years which means he'll be out in time to see his ex-wife before her panto finishes later this month.' They went on to suggest that to complain about Ronnie using the Windsor name to move vast sums of money out of the country was unreasonable – 'The Duchess of York's been doing it for years.'

I remember vividly Barbara's distress back in the early seventies when her brother-in-law, Ronnie's brother Colin, was shot dead. We were between playing *Sing a Rude Song*, the show in which she was Marie Lloyd, at Greenwich and bringing it to the West End at the Garrick. I rang to sympathise. Barbara was deeply upset. Through her tears she sobbed out, 'He was such a dear boy, never done nobody no 'arm. Why did they do it? Now if it had been my husband Ronnie, I could understand . . .'

As always with live interviews on radio the best bits crop up in the breaks for music, recorded inserts or in the pub afterwards. John Neville is in London for Strindberg's *Dance of Death* at the Almeida. Surprisingly the BBC has a pirate recording of *Lolita* in its archives. It is not noted for these piracies. This is not the opera premièred in

Scandinavia at the end of last year but the disastrous Alan J. Lerner/ John Barry musical. Neville, who played Humbert Humbert, is still devoted to the score and puts the problems of the show down to Lerner's book – as so often. After he brilliantly adapted Shaw's *Pygmalion* why did Alan insist on doing his own books? Tony Hancock wanted to prove above all to himself that everything stemmed from him, and removed his collaborators, be they writers, fellow actors, directors or, eventually, broadcasting companies, to that end. Some similar instinct possessed Alan; on the Lerner/Barry *Lolita* they had three Lolitas, three choreographers and three directors. Neville survived all the changes. They were due to play five weeks in Philadelphia. They played three weeks and came back to New York to re-cast and re-rehearse. John felt that Noel Wilman, the last director, had solved the problems of Act One; but he could not make Act Two work. Alan would not re-write. The stalls, when they got to Boston, were littered with his bloodstained white gloves: he was a compulsive nail-biter. Then there was a bomb scare. The theatre was evacuated. The cast huddled in the car park. One member was missing. It was Dorothy Loudon, who played Lolita's mother. She finally emerged from the stage door, 'Where is everybody?' she called. Spotting her colleagues she yelled, 'Why are you out here?' Someone shouted, 'There's a bomb in the theatre!' 'You mean there's another?' she cried.

Sunday 8th January

To Salcombe and the Marine Hotel to try to finish off this bloody novel, *Scratch an Actor*. To use a Polonius-ism, it's a Theatrical-Dynastical novel and writing it is the only thing in an increasingly long career which has given me no pleasure. I hope it finds one happy reader. I have done about 90,000 words typed up and about another 10,000 still in longhand. The only hope is that it looks slightly better when the writing is unjoined. I have still to decide on, arrange and write the dénouement. Solitude in Salcombe is an attempt to crack it. As I was driven down Cliff Road into the town, it looked its loveliest. Bright sun had followed rain and sparkled on the Estuary. It lit the sandy bays, the hills opposite and the toy sheep which dotted them. I dined in my room. It was staff party night and judging by the noise it was a riot.

Monday 9ᵗʰ January

I started work early with the best intentions – hearty breakfast, pens at the ready, A4 pad on the desk before me. I had hardly put pen to paper before being distracted by the first of the phone calls I had come to escape. There was a sad reason for it. The first call announced that wonderful Peter Cook is dead. I knew he was in hospital but it is always a shock. I started counting after about ten calls and clocked another fifteen before the day was done. Three papers – *The Times, Express* and *Mirror* asked for written pieces – not a possibility when you are desperately trying to write something else. The rest were interviews for papers or radio stations. On the recordings I caught I was embarrassed to hear them describing me as 'one of his oldest and closest friends'. We were never that close although I had known and admired him since his *Footlight* sketches started to delight London. Peter went to America with *Beyond the Fringe* before we launched *TW3 (That Was The Week That Was)* and was, I think, a little disappointed by its success in his absence.

Although all the *Beyond the Fringe* team were hugely talented he was the standard bearer. He was the one principally identified with the frontal attack on the sacred cows – The Establishment, Politicians, Royalty and Religion. On *TW3* our guide rule was always 'If something is worth being serious about it is worth making a good joke about'.

Towards the end of the day, as Los Angeles woke up, Dudley Moore came on the airwaves. I wondered why no Miller, no Bennett? Both eloquent. Perhaps they were away. No, Jonathan arrived on the *Late Show* in a splendidly genial chat with John Bird, amused and amusing, nothing mawkish – the best of the tributes, along with Russell Davies's piece in the *Telegraph* the next day. Russell added a telling last sentence about Dudley: 'Out there on the California coast somewhere there's a Dagenham boy who's lost the geezer who used to make *him* laugh.'

They played the sketch – ascribed to *Not Only But Also* – in which Cook, as an agent, interviews Moore, who only sports one leg, for the role of Tarzan. Cook admires the leg. 'I like it,' he says, 'I've got nothing against it – trouble is, neither have you.'

The sketch has a much earlier pedigree. When they were trying to bring *Beyond the Fringe* from the Edinburgh Festival to the West End they played it to Donald Albery, a powerful theatre owner who had only one leg. This they did not know. Albery saw the first act which included the sketch and then had to go to an appointment. The boys performed the second act before him later in the week. By this time they had rejigged the running order. The one-legged Tarzan sketch now appeared in Act Two. Albery did not take the show which went to the Fortune Theatre, not one of his.

A sad day – but, somehow, 2,000 words. There was a humiliating postscript to the Peter Cook business. Caught off guard by the first call, from a press agency, I heard myself saying, 'He started it off. He was the Guv'nor.' I did not repeat the phrase; but it seemed to crop up in every paper next day and then later in most sayings of the week. I have never sounded more like a third-rate professional footballer. I'm surprised I didn't add, 'I'm sick as a parrot.'

Tuesday 10ᵗʰ January

I have learnt three things:
1. The rules of University Challenge.
2. In an hotel out-of-season the lift is almost invariably waiting for you where you left it.
3. The Victoria pub, on a regular basis, does:
    Apple pie and custard
    Spotted dick
    Treacle pudding
    Apple and sultana pudding
    and Bread and Butter pudding
I've only tried the last – excellent.

There is a wonderful elderly pianist in the lounge whose repertoire is classic. Novello, Coward, 'My Way', Lloyd Webber, even ' . . . any umbrellas to mend today'. Dining next door we applauded politely at the end of each selection.

Thursday 12ᵗʰ January

Keith Waterhouse in the *Mail* had the last word on the crop of 'gatherings' over the last weeks. I and my sixties contemporaries can all look forward to this sort of obituary:

> While still in his twenties he rocked the nation with work that made history. But he was never to fulfil that early promise.
>
> Younger people were coming along and copying his style but he was unable to adapt and copy theirs in turn. Sadly, not everything he produced was as successful as his first efforts, or even his last. As long ago as last Tuesday, friends were saying that there was a falling-off in his talent.
>
> With his premature death, it was obviously that whatever remaining spark there was had gone out . . .

What a contrast to George Abbot, the Victorian Broadway director. He was a professional actor in New York before Lilian Baylis founded the Old Vic. I wrote his obituary for *The Times* some seven years ago when he was a hundred. Last year he revived one of his old shows on Broadway. Now he's planning another!

Last day at Salcombe. Beautifully bright and a wonderful sunset. I've never seen an aubergine sunset before; but this was the effect of the pink, sinking light on the skinny blue herring-bone clouds.

I haven't finished the novel but I'm not far from the last fence and the home straight. I have to arrange a trial for the leading character. He is opening a musical in Bristol in 1953 and is charged with indecency. Will he be acquitted? Will his show be a hit?

Friday 13ᵗʰ January

Early train to Paddington. Full fry-up.

I am not a triskaidekaphobe. Does the superstition about number 13 date from Norse mythology? Twelve Norse gods were gatecrashed by a thirteenth god, Loki – the God of Mischief. Or does it come from the thirteenth present at the Last Supper?

In *The Times* on the way up I read that applications for the Royal Enclosure at Ascot have opened this week. In 1952 a peer who had been recently divorced asked the Earl Marshal – the Duke of Norfolk

– whether he was eligible to attend the Coronation. 'Good God, man,' the Duke snorted, 'this is a Coronation, not Ascot!'

The Parker-Bowleses announced their divorce. His solicitors have a fine P.G. Wodehouse name – Boodle Hatfield. At home I looked up a quotation:

'She is a woman of charm, sense, balance . . . with dignity and taste. She has always been an excellent influence . . . her reserve and discretion are famous, and proved by the fact that no one knew of her impending divorce, and also by the fact that she never confided in anyone her hopes of being Queen.'

Can this be about Camilla P-B? No. It's Chips Channon writing about Mrs Simpson in 1936.

Then there is an enjoyable Oxford row – sparked off by David Butler whose wife is now Rector of my old college, Exeter. It continues to reverberate. Butler resigned from the Oxford and Cambridge Club because it won't have women on board. I'm with the Bishop of London who, when women were first admitted to full membership at Oxford, pronounced at a special service, 'All are destined to become the wives of some good *man*.'

Saturday 14th January

A shock to open *The Times* at 6.30 over my early-morning yoghurt, roughage and grapefruit juice, and read of Mervyn Stockwood's death yesterday in hospital, in Bath. He gallantly came up for the recording of my *This is Your Life* less than a month ago, just before Christmas and wasn't rewarded with so much as a close-up. I first met him through Caryl Brahms who had encountered him at the bedside of Dr Bradfield, Bishop of Bath and Wells when Mervyn was a parson in Bristol. Back in the late sixties he was a witness on the first substantial television programme on which I appeared, *Your Witness*. It was devised by Tony Smith and the other 'counsel', who debated various topics over ninety minutes, were all distinguished lawyers. I *just* qualified, having been called to the Bar. Sir John Hobson, until recently a Tory Attorney-General, and I debated censorship. Along with Mervyn I called Michael Foot and the playwright Ben Levy but my star witness was Benjamin, the twelve-year-old son of Margaret Daniel, a parson's wife who worked for Caryl. Ben claimed to have read *Lady Chatter-*

ley's Lover and not to have been corrupted by it. Hobson wisely decided not to cross-examine him. His witnesses included Donald Wolfit and Denise Robbins, the romantic novelist. Ironically, although my side won I was looking so modestly serious when the vote was declared and Hobson was smiling so sportingly at his defeat that most of the viewing audience thought my case had been lost.

When he was Bishop of Southwark Mervyn gave splendid mid-Lent drinks parties until Eric Roberts, a voluble black American cabaret singer to whom I introduced him waxed innocently lyrical about the lavishness of the entertainment to the *Sunday Express* and outrage broke out. There were also particularly jolly dinner parties for royals, politicians, and actors, with everyone loyally enthusing about the burnt meat which used to emerge from the kitchen hideously over cooked by Mounia, a Palestinian refugee whom Mervyn had imported from the Mount of Olives.

The Bishop loved to keep a scrapbook. At Hywel Bennett's wedding to Cathy McGowan I was in charge of the *placement* at the breakfast at San Lorenzo. I sat Mervyn next to Roger Moore and the papers next day duly spread the pictures captioned 'The Bishop Meets the Saint'. A couple of years later I was producing *Up the Front* with Frankie Howerd and Zsa Zsa Gabor. I gave a party at Inigo Jones on Zsa Zsa's arrival and Mervyn's presence produced another slew of 'The Actress and the Bishop' pictures. They all finished up in his scrapbook.

Mervyn came to dinner once at my little house in Bywater Street, in Chelsea. He arrived in the full purple, straight from a confirmation, surprising Kenneth Williams and Vincent Price. Vincent said bitterly, 'If I'd known it was fancy dress I've got much grander drag at home.'

When *A Passionate Woman* opened in Bath, Mervyn came, as always, on the Thursday night. Stephanie Cole, a Bath/Bristolian, had been dying to meet him so I asked them both to dinner at the Olive Tree – Bath's best restaurant in the basement of The Queensberry, Bath's best hotel. Unfortunately she was called to London at the last moment to appear early next morning on a bed with Paula Yates. I asked James Gaddas and Neil Morrissey instead and they had a wonderful time, emerging in awe of Mervyn. He took particular interest in Gaddas, who was trembling on the brink of a second marriage, and offered to pull strings to arrange for a church wedding if that was what James wanted.

Michael De-la-Noy's obit in the *Independent* gets over the suggestions of homosexuality – 'Merv-the-Perv' – with the neat phrase, 'His relations with women were more ambivalent . . .' I cannot remember discussing it with him. I always assumed that his instincts were gay but that his vows required celibacy. I have no authority for one view or the other.

I liked De-la-Noy's anecdote about the way Stockwood disciplined a lazy clergyman while he was at Southwark. 'You are only treating me like this because I am black,' protested the man. 'Indeed I am,' said Mervyn. 'If you were white I should have deprived you of your living.'

On *Loose Ends* the MP Rhodes Boyson peddled a sort of autobiography. As so often with popular 'monsters' he shows a disconcerting desire to be loved. And he is much smaller than his ogre image; but he did run his schools efficiently. I liked particularly his treatment of some girls he discovered were smoking in roofless lavatories. He had the hoses turned on them. When they emerged protesting he said he assumed they were on fire and did it to save their lives.

We also had a strange man who has programmed a computer to produce anagrams. 'Ned Sherrin' produced nothing wittier than 'her dinners' and 'rend shrine'. But 'Ned Sherrin's Loose Ends' did at least yield 'so he's nonsense riddler' – and even more pretty meaningless rearrangements.

Michael Howard is becoming a popular monologue villain. The Isle of Wight escapes and Parkhurst Governor's dismissal. John Marriott (the Guv) was told by the Home Secretary that he had been removed from his job and that he 'would not be running any other prison in the Prison Service' and then reassured that 'this did not mean he had been sacked'!

Monday 16ᵗʰ January

Anthony Powell has made a feature of his visits to the dentist in his newly published diaries, so I suppose I must record mine. For years I have been tended by David Sigaloff in Shepherd's Bush. I used to go there when I worked at Lime Grove in the late fifties and he was always kindness personified. He had only two faults. Like all dentists he would cram your mouth with pieces of apparatus and then ask you a question. More originally, he used to cradle your head fondly and bestow a kiss on the balding pate, exclaiming how brave one was being. Poor David died at the end of last year. It was not unexpected. He has been ill and off work for a long time and I have been in the hands of Byzanti – I have no idea how it is spelt – a beautiful Pakistani receptionist/assistant, and a passionate viewer of TV soaps; and Anita who is still taking dental exams. They have been extremely kind and concerned but Shepherd's Bush is too far to go and I have just moved to David Croser who used to be a neighbour in Pimlico. His surgery is in Victoria. It is very high-tech and ultra-efficient and very good for food shopping in Elizabeth Street and Ebury Street when the torture is over.

No torture this morning. A cap fell off and had to be replaced. I had a mouthful of some sort of plasticine substance to make a mould for a more ambitious double cap. There is talk of an 'implant' which sounds very expensive and not a little painful. It appears I have no back teeth and am putting altogether too much responsibility on my front teeth which are cracking under the strain.

We discussed Elaine Paige's appearance in *Sunset Boulevard*. She is easily the best Norma Desmond I've seen, and I've seen them all, witty and poised. She sings it spectacularly.

To Peter Hall's disappointing *Hamlet* in the evening. Stephen Dillane's 'Hamlet for the nineties' was pale after David Warner's 'Hamlet for the sixties' under the same director. The verse went for nothing in a staccato Dalek voice. The women were ill-at-ease, the pace leaden. Donald Sinden's Polonius livened things up. I did not like Hamlet's Polonius/Sinden impersonation, sending him up to his face. Act One lasts two hours. Sinden, dead, is given leave to go home after Act One and miss the curtain call.

It's the first time I've been to the Globe since it became the Gielgud. When Sir John opened it last year he said, 'I've been walking down Shaftesbury Avenue for so many years now without seeing a single name in lights that I know. It'll be a relief to spot one I can recognise.' In his *Writing Home*, Alan Bennett remembers that when Gielgud was at the Apollo in Bennett's *Forty Years On* he urged Alan to write a

Noël Coward parody. 'You know the sort of thing – lots of little epigrams. Smart, witty remarks. It wouldn't be at all difficult.'

'I couldn't possibly,' protested Alan.

'Why not? Terribly easy. Noël does it all the time.'

I went with Glen Roven. Knowing how the play ends, we did not stay the course.

Tuesday 17ᵗʰ January

I spent the morning trying to avoid work. The papers were a beguiling distraction.

The Pope has drawn bigger crowds in Manila on Sunday (four million for a Mass) than Rod Stewart's recent three and a half million for a beach concert in Rio. Reports say that the weakened Pope 'waved his cane in the style of Maurice Chevalier'; while lusty Rod Stewart was so fatigued that he had to be removed to an ambulance and given oxygen – presumably the oxygen of publicity.

Prince Charles has another ratting valet. The nation is up in arms about green stains on his pyjamas after he romped with Mrs P-B in the garden among the cabbages. I hope this chap is more accurate than Crawfie, the original breacher of royal privacy. One of the highlights of her royal memoir was a colourful description of 'Trooping the Colour' the year it was cancelled . . .

Wednesday 18ᵗʰ January

Last year I got a letter from Colin – a prisoner in Whitemoor, the maximum-security prison near March in Cambridgeshire. Colin belongs to a longtermers/lifers group who meet in the Education Department every Wednesday from 2 p.m. until 4.30. He invited me to talk to the group. He enclosed a letter from Trina Warman, who is on the staff of the department and an information sheet listing the people who had already spoken at Whitemoor. They range from a Buddhist monk to John Peel and Benjamin Zephaniah – who were all great successes.

Whitemoor has recently become notorious because of Paul Magee's escape, aided by a gun which he concealed in his cell. One prison warder was shot and injured during the attempt. I have never been inside a prison before so a mixture of curiosity and manners made me say yes. I am aware that the curiosity can be dismissed as simple nosiness. The manners come into play because it was such a pleasant letter. Colin pointed out that both he and Trina Warman were regular *Loose Ends* listeners and speculated that she might therefore be handing out chocolate biscuits at the meeting, 'instead of the usual plain ones'.

My letter agreeing had Colin 'gobsmacked', as he replied by return. He gave instructions for the journey by train and by car – 'You've probably got a fleet of chauffeur driven Rolls-Royces!!' He went on 'If you come via Huntingdon, don't make too much noise as our leader John Major lives there and you wouldn't want to wake him up, would you?'

I phoned Trina Warman who warned me that I must bring some identification with me and that I would be thoroughly searched on arrival. I went by train, changing at Peterborough. I was met at March by Trina and a couple of jolly teacher colleagues. Whitemoor, just outside the town, stands on a flat, barren piece of East Anglian turf. It looks like a small walled city, isolated and grim. The security checks were very thorough. I was carrying my old Gladstone bag which goes everywhere with me. All my pill bottles – containing nothing more exciting than a few temazepam and Valium tablets and some for tightening or loosening the bowels – were removed. Even more interest was shown in a metal punch. One of those gadgets with which you can make holes in papers you want to file. There was some excitement at the gate as Princess Anne was on a visit and was expected to emerge at any moment. As it happened she was shown out by another exit so we did not clash.

After a lot of clanging doors and clinking chains we arrived at D Wing and the Education Department, where the staff room looks like any secondary modern school staff room. There are timetables and graphs on the walls. Papers and magazines are strewn around. Kettles and coffee makers are in constant use by the sink. The teachers chatted in a desultory way about their charges, much as they would about naughty boys – with the occasional grim joke about the unwisdom of accepting a cup of tea from one prisoner who was being detained on account of a slight case of poisoning.

We went into the empty classroom at two and arranged a dozen or so chairs in a semicircle. The corridors outside were beginning to buzz with activity and eventually a dozen or so prisoners wandered in. Colin is a frail-looking, prematurely aged man, balding and stooped. He was holding one of those hand-rolled cigarettes so thin you wonder if it has room for any tobacco at all in it, which I shall always associate with prisoners. The rest were a mixed group. Two or three black men, one dark young man with heavy shoulders and a low brow under thick dark hair who looked like one of nature's security guards or bouncers. I did my autobiographical ramble through television, movies, theatre and radio to give them an idea of the areas we could talk about and questions came fairly freely. One prisoner has 'got religion' since being given life and has virtually gone into competition with the prison padre. Another is corresponding with a television playwright about the subject of suicides in prison. There was a general feeling that 'there's too much crime on TV' and some curiosity about the sex lives of the stars. 'That Benny Hill, 'e was a poof, wan'ee?' I said I had no first-hand knowledge, except that he once made a pass at an ex-lover of mine. This caused a lot of raised eyebrows and surprised glances. The born bouncer's brow furrowed deeply and about three questions later he got round to asking, 'What you said about . . . does that mean that you . . .? With that out of the way we talked of other prisons. Most of them had been to several. In some cases they had been to Whitemoor before and then returned. The general consensus, in the light of the Isle of Wight escapes, was that Parkhurst was a 'good' prison. Albany, also on the island, was 'bad'. They were dismissive of Ronnie Knight's sentence compared to the lengths of theirs. They apologised for having 'a prison language' which enabled them to communicate with one another but which I might not understand. This puzzled me as I didn't think anything had escaped me. We got our chocolate digestive biscuits and Trina, who drove me back to Peterborough station, judged it a success. 'It'll give them something to talk about for weeks,' she said, pointing out other things I hadn't noticed like the fact that they had all put on best jeans and smartened themselves up for the visit. It must be hard to maintain one's self-respect in those conditions. I suppose putting on best jeans and a clean ironed shirt does give a man an infinitesimal lift.

I've agreed to encourage other speakers to visit. Who? I'll try Arthur Smith and Stephanie Cole.

Thursday 19th January

Understudy rehearsal for *A Passionate Woman* at the Comedy. Gordon Alcock, who is covering Alfie Lynch, is particularly good. He and David Conolly, who stands in for Neil Morrissey and James Gaddas, both had a chance to work with Stephanie Cole. Having spent the previous weeks with Maggie Guess, Stephanie's excellent understudy, they got to grips with the real thing. She is admirably diplomatic about rehearsing with them and making sure that their performances mesh with what has become smooth and precise.

We recorded two *Counterpoints*, the Radio 4 music quiz which I chair, at the Paris Cinema and then back to the Comedy to see Act Two. On to the Ivy. Poor David Pugh (the producer) was to give Steph and me supper. However Kay Mellor (author) her daughter and Morrissey all tagged along and a table booked for four expanded to eight.

Stephanie volunteered to talk at Whitemoor but can't do so while the play runs as she has a Wednesday matinée.

Friday 20th January

A terrible shock.

Edward Bunn called to say that Lorna has hanged herself. Poor Douglas. Poor children. Poor Lorna.

Saturday 21st January

Annie Ross on *Loose Ends*, looking marvellous. It was too early for her to sing. We played a bit of her 'Twisted' largely because there is a whole generation which doesn't know it is hers and assume that Joni Mitchell or Barbara Streisand, who have both recorded it, originated it.

One of the irritations of doing an interview programme over a long period is having to ask routine biographical questions of people simply because a new generation has grown up in total ignorance of someone's early achievements. Annie must be bored stiff recalling her Hollywood childhood, school with Garland, touring with the innovative jazz trio Lambert, Hendricks and Ross, and her Paris days with Dizzy Gillespie and Gerry Mulligan; but she manages to attack the over-exposed topics with fresh enthusiasm and wit. Will Durst, a very engaging left-wing American stand-up born in the Midwest who moved to San Francisco because in his home town 'comedy was illegal', was politely in awe of *TW3* – even though he only saw the watered-down American version.

John Hegley was very funny singing with his guitar-playing accompanist Nigel. I confused two publicity handouts and called him Nigel Charnock who is an extrovert, camp dancer-actor who used to be with DV8 and is about to open a season at the Drill Hall.

Douglas (Bunn) called to ask if I would speak at Lorna's funeral. Monday afternoon at a crematorium near Crawley. It is not a request I can, or would, want to refuse; but it is not a task to which I look forward.

Sunday 22nd January

I was due to meet Glen Roven outside the Curzon cinema in Shaftesbury Avenue to see a screening of Ronnie Shedloe's movie *Carrington* – written and directed by Christopher Hampton. It's about the Bloomsberries. I was so nervous about the address for Lorna that I forgot about it completely as I struggled to find the words. Then Glen phoned at noon and said, 'Weren't we going to see a movie?' He was very understanding.

In the evening to the Savoy to a Globe Theatre Awards ceremony introduced by Zoë Wanamaker and compered amusingly by Henry Kelly. I took Stephanie Cole who had a great reunion with Maggie Smith – they had been in *Memento Mori* together on television. Maggie was there to support her son Toby Stephens who got 'most promising newcomer' for his Coriolanus at the RSC. When his mother heard he had got the part she is supposed to have rung his father, Robert Stephens, and said, 'Toby's got Coriolanus – and it's not infectious!'

Monday 23rd January

I drove down to Crawley with Neil and Ann Benson for Lorna's funeral. Neil is Douglas's accountant and a good friend to both of us.

It was a cold, grey, damp day. Real funeral weather. There was a huge turn-out and we all had to wait outside, until an earlier ceremony was over. Then the crowd overflowed the little chapel, so many had turned up who loved Lorna – and to support Douglas. It was a short and very simple ceremony with the order of service on a typed sheet. Speaking at a funeral is much harder than at a memorial service. The grief and shock are still present and all-pervasive. At a memorial service the convention is always that it is the celebration of a life. An occasion for joy. Lorna's daughters Chloë and Daisy were there. Although they are only fourteen and eleven they looked beautiful, poised and brave in the smart black suits that Douglas had bought for them before Christmas at Fenwicks; but their eyes were full of tears and I was concerned for Chloë who had courageously decided to speak. In fact she did it beautifully, remembering her mother's injunction that 'every cloud has a silver lining'. She said she found it hard to see one on this particular day but perhaps, if her mother was happy at last and at peace, that was it. Almost everyone came back to Hickstead Place afterwards – where Lorna had so often presided over huge parties. Charlie Bunn, my godson, who is just coming up to eight, raced round and round the house. He has not quite realised or registered his loss, which is comforting.

The Bensons drove me back and I recorded two editions of *Counterpoint* at the Paris in the evening. *Counterpoint* contestants are lay people, not celebs, and often show a huge range of knowledge. When they don't it is hard going!

I usually finish *The Times* (reading it, not doing the crossword) before breakfast but I picked it up at the end of the day and strayed to the anniversaries. On this day in 1924 Ramsay MacDonald formed the first Labour Government, and King George V wrote in his diary 'Today, 23 years ago dear Grandmama [Queen Victoria] died. I wonder what she would have thought of a Labour Government. Not amused, I dare say.'

It is also the anniversary of the death of William Pitt the Younger who made only one recorded joke in his short, famous but lonely life. 'Take a wife, Mr Pitt,' advised a kindly colleague. 'Whose wife shall I take?' replied Pitt.

Tuesday 24th January

A meeting at the Marriott Hotel to judge the Lloyds Private Banking Playwright of the Year Award. Some £25,000 will go to one of a shortlist of ten plays. The judges, chaired by Melvyn Bragg, are mainly critics, Sheridan Morley, Jack Tinker, Clive Hirschhorn, etc., with Nanette Newman, Tim Rice and me thrown in as media bimbos. Judging amicable. We filled in slips of paper with our first, second and third recommendations. These were taken out by the ebullient Tony Ball, the PR who organises it for Lloyds. He returned to say that we had a result but that they were not going to reveal the winner until the presentation day in March. My money is on Terry Johnson's *Dead Funny*.

I approached Melvyn about a suggestion from Stephen Sondheim that the South Bank Show should mount a programme about Revue – using as the core a show the Mercury company produced. They are largely graduates of Stephen's year of professorship, teaching at Oxford. It was quite a success in the tiny Jermyn Street Theatre just before Christmas. Julia McKenzie directed it and George Styles and Anthony Drewe entered their two funny numbers – the one about navvies' cleavages (rear view) and their slightly dated, but very funny attack on nouvelle cuisine.

Victoria Mather has written movingly in *The Daily Telegraph* about Lorna, the earlier tragedy of losing little Douglas, her second child, in a cot death and the devotion and care she gave to raising money for the study of Infant Death and to comforting other victims. Angela Perry, committee chairman for the fund, is quoted saying, 'She never got over her baby's death. It has been the root of everything that has happened.'

Wednesday 25th January

I made a rare foray into the financial pages today, my eye drawn there by the word 'Wellcome' in a headline. The disappointing sequel was the news of a merger between Glaxo and Wellcome into the world's largest drugs combine. I think I had been hoping for belated dirt on another doomed Wellcome merger – that, nearly 80 years ago, between Syrie Wellcome and Somerset Maugham in 1917. The vitriol was still flowing forth five years later when Willie Maugham published a memoir 'Looking Back' in the *Sunday Express* vilifying his dead wife. His nephew Robin Maugham recalled that when news of Syrie's death reached Maugham at the Villa Mauresque he chanted, 'Tra-la, tra-la. No more alimony. Tra-la, tra-la.' Staying at the Villa Mauresque must have been fraught with danger. Cyril Connolly was accused of stealing avocados. When Evelyn Waugh stayed with Maugham at Cap Ferrat Maugham asked him what someone was like. Presumably without thinking Waugh replied, 'a pansy with a stammer.' In a letter to Harold Acton in 1952, Waugh recorded that 'All the Picassos on the wall blanched. Noël Coward fared no better when he visited. Maugham had just returned from Switzerland after one of those rejuvenating injections which were fashionable at the time – goats' glands or something similar were injected. Coward was on his best behaviour and determined not to mention it. However, as Maugham hopped nimbly down a rockery to greet him he found himself saying, 'Ah! There you are, Willie. Skipping about like a mountain goat!'

Rose Kennedy has died at 104. When she and her husband Joe arrived in Britain in 1938 for his disastrous period as Ambassador they spent a night at Windsor Castle. 'Well, Rose,' said Joe Kennedy, 'this is a hell of a long way from East Boston.'

Thursday 26th January

I am doing a restaurant column for *Harpers & Queen* – just a one-off. I am a great believer in the late Nubar Gulbenkian's idea of how to define the perfect luncheon or dinner table – 'myself and a good head waiter'. I am in favour of Gulbenkian anyway. When he appeared on an edition of the old BBC *Tonight* programme which I was directing, he arrived at the studio in a London black cab decorated with gold leaf and with a Rolls-Royce engine inserted. Derek Hart asked him why he had bought it and Gulbenkian replied (I think for the first time – it was much quoted afterwards), 'Because I am told it can turn on a sixpence, whatever that may be.' Come to think of it, I recalled neither of these remarks when I edited the new *Oxford Dictionary of Humorous Quotations* last year, which just shows how hard it is to be a good lexicographer.

Lou Pescadou, primarily a fish bistro in the Old Brompton Road, was my first venture for the *Harpers* column. Patrick Tako, the head waiter, is my favourite waiter in London. I once made a pass at him only to be brushed aside with a chortled 'You must be joking, Ned!' Since my chosen guest, Keith Waterhouse (*The Theory and Practice of Lunch* by Keith Waterhouse), was once rudely handled at Lou Pescadou and will not return, I knew I would have a peaceful, solo meal. Patrick was very keen to reclaim Waterhouse as a customer and explained that his senior – Daniel – who has always been scrupulously polite to me but who some allege established Lou Pescadou's reputation for brusqueness early on is rarely there these days. He is supervising Stratfords, his new establishment near Marloes Road.

People always say go to a Chinese restaurant where there are lots of Chinese eating. Lou Pescadou (as French as Cantona and, in the old days, as temperamental) claimed many French tables the day I was there. I know the French are thrifty, but they do have an eye for a bargain. There was an £8 lunch, offering a starter of mussel soup or tomato salad *provençale* a main course of pork chop or *assiette* of fish; and, for pudding, a sorbet or a *tarte aux pommes*. As *Harpers & Queen* was in the chair, I had six delectable native oysters first. Then I snapped up the mussel soup, the chop and the *tarte*. I confess to a bottle of Pouilly Fumé and a double espresso, otherwise the bill would not have been anything like £44.50, service included.

Patrick would have made Gulbenkian a proud and happy man and I must regain Waterhouse, the inveterate luncher-out, as a regular at his neighbourhood trough. To soften him up I took him to Bibendum in the Fulham Road, where we have launched several successful plays.

Keith has a habit of choosing the same dish at his favourite restaurants wherever he goes so that he does not have to pay too much attention to the menu. At the Ivy, unless he is in a cantankerous mood, it is Eggs Benedict. At Bibendum, it is deep-fried fish and chips, upon which Simon Hopkinson's brigade lavishes great care. This day Keith had a sorrel soup which had 'bits' on it. 'I don't usually like bits in soup,' he said, 'but these are delicious. They could be avocado.' We shall never know.

Then he had fried plaice and chips; no greens, not even mushy peas, which I think were not offered. 'Green doesn't go with fish and chips,' he pronounced, *ex cathedra*. The idea of Waterhouse as a colour consultant was a new one; but he judged the whole dish 'gradely'. He then confessed that he had never heard a Yorkshireman alive or dead use that word outside fiction.

Simon Hopkinson is one of the high priests of offal and he memorably fried delicious chitterlings for me at my home for the 400th edition of Radio 4's *Loose Ends*. I attacked his andouillettes with high optimism because when I have tried to cook them myself I have organised disaster. Of course, Simon's is in a different class; but I am not a convert. I shall not call for them again, especially as there are so many treats on Bibendum's menu (I shall rush back whenever tripe or *tête de veau* is rumoured to be available). The passion fruit sorbet was delicious. Keith obliterated a lemon cheesecake.

Waterhouse's book teaches one to avoid phrases like 'Can we manage with a half between us?' and 'I don't think we need another bottle, do you?' So I report only the *prix fixe*, £54 for two, and the attentive service.

There was a contretemps at the end of lunch. *Harpers & Queen* sent a photographer. His equipment was coming from elsewhere and it hadn't arrived. Keith wisely decided there was going to be a long wait and he wasn't staying so he paddled off. I had a book to read for *Loose Ends* so I had a glass of port and ploughed on, finally emerging at about four o'clock.

Writing about food reminds me inevitably of last year's tour of *A Passionate Woman*. The publicist, the indefatigable Peter Thompson, persuaded *The Daily Telegraph* to let me do a tour diary and of course it finished up as a catalogue of meals enjoyed on the way. David Pugh, the producer, had been looking for a vehicle for Stephanie Cole, a great actress and an immense TV star from *Tenko* and *Waiting for God*. We thought we were going to do Ben Travers's *The Bed Before Yesterday*; but it was snatched from our grasp at the last moment by the Almeida, who had one of their few resounding flops with it. As we despaired of finding the right play he threw in a script which he optioned last year when it was a triumphant success at the lively West Yorkshire Playhouse, Leeds.

A Passionate Woman by Kay Mellor deals, with exceptional insight and humour, with the mid-life crisis of a woman whose marriage has become a shell. She has invested all her emotion in her son. On his wedding day her despair at losing him drives her first up to her attic and finally on to the roof of her house.

Stephanie and I jumped at the chance – knowing that it will be a candidate for Best Play, Best Comedy or Most Promising New Playwright when the Awards Ceremonies come around.

It is rare to find a producer brave enough to take a chance on a new play in the present theatrical climate; but here we were happily faced, not with a touring revival, but with a West End opening eight weeks away at the Comedy Theatre.

I thought *A Passionate Woman* was such a good play that I got rid of earlier superstitions and had my first go at keeping a diary. There is so much of the play in this book that I reproduce it to introduce the cast.

Monday 5ᵗʰ September 1994

First read-through: strangely appropriate. My diary says it is Labor Day in America – the traditional week for starting rehearsals for the Broadway autumn season. We are in a large room off The Cut rented out by the Cambridge Theatre Company. The producers, David Pugh and William Russo, bring champagne and sticky cakes. Food is clearly going to be a feature of this production – not on stage but at lunchtime during rehearsals and after the show on tour.

Stephanie Cole stars; with her are Neil Morrissey, James Gaddas and Alfred Lynch. Gaddas has the biggest appetite, especially for puddings!

Tuesday 6ᵗʰ September 1994

Serious work starts, exploring Betty/Stephanie's relationship with the son on whom she dotes. The role is a splendid change for her. An attractive 53-year-old, she can now play her age – knocking off the 20-odd years she has to add on to play Diana in *Waiting for God*. She moans that it will take days to shake the older character off. Neil Morrissey on the other hand has to find a softer character than his flashy television persona. They have an immediate rapport which helps.

I introduce our gourmand cast to Bar Central, a new restaurant where the pub used to be next to the former stage door of the Old Vic. It is now run by Stewart who was Maître d'Hotel at Joe Allen.

Nicknames and catchphrases emerge early on in rehearsal. I can't remember Morrissey's name at one point and call him 'Mulrooney' which sticks. Later he boasts that he can move on the roof that takes over the set in Act Two 'like a gazelle'. From then on he becomes Bambi Mulrooney. Stephanie Cole, most generous actress and woman, never speaks of one long-gone actor who could not remember his lines without a qualifying 'bless his heart'. This phrase becomes essential whenever anybody screws up in rehearsal.

Friday 9ᵗʰ September 1994

We have been bedevilled by rail strikes, particularly irritating for Alfie Lynch who commutes from Brighton. Fortunately most of his scenes are in Act Two. He is such a pleasant man with a Stan Laurel face that we have to push a bit to move him towards the strutting, Leodensian little Hitler, Stephanie's husband in the loveless marriage.

Disaster at Bar Central. It is crowded and they can't find us a table. Morrissey particularly distressed as the day's specials include roast hind which neither he, nor the rest of us, has ever tasted. We drift down the road to The Fire Station with ill-grace.

The play is solidly blocked by the end of the week. We don't rehearse on Saturdays as I have to do *Loose Ends*.

Monday 12ᵗʰ September 1994

We have moved to the upstairs rehearsal room at the Old Vic where a huge mock-up roof has been erected so that Mulrooney can fall up and down it (like a gazelle). Stephanie ('bless her heart') can emote from a chimney stack, James can perform ghostly tricks and Alfie can emerge unexpectedly. James is playing the ghost of Stephanie's indiscretion – early in her marriage. He enters enthusiastically into planning the various tricks which help him to materialise, appear transparent and walk up walls. It's a huge help to have an actor who uses his own imagination to solve practical problems. The weekend has produced a big advance in familiarity with the lines. Stephanie gives a hint of the power she will bring to one chimney-potty aria and we have a happy author. Spicy sausages are most popular, also grilled chicken. Gaddas has run through the pudding choices. The big news is that there's a new menu on Monday. Suspect that they are trying it out in Daily Specials. Make sure Friday's table is booked. Roast hind off.

Monday 19th September 1994

We are joined by three amazingly adept understudies who swell the ranks and appear to be word perfect. New menu not quite ready.

Much time usefully spent in examining the relationship between Betty/Stephanie and Craze, her ghostly ex-lover. We have to explore the comedy of a character whom the mother can see and hear but not her son. More delicate is the scene Stephanie and the ghost have to play at the end of Act One in which she wants him to take her away. James suggests a useful exercise for the ghostly comedy speaking his lines from off-stage so that Neil gets some idea of the ridiculous conversation his mother seems to be having with thin air. The romantic scene will take longer.

Tuesday/Wednesday 20th/21st September 1994

Chef still not happy with new menu. Thursday new menu arrives. Chef congratulated (bless his heart). Am amused to watch restaurant's and street's glances from TV fans of Steph (*Waiting For God*), Mulrooney (*Boon* and *Men Behaving Badly*) and James (*Medics*). The latter two mainly stared at by young women. Mulrooney – voluble on the effects of testosterone and oestrogen – coins a new catchphrase which sticks – 'Begging for it'. Company noticeably less than politically correct.

The best monologue line in this week's *Loose Ends* was in my view Neil Shand's 'Lord Archer of Weston-Super-Mare – the only seaside pier on which Danny La Rue has not performed.'

Monday 26th September 1994

We have said goodbye to the Old Vic and Bar Central and moved to the Groucho Club for food and the stage of the Queen's Theatre for rehearsal on the full set – revolves, flying equipment, special effects. We have three more days to play with our toy-set before shipping it to Bath. It is of course far more expensive to instal the set on a West End stage but it pays off. All sorts of problems present themselves with the revolve, various bits of flying gear and special effects tackle. In Bath we shall move in on Sunday and must open on Tuesday night. We would never have solved these difficulties in time. Teams rush up from Guildford where the set was built and by the end of the week all the machinery is in working order. A sigh of relief.

Groucho lunches are well up to scratch. We play a wicked trick on Mulrooney when he misses one, pretending that Catherine Zeta Jones was there oozing oestrogen and asking about him.

Sunday 2nd October 1994

We arrive in comforting Bath. The set is up at the Theatre Royal. The Queensberry Hotel welcoming. Its celebrated restaurant, the Olive Tree is now opening on Sundays. I feed Keith Waterhouse who has moved his second home to Bath. If the post-war food revolution can claim a birthplace, it is probably Bath and the Hole-in-the-Wall. That restaurant is now regaining a reputation; but the Olive Tree, which Stephen Ross started after abandoning his country house hotel outside the city is still my favourite.

Monday 3rd October 1994

Hectic schedule with lighting, technical rehearsals and jovial tuck-in at 10 p.m. at nearby Beaujolais restaurant. The set works. Spirits high.

Tuesday 4th October 1994

Discover excellent brasserie, the New Moon opposite stage door. Fortified for smooth dress rehearsal and imminent first night. London friends, lovers and followers descend. Cast on terrific form, much laughter and applause. Keith Waterhouse declares one of Stephanie's Act Two speeches has authentic Broadway-bound ring. Nagging problem: however we stage James's first ghostly entrance it seems wrong. Various lighting changes don't help. The audience need to feel he has materialised through the attic wall. Perhaps we need David Copperfield!

Thursday 6th October 1994
Stephanie had to rush to London to be 'in bed with Paula Yates' in the morning, so I ate with the two boys. A great deal of roast loin of venison, compôte of peas and quince and black pepper and port sauce and red wine fuelled the conversation. Local press good. Cast happy. I leave on Friday (7th) for *Loose Ends* (favourite monologue line (Neil Shand); 'John Gummer came out in support of Organic Vegetables – it takes one to know one').

Monday 10th October 1994
Still not happy with Ghost's first entrance. More lighting changes do not quite solve it.

First tour move to Richmond. Complicated set moved efficiently. Cast finding new subtleties. Talk to Lloyds Private Banking clients who are sponsoring the week. Response reassuring. We agree a couple of minor re-writes with Kay Mellor – to be rehearsed and included next week at Guildford. Excellent Italian restaurant opposite stage door. Access through kitchens. Warm welcome. Ideal for post-mortems. Leave Friday for *Loose Ends* in Taunton with Leslie Nielsen and Gary Glitter. Castle Hotel food sensational as ever. Share wine bill with Emma Freud.

Monday 17th October 1994
Guildford: we start our last two weeks out of town. The re-writes slot in happily. James and Stephanie have found a wonderful new way of playing their scene at the end of Act One. Suddenly sitting at the front of the stage and echoing

their early romance adds a whole extra dimension of poignancy and drama. Kay Mellor, who suggested it, is thrilled. She has been a constant support throughout. Always watchful and thoughtful. She knows every nuance of her play but insists that Stephanie is finding subtleties she never thought of. The theatre wine-and-quiche us afterwards. Patrons very enthusiastic; also perceptive local critic who spots the substance of Kay's play beneath the laughter. Business, slow at beginning of week, picks up sensationally on word of mouth.

Monday 24th October 1994

A woman materialises in Stephanie's dressing-room to announce that her performance has confirmed her decision to leave her husband. Cast spirits, already high, bolstered by praise from Albert Finney and Cameron Mackintosh. Nonagenarian lady complains opening music too loud ('I should know, I'm deaf'). Octogenarian falls asleep on Cameron's shoulder at matinée.

My favourite monologue line from this week's *Loose Euds* is Debbie Barham's 'Radio 1 has now lost so many listeners that Group 4 are rumoured to be putting in a bid for it.'

Tuesday 1st November 1994

First preview in West End. At last we have got James's entrance right by having him come on ten seconds earlier in darkness. The audience gasps. Why didn't I think of it before?

Five restaurants adjoin the theatre. Hooray! Producer takes us to the Ivy to celebrate. We open at the Comedy Theatre on Monday.

Thursday 26th January

This Thursday we rather carried on the tradition. More or less the whole cast and backstage crew went on to the Pizza on the Park where Annie Ross was holding court. She split her act tonight so that we could get along after curtain.

Saturday 28th January

A very jolly *Loose Ends*. Peter Shaffer was in to talk about his re-writes on *Yonadab*, a play based on the Bible's account of the House of David, which flopped at the National in Peter Hall's production a few years ago with Alan Bates in the title role. Shaffer has revised it extensively, first of all for the printed text and then again for a new undergraduate production by the OUDS at Oxford Playhouse. I read it last night and was amazed that it could have failed. It cries out for John Wood. Peter is very enthusiastic about his student cast and particularly Elliot Levey who plays the title role.

I got him to retell (there are so many bastard versions) the story of the reaction of Hugh ('Binkie') Beaumont, the powerful West End impresario who produced his first play, *Five Finger Exercise*, when he gave him *The Royal Hunt of the Sun* to read. He was staying with Beaumont and his partner John Perry at the country home near Cambridge, Knott's Fosse. Peter was coming down to breakfast when he heard the two producers discussing the script. Perry was the one who had taken it to bed to read. Beaumont was asking what it was about. Shaffer came into earshot as Perry was saying, 'Now they go up the Andes, dear.' Binkie asked in his silky voice, 'Then what happens?' 'Now they go down, dear.' 'Fancy!' It was clearly a production on a scale outside their reach; but Binkie was helpful in getting it staged at the National.

Martin Clunes, son of Alec, and the endearing, puppyish TV star of *Men Behaving Badly*, had a late Rex Harrison anecdote. He had been in Rex's last play at the Haymarket. The play was Barrie's *The Admirable Crichton*. Rex was playing Lord Loam and hating it. He was ill, virtually blind and very unsure of his lines. He also farted a great deal on stage. Martin particularly cherished one exit when Rex was steered off-stage by Margaret Courtenay, playing his wife. They were going in for dinner and when another member of the cast asked what was for dinner Rex enunciated clearly and loudly, 'a turkey in three acts'.

Eric Cantona's assault on a spectator at Crystal Palace who had provoked him beyond reason dominated the news and Mike Coleman's monologue. Cantona's new book of his metaphysical observations, *La Philosophie de Cantona*, contains such gems as 'Life is always too cruel. All we can do is say Let's try to pass the ball and let the sun shine.' Can't wait for the novel, Eric.

Sunday 29th January

I took Glen Roven to the *Evening Standard* British Film Awards at the Savoy. Hugh Grant won the Peter Sellers Award for Comedy for *Four Weddings and a Funeral*. He was on satellite from Los Angeles and made another of those inverted modesty speeches like the one he gave a few days ago when he referred to himself as 'easily the nastiest, most ill-tempered, prima-donnaish actor in the English cinema'. Jane Asher was an incredibly cool and fluent compère.

Monday 30th January

Another two *Counterpoints*. This time we were playing away at Bury St Edmunds in the lovely old theatre where we played our penultimate out-of-town audition for *Side By Side By Sondheim* twenty years ago. I was thrilled to find that in the interim they have installed central heating. When Millicent Martin, Julia McKenzie, David Kernan and I appeared there on a cold, damp, winter Sunday night in a half-filled house, the chilly fog seeped up through the floorboards and cast and audience shivered. The biggest laugh came with the encore: 'Isn't it warm/Isn't it cosy/ Side by Side by Side.' It was still called *A Sondheim Songbook*' at that time. Burt Shevelove suggested the new title on the drive up.

We had high hopes that Michael Codron would bring the show into the West End. I knew from the moment he came round to the dressing-room afterwards that there wasn't a chance. He threw open the dressing-room door, flung his arms wide and said, 'Tell me where I shall find three such talented musical performers?' The others thought it meant he was going to produce us. On Monday morning he told the Business Manager 'No.' Michael keeps saying that 'one day he will tell me the whole story . . .' I'm still waiting.

I had a letter from Sondheim this morning. He told me in December that he was excited about a new project (he has already completed a new thriller with George Furth of which Mike Nichols thinks highly). Now he's working with John Weidman on a musical about the Mizner

Brothers, Wilson and Addison. Wilson was a Hollywood wit. Addison invented Florida. I had written to ask if he knew that Irving Berlin had once worked on the same subject.

Steve replies that he not only knew about the project, but he read what had been written (five scenes) in the early sixties when David Merrick, who was planning to produce it, showed it to him. The book was by S.N. Behrman, 'and quite graceful, as one would expect, but in no way a musical'.

'Hope you are the same,' he concluded. I wondered for a moment if that meant that he thought I was 'graceful, but in no way musical' – but decided that it was just a routine enquiry about my health. Pity.

An odd letter from Lucien James. I can't remember what his real name is. I met him some years ago when he was an Oxford undergraduate who interviewed me for the *Isis*. I was doing a charity show at the Playhouse. It never got printed but he writes out of the blue occasionally. He didn't like his real name so he has simply become Lucien. He wants to know if I can point him towards any celebrity gardeners. He is researching a television series for Channel 4. 'I understand that Barbara Windsor has a lovely garden and I'd love to use her in the show. But apparently we are aiming for people who might know some Latin plant names.'

I rang him to say he'd drawn a blank. He spends his days bizarrely watching Channel 4 programmes which might be exported to the Far East. His brief is to look out for pigs in the background (or, even worse, foreground). The presence of pigs in a shot makes them unacceptable to many Far Eastern viewers. I wonder if the producers were aware of this when they made *Leon, the Pig Farmer*, or Alan Bennett when he wrote *A Private Function*, for that matter? Or Orwell embarking on *Animal Farm*?

February

Wednesday 1st February

DID A VOICEOVER for a trailer for a BBC *Arena* documentary series about Peter Sellers. It is to run over three Saturdays and features miles of Sellers home videos. The material in the trailer was unremarkable, except for a brief, almost subliminal, shot of Princess Margaret leaping out in front of the camera, pulling a face and disappearing again.

Thursday 2nd February

Back to David Croser. My double cap has arrived and fits nicely. Now I have to go to see a Mr Bashaarat in Chelsea. He will tell me if I can have an 'implant'. He will also tell me how much it is going to cost. I get the impression that it will be both painful *and* expensive.

I hope I don't get into the Martin Amis class. He spent £20,000 of the advance his new agent has secured for him on dental work. One single false tooth made of gold and porcelain cost £1,000.

Apparently 'Dentics' in the King's Road has 'a trendy boutique atmosphere'. Mr Croser's premises are quite chic enough for me.

Friday 3rd February

Dinner at Deke and Jill Arlon's. Deke is my 'manager/agent'. His name is manufactured. When he was a teenager he became a rock singer. 'Deke' was the name of someone Elvis Presley played in a movie. 'Arlon' – which sounds like a manmade fibre – he got from the phone book. I suspect he got bored while he was still in the 'A's'. The idea was to float the idea of Keith Waterhouse's new play to Dennis

Waterman. Keith and Dennis were there too. *Bing Bong* is a very fine, very dark comedy about two ageing sitcom writers, their agent and their secretary. It is proving not at all easy to cast but Dennis would be excellent as one of them. *Bing Bong* because that is the noise which always heralds a new arrival on the scene in sitcom-land. He likes the idea and took it away to read.

Saturday 4ᵗʰ February

A rather crowded *Loose Ends*. Paul Merton who is opening in Arthur Smith's *Live Bed Show* next week was fun. So was Patrick Marber who is dazzling as various characters interviewed by Steve Coogan in his 'Alan Partridge' guise. Marber has written a very fine first play, *Dealer's Choice*, which he is directing himself after some workshop performances. It is at the Cottesloe. The subject is an all-night poker game in a down-market restaurant. It owes a lot to David Mamet and not a little to Marber's own passion for gambling when he was at Oxford. I didn't find out until after the the programme that he is the son of Brian Marber, who was a leading Footlight in the Jonathan Miller, Frederic Raphael, Leslie Bricusse era. Brian did a very funny solo act with a malleable standard lamp. I should have identified Patrick as Brian's son. They are both pear shaped. I gather Brian always regretted going into money and not entertainment. Still perhaps it enabled him to bail out his son during his early gambling sprees.

Dan Freedman and Nick Romero were on the show. They are very young and do a double act for us which is often very funny. Dan had pleaded to be on this week because Nichelle Nichols was coming. Never having seen *Star Trek* to my knowledge, I knew nothing about her but Dan is an abject fan and was thrilled with a passionate embrace after Emma Freud had interviewed her. Cherie Lunghi talked about her new mini-series, Edith Wharton's unfinished *The Buccaneers*. It is another lavish costume drama. Cherie refused to be drawn into the controversy aroused by the way in which the adapter, Maggie Wadey, has added a dash of homosexuality and a rape.

As I was scanning the papers before doing *Loose Ends* I was confronted by a nicely vicious article and caricature in the *Independent* magazine.

THE GOOD, THE GREAT & THE UGLY
No. 96. Ned Sherrin

I see Ned Sherrin is presenting the 'Nibbies' this year. What on earth are they?
They're awards for people in the book trade: booksellers, publishers and so on. They're spiffing little objects in the shape of a nib, hence the name.

And what's that got to do with Ned?
Nothing much, except that, like the British book industry, he has been more successful producing books – novels, short stories, humour, autobiography – than selling them. he's probably best known for his collections of anecdotes, such as *In His Anecdotage*.

Very droll. And what kind of anecdotes are they?
Familiar ones. For instance, there's the one about the time when Madame de Gaulle was asked what she most wanted in life and she replied 'a penis'. And then the General stepped in and told her, 'In English, it is pronounced "'appiness".' That's the sort of thing.

There must be more to him than that, surely?
Well, he is an energetic broadcaster, in which capacity he gave Esther Rantzen her first break in broadcasting. His Radio 4 *Loose Ends* survives year in, year out, even though it's mostly Ned droning on about 'Binkie' Beaumont with the three or four other people left in Britain who know who he was.

And he does a panel game, doesn't he?
Yes, *Counterpoint*, a musical quiz show covering everything 'from Boney M to *La Bohème*', as *Radio Times* puts it.

Very upmarket. But how did he acquire this breathtaking command of show-business?
It started after he arrived at Oxford, the star-struck scion of a down-to-earth Somerset family, and immediately got stuck into student theatre. *The Sleeping Beauty* he directed for the Oxford University Dramatic Society was widely considered a great improvement on the previous year's effort.

Why?

Because that had starred Ned Sherrin as the Fairy Queen. And Nigel Lawson was in the chorus.

I see. Was that the end of his acting career?

It seems to have been. After Oxford, he read for the Bar, but changed his mind and went into television. He created *That Was The Week That Was*, of course, along with Bernard Levin and David Frost, and has produced and directed films, plays, musicals, radio and television programmes ever since. Prolific is his middle name.

I thought that was George?

Don't be so literal-minded.

The 'Whipless' Tories continue to be vocal. In his *A Bag of Boiled Sweets* Julian Critchley recalls the brief and legendary career as a Conservative Whip of Sir Walter Bromley-Davenport, the exuberant MP for Sevenoaks. In the 1950s Whips were posted to discourage MP's from sneaking off home. Sir Walter pursued one errant member and booted him up the arse. It turned out to belong to the Belgian Ambassador. War was averted but Bromley-Davenport was replaced by a younger member – Edward Heath.

There is a new edition of *Who's Who*. Some are more Who than others. David Frost's entry mentions his own name 45 times. Barbara Cartland lists the 22 novels she wrote *in the previous year*. As far as I can see Pat Arrowsmith is the only entrant to admit to having been in prison. Kurt Waldheim and President Mitterrand both appear to have had very uneventful wars.

I got into *Who's Who* in 1970. Caryl Brahms and I were being interviewed by the *Sunday Times*. She boasted that I was only in the book as a footnote to her entry. The remark was printed and I received a form from the publishers of the book on the Tuesday morning after the article came out. Caryl was furious!

Seventy-seventh birthday of Sir Clive Bossom, former MP. I never see Clive without remembering Churchill on his father's name: 'Bossom? It is neither one thing nor the other!'

Sunday 5th February

A quiet day at home. Magdalena Buznea, the émigré Romanian actress, came to see me. She usually comes on Saturdays. She brings me a loaf of homebaked bread. However, yesterday she was in Chichester with her friend Lizzie Hunter. She is always 'Lizzie Hunter', never 'Lizzie' or 'Ms Hunter'. Magdalena has become fascinated by LH's new computer. She has also discovered Schopenhauer. She has run through Aristotle, Plato and Descartes. Schopenhauer suits her mood this week. As Lorenz Hart wrote for his culture-snob stripper in *Pal Joey*:

'I was reading Schopenhauer last night;
And I think that Schopenhauer – was right.'

Keith Waterhouse's birthday. Sixty-six. That shock of white hair over bland, pink cheeks reminds me of David Hockney on the wrinkled old W.H. Auden. 'I kept thinking, if his face looks like this what must his balls look like?'

Monday 6th February

A crowded afternoon. The final of *Counterpoint* at the Wigmore Hall at three. Poor Sarah Tompsett, the PA, fell down the stairs and twisted her ankle which swelled up to the size of a cricket ball. She was far too faint to score so Jo Clegg the producer, had to. It was an exciting final played with the usual good humour: *Counterpoint* contestants are invariably keen but chivalrous.

On to the Theatre Museum (I'm on the Development Committee) for the opening of the exhibition 'Picturing the Players' – the collection of Somerset Maugham's Theatrical paintings which he left to the National Theatre. They don't have a good space to exhibit them and during their custodianship a couple disappeared. Everyone was keeping tactfully quiet about this. There was a big establishment turnout and a lot of Maugham relatives and descendants. Maugham sold his main art collection – Picasso, Monet, Matisse, Renoir, etc. – in 1961 because he was weary of storing the paintings in a bank in Marseilles when he went travelling. Art thefts were just becoming fashionable on the Riviera. He replaced them with the Zoffanys, De

Wildes and Hamiltons. Rumbling in the background was an acrimonious dispute with his daughter Eliza about the ownership of the main collection.

It was splendid to see the bravura theatricality of the Zoffanys, especially in 'the flesh' as it were – particularly the *Venice Preserved* and Garrick in drag as Sir John Brute in *The Provok'd Wife*. Mary Soames made a brisk enthusiastic speech.

Michael Codron (producer) was there. They have just started rehearsing his revival of *The Killing of Sister George* with Miriam Margolyes in the old Beryl Reid role. Michael said he had been teasing Miriam about a new romance with an older person and had expressed surprise thinking that her tastes ran to younger things. 'Oh no, Michael,' she denied, looking at his shock of white hair, 'I should find you very handsome if you were a man . . .' and tailed off in apologies realising what she had said.

Coincidentally a play of Robin Maugham's novel *The Servant* is to be staged in Birmingham. The novel was based on fact. Robin had a servant in his house in Fulham in the 1950s: '[He] was an excellent servant, softly moving and soft-voiced, he would glide silently around the house' he wrote in his autobiography, *Escape from the Shadows*. 'But there was something about him which made me shudder each time he'd come into the room.' On one occasion in his basement room he offered Robin his naked 14-year-old 'nephew' – an incipient blackmail attempt which Maugham refused.

When the novel came out Robin's dreaded father, Viscount Maugham, the former Lord Chancellor, was so shocked that he suggested buying up all the copies to be destroyed. Only the intervention of Harold Nicolson saved the day.

After the pictures I went on to the Shaftesbury Theatre to see the much-vaunted Théâtre de Complicité in *The Three Lives of Lucie Cabrol*. It has been lavishly praised and there is a certain energy in the way the actors bang around on the stage and crash planks and pretend to be peasants. However, the dialogue they have extracted from John Berger's book is naive and unfocused. It was a bit like an underpowered Gallic *Cold Comfort Farm* and I longed to close my eyes and listen to the omnibus version of *The Archers*.

I escaped in time to have a bowl of stracciatella at Giovanni's before taking Stephanie Cole to the Pizza on the Park to hear Ann

Hampton Calloway. 'Ah,' said the Maître d' at Giovanni's sunnily when I told him I was collecting Steph, 'you are Stephanie 'usband!' I disabused him. Ann only got in from New York on the Sunday and was still jet-lagged. She's a game girl with a great range and a bubbling sense of humour. She bravely ploughed on and won over the second house. She was somewhat handicapped when it came to her virtuoso improvisations in a song constructed around names yelled from the audience. Never having heard of Camilla Parker-Bowles proved a definite handicap.

Fran Landesman (the American poet and lyricist of 'Spring Can Really Hang You Up the Most' and 'All the Sad Young Men') was nearby. She's been away and didn't know about *A Passionate Woman*. I said she would enjoy it – and empathise with Stephanie's role – a wife whose husband constantly disappointed her. Fran looked me sternly in the eye and said firmly, 'Mr Landesman has never disappointed me!' I was rightly rebuked and wondered what the word should have been. Surprised. Astonished? Exasperated?

The *Sun* has reported that Jeremy Paxman is Europe's new heart-throb 'because of his huge conk'. It's a good job the news wasn't broken in the *Guardian*.

Tuesday 7th February

Ugh! To Finchley Road with Frank Coachworth, who tries to make sense of my accounts, to talk to the accountants who try to keep the Inland Revenue at bay. The problem is always having a high profile and a comparatively small income. Apparently life has become a bit easier since I got rid of a company and divorced, at a stroke as it were, a particularly suspicious inspector. However there's an awful lot of tax to pay, although by the end of the meeting it began to seem as though we might, with luck, be able to find most of it.

To Arthur Smith's new play *Live Bed Show* at the Garrick. I saw it in Edinburgh a few years ago when Arthur played it himself with Caroline Quentin (married to Paul Merton). He has added about a half an hour for Paul Merton who replaces him: Mrs Merton is still in it. It's still funny – almost a revue set around a bed, dealing with all sorts of aspects of love, sex, marriage and relationships, with some very good one-liners. However, the extra thirty minutes, taking it to an hour and a half (no interval) cries out for some suggestion of a story line to hold one's attention. I was dozing soon after the curtain went up – I like to get my sleep over early – when through the snooze I heard my name called from the stage. I awoke quickly. In one of the episodes Paul had to wake from a nightmare and say, 'What's Ned Sherrin doing in my dream?' At least it got a laugh. Caryl Brahms and I once went to see a revue at Richmond in which we heard we were being sent up and found ourselves the subject of a *This is Your Life* sketch. Caryl was played by Jimmy Kenney with an enormous false nose and I was 'given' by Charmiane Innes who, for some reason we never fathomed, was wearing a white naval officer's uniform. The packed audience plainly had no idea who either of us was and refused to laugh even once during the six- or seven-minute débâcle. The sketch had long gone when the revue came to London and flopped at the Mayfair.

On to a party in Neal's Yard where Arthur had gathered most of the New Comedy Establishment. I teased Vernon Laurence who now seems to control the whole of commercial television about the ridiculous policy of only booking new series if they have established stars; and Annabel Giles. She has a new boyfriend who runs a despatch rider service and looks like one of his employees.

Yippee! The novel is finished. I've never been more thankful to write 'THE END'. It has ended happily. What will be the fate of the book? The last package has gone off to Christine Motley to type. It does always look *slightly* better in typescript than in longhand.

Eric Cantona has been seen at Manchester Airport with that other top striker, Arthur Scargill. Will police bring the additional charge – consorting with a miner?

Wednesday 8th February

A small sensation at PM's Question Time. Major calls Blair a 'dimwit'. According to the *OED* a fairly modern word of US origin. In 1925 the *New Yorker* discredited an 'archduke as a sort of royal dim wit'. My dictionary of American slang simply says '= boob'.

On its property page *The Times* oddly describes a thatched house in Ibsley, Hampshire, which they say Nelson bought for his mistress, 'Josephine' . . .? '*Pas ce soir, Emma*'?

Tomorrow is the National Book Awards prize-giving at the Hilton, the Nibbies. I went to GLR to give it a plug on the Johnny Walker mid-morning show. An amiable DJ whom I had not met before. An enjoyably vacuous twenty minutes. The best thing about going to GLR is Blagdons – the fish shop round the corner in Paddington Street. I collected some fish and a bottle of lobster bisque. The hire-car man got very stroppy and insisted it all went into the boot. I gave in with ill grace.

To the Theatre Museum to hear a rehearsed reading of a musical of *Mapp and Lucia* with Fenella Fielding and Gaye Brown. Met at the door by a downcast Margaret Benton who runs the Museum. The do was heavily oversold and there was no room for me or Robert Meadmore and Mark Greenstreet who arrived at the same time. We went across the road to Brahms & Liszt and got through three bottles of Chardonnay instead. One person who did get in reported later that the book was splendid but the songs had little to do with it. Good decision!

I went on to the Donmar to see Jeremy Sams's new translation of *The Threepenny Opera* sprawling lackadaisically across the stage. It is set in the next century on the eve of Prince William's coronation and slackly staged by Phyllida Lloyd who did such a good job on *Six Degrees of Separation*. Two good performances, the wide boy Macheath, Tom Hollander, and Tara Hugo as Jenny, who had a good and gutsy go at 'Mack the Knife'. Give me *The Beggar's Opera* every time.

Tonight they are due to transmit my *This is Your Life*. It was recorded before Christmas. I had got off the plane from Singapore at 5.30 in the morning, gone home, washed, picked up the mail and phone messages, and prepared to go to Broadcasting House to have lunch with Ian Gardhouse and David Hatch, a radio panjandrum, to discuss 'my future'. My manager Deke Arlon was to come too and we were meeting at my house at 12 to get to Broadcasting House at 12.30. The taxi came early, Deke was late. I should have suspected something when the driver started to talk about having to arrive at 'exactly 12.30' but nothing was further from my mind. Deke eventually panted up having come out with no money. I lent him £10 to pay off his taxi. I had two huge boxes of Singapore orchids and apparently caused more anxiety by insisting on dropping one off at the Comedy Theatre for the cast of *A Passionate Woman*. We eventually got to BH at 12.45 – murderous traffic in Regent Street – and I made for reception to hand over the *Loose Ends* orchids. Here I was diverted to a screened-off corner by an anxious Gardhouse to be confronted by most of the radio regulars past and present screaming like banshees. I couldn't understand why we were having another 400th edition celebration party until I saw a distinctly grey-looking Michael Aspel emerge from the throng with his bloody book. My first thought was that I had arranged to see the Mercury Revue that night at the Jermyn Street Theatre and someone would have to cancel the tickets.

It is a very odd procedure. You are isolated from the moment of 'the snatch' until you walk on to the set and no hint is given of who is to be on the programme. I did manage to squeeze a bottle of vodka and some smoked salmon sandwiches out of John Gordon, the pleasant Thames producer who was chaperoning me along with Deke. I had been asked about five years ago if I minded and decided I didn't particularly if there was something to plug.

I should have rumbled something when I was asked on to Stephanie Cole's *Life* just before I left for Singapore and not asked to pay vocal tribute; but I just dismissed it as bad programme making. I gather it took five years for them to get an agreed cast together. It is quite a good game speculating about who is going to turn up and I got almost everyone right – except that I hadn't expected such a large contingent from Somerset – plus Kay Mellor, Douglas Bunn and Mervyn Stockwood. At least Stephanie got a chance to meet her idol Mervyn at last before he died.

My brother Alfred stole the show as usual. He was followed by Cliff Michelmore and Alan Whicker generously remembering the old *Tonight* days. By now I was becoming very bossy, correcting poor Aspel about where I started my TV career and embarrassing Whicker with a story of how we once went together to a Heather Jenner St Valentine's Day party for eligible bachelors and were mistaken for 'an item'. Michael Upsall from my old school, Sexey's Bruton, was wheeled on to cover that bit. Willie Rushton, Ken Cope and Lance Percival rolled in together for *TW3* with Frostie on film. Similarly David Kernan and Julia McKenzie represented *Side By Side By Sondheim* with Milly Martin pre-recorded.

Kernan told the story of the ample black maid, 'Lily', who looked after us in New York – once she knew we were working in a theatre she always called us 'You actresses'. Julia had tried to start on one of my favourite stories so I decided to take it over. It's better as a story against the teller. Coming out of the stage door on 44th Street one night I fell arse-over-tip into the gutter. Two emerging playgoers – in retrospect vicious queens – looked down on me in contempt. The one said to the other, 'Funnier than anything she did on the stage!' Poor Julia. It meant that after editing she had said nothing and was left to get off mute. Marion Montgomery and Lis Welch represented the *Song By Song* TV series. Leslie Thomas and Ray Davies (of the Kinks) turned up for *The Virgin Soldiers*. Dennis Waterman was on film to talk about *Jeffrey Bernard is Unwell*. Poor Jeffrey, in a wheelchair, minus one leg, was in the studio and furious afterwards at not being allowed to say anything. Dennis was ribald about my directing skills, and quoted me along the lines of, 'Try and do it more like Peter, dear, I think it's time for a Chardonnay.' Pat Hodge, looking lovely, evoked *The Mitford Girls*, and the final guest was Sondheim.

This was hardly a surprise. Although the traditional 'Specially flown in from New York' phrase was used I knew he was in the country. This is the spot usually reserved for tiny grandchildren 'specially flown in from New Zealand'. The audience goes 'Ah!' as the little tots totter towards grandpa's embrace. As I have no grandchildren in New Zealand or anywhere else I shall now look on Steve as my honorary grandson.

It was all very jolly. I had been asking for a Valium, usually effective at stopping my upper lip quivering in moments of emotion. However, there weren't any and I did not notice the lack. We partied in the canteen afterwards. Red and white wine, cold cuts and quiches. The Somerset contingent tucked into the food with gusto, particularly admiring the beef. Dear Lis Welch was a little disorientated and when David Kernan asked if he could give her a lift home said, 'No, honey, they've got me a room here at the Savoy.'

It all broke up around seven so that the West Country party could get to Paddington. I gather that Alfred sent my nephew David to the buffet car to round up all the available whisky miniatures and they had a triumphant journey home to Castle Cary station.

It's a bit like being 'Queen for a day'. They give you a driver who stays with you until dismissed. Mine had a lucky night as I was home by eight and he was free. When we recorded Stephanie's (after the play) he didn't get home until five a.m.

It was a bizarre experience to watch it back when I got home from *The Threepenny Opera*. I was acutely conscious that Mervyn has died since we recorded it. So has Lorna. So have John Osborne and Peter Cook. For once I had managed to get the taping right. They did a good job of the editing, though the director might have managed one slow pan across the 'home team'. No close-ups of Mervyn, Stephanie, Douglas or Kay Mellor and no group shot in which the Somerset contingent could recognise themselves. Half a dozen encouraging calls on the answerphone.

Thursday 9th February

TIYL much admired in the King's Road shops. Two old ladies stopped me separately to say how nice it was to see 'somebody dignified. Not all that kissing!'

'Nibbie' time at the Hilton. The award turns out to be cast in the shape of a pen-nib – which shows just how foolish I have been to try to work out the acronym. The place was packed with Folletts and Delia Smiths and all manner of authors, publishers, agents and hangers on all sounding very pleased with themselves. It was apparently the biggest turnout they'd had, with 715 of them in the ballroom. Frostie did the prizegiving in 1994 and I was briefed 'not just to do the old jokes like the man last year!' Neil Shand came to my rescue. So did the revelation that John Major in his toy boy days had bought Mrs Kierans a subscription to *Reader's Digest*. It's almost more pleasurable to provoke a shocked gasp than a laugh. We certainly managed it with the news that P.D. James was in America – 'She's working on a gardening book – plenty of advice on how to turn over an old plot.' (She has pleaded innocent to the charge that her new novel echoes a much earlier thriller by Michael Innes.)

Martin Amis was an obvious target. 'Naturally Martin Amis hasn't got back from his New York dentist in time. I had a preview when I was over there. I've seen better caps at a miner's gala. An American friend said, "The last time I saw a bridge like that Edward Kennedy was driving off it." Amis's new piranha team of agents were said to have come straight from a special screening of *Jaws*. It was played backwards. That way they got a happy ending.' Neil also had a good list of celebrity books. 'Bruce Forsyth's wigmaker heads the charts with *From Rugs to Riches*, Boris Yeltsin has a new travel book, *Europe on Five Bottles a Day*, and Elizabeth Hurley is working on a fashion volume – that's a pop-out book.' We welcomed the poetry revival. Before *Four Weddings and a Funeral* most people thought that Auden was a German car.

It went rather well, I think. When I got back to the Virgin table – I'd had a choice of three publishers with Christopher Sinclair-Stevenson and OUP in the room as well – my neighbours seemed pleased.

Alan Bennett, as usual, stole the evening. He got Book of the Year, winning, I would guess, over Jonathan Dimbleby's Prince of Wales tome with his *Writing Home*. Funny and graceful, he evoked the book-plugging tour and the soulless staff rooms in countless Waterstones shops where he had been condemned to sit signing copies 'for stock'. Always there was a nylon shirt drying on a hook, socks on a radiator and a half-eaten pizza. He shared some dates with Peter Carey, the Australian novelist who had 'a much more Calvinistic attitude than mine'. Carey refused to sign 'for Mum and Dad' on the grounds that the parents in question were not *his* mum and dad. Alan had no such scruples. On one occasion, to the often-reiterated question 'will you put . . .?' Alan found himself writing 'Sorry about last night, I won't do it again, Alan Bennett.' He is now haunted by the dreadful fear of what some future biographers, some eager Humphrey Carpenter, will one day make of it.

Rob Shreeve of Virgin asked hopefully of this diary, 'Will it be scandalous?' Small chance. And I met one of Virgin's new editors. A pleasant, keen young man called Mal. I felt a bit guilty as in *A Passionate Woman* Kay Mellor's leading character, Betty, is relent-lessly contemptuous of her sister's younger 'fancy-man' and of his name – which is also Mal. Virgin Mal worships at the shrine of Tony Parsons. A perfectly good shrine. But do we both pray facing in the same direction?

Friday 10ᵗʰ February

Another radio station to talk about the Nibbies. God knows what good it does anyone. This time it was London Talk Radio in Hammersmith. The interviewer was Petroc Trelawney, who also does Classic FM. He is one of those eager, young, puppy-dog interviewers who you can imagine shagging your leg and wagging his tail while he lobs comments enthusiastically at you instead of questions.

At the *Loose Ends* office I found a very fiery, disapproving letter addressed to 'someone called Ned Sherrin' from Joan Plowright. I had rudely referred to her friend Maggie Wadey (the adapter of *The Buccaneers*), as 'someone called...' last week. I was in the wrong and wrote a crawling apology. Joan had signed herself 'someone called Joan Plowright (Lady Olivier)'.

Freddie Forsyth and James Elroy, both came to *Loose Ends* bearing books. That meant a lot of words to read. Both books weave fiction around world events. Forsyth's *The Fist of God*, the Gulf War. Elroy's *American Tabloid*, the build-up to Kennedy's assassination. I found his staccato, violent style particularly hard to follow. He has two separate lists of Marilyn Monroe's alleged lovers: 'Allan Freed, Betty Eikstein, Freddie Otash, Rin Tin Tin's trainer, Jon "Rumar of the Jungle" Hall, her pool cleaner, two pizza-delivery boys and her maid's husband.' Thirty pages later he adds 'Louis Prima, two off-duty marines, Franchot Tone, Yves Montand, Stan Kenton, David Seville of David Seville and the Chipmunks. Four pizza-delivery boys, bantamweight battler "Fighting Harada" and a disc-jockey at an all-spook R & B station.' Is it coincidence that almost all the suspects are either dead or unidentifiable?

His next book – a factual investigation of the murder of his mother when he was ten, so far unsolved – sounds more interesting.

There was an extraordinary young actress, Kate Winslet, who plays one of the two teenage murderers in a New Zealand film, *Heavenly Creatures*. She was amazingly articulate and composed – and, like her co-criminal, very good in the film amidst a mass of school-of-Ramsay-Street Antipodean writing and acting. I hope she sticks to acting and doesn't dwindle into being a TV presenter. She thinks she's got a part in Emma Thompson's *Sense and Sensibility*.

Peter Greenwell sang 'Mrs Worthington' and the recently unveiled male verse 'Mad About the Boy' which Graham Payn publishes in his new Coward *Memoir*. It was written for the 1935 New York revue *Set to Music* – the US version of *Words and Music* – to be sung by a dapper businessman in formal black coat and striped trousers in a smart office setting. All the verses are sung to or about a screen idol. It was dropped as 'too shocking'. Coward had fun with his rhymes:

> ... And even Doctor Freud cannot explain
> Those vexing dreams
> I've had about the boy ...

Getting desperate for 'boy' rhymes, he comes up triumphantly with:

> ... People I employ
> Have the impertinence
> To call me Myrna Loy ...

It sounded like a perfect encore for Peter's Chichester concert.

I told Freddie Forsyth of Denis Thatcher's admiration for his books – a fact of which he is all too well aware. Denis is impressed by the mixture of real and fictional characters. I suggested that Mrs Thatcher was his most vivid creation and his hero, Mike Martin, more of a real person.

It was Mike Coleman's last monologue on this stint. He came across a Mr Michael Howard in Leeds who, having been charged £20 for a £10 overdraft changed his name by deed poll to 'Yorkshire Bank are Fascist Bastards PLC'. In the present political climate it sounds much nicer than being called Michael Howard.

Mike also noted that Club 18–30, who have been told to advertise other attractions on their holidays besides sex, have failed to come up with any.

I got home to receive a telephone call from Foyle's. Christina generously wants to give a lunch for me in March. The suggestion was that it should be a general 'honouring' one. I think she must have seen *This Is Your Life*. I pointed out that the *Oxford Dictionary of Humorous Quotations* will be out any day so we can deal that into the equation. I hope someone turns up. I've enjoyed my other two Foyle's lunches.

Sunday 12ᵗʰ February

To Chichester to see Peter Greenwell's one-man show *A Talent to Amuse*. Undiluted Noël Coward and the better for it. Greenwell has most artfully put together two hours of vintage and unfamiliar Coward. The 1350-seater was full. The performance was precise, musicianly and very funny. There was no attempt to force the pace or flag the jokes and the personal anecdotes were cleverly chosen. He was Coward's last accompanist and won the old boy's confidence by doing his homework. When Coward asked him to play 'Mrs Worthington' at his 'audition' he inquired brightly, 'In E flat?', knowing it was Coward's favourite key. 'Ah,' said Coward, 'I knew we were destined to be lovers.' Peter says that one night after a show a spooky man met him at the stage door and said, 'Were you really Coward's lover?' 'No,' said Peter. 'I was,' said the man and vanished into the night.

Coward had a neat way of giving critical notes. After one rehearsal at the Savoy he said to Peter, 'I'm going to have a shower. Why don't you amuse yourself looking at those chords?' Turning back at the bathroom door he added, 'The old boy wrote some rather good ones,' and then lethally, 'and you're not playing them.'

Another day Peter brought in an *Evening Standard* with a prominent article about people 'coming out' sexually. Coward digested it, looked up and said, 'Well, here's one person who won't be coming out. There are a lot of old ladies in Goring-by-the-Sea who still harbour designs on my body and I have no intention of disillusioning them now.'

One afternoon Marlene Dietrich was there when Peter arrived. Coward urged him upon her as an accompanist. 'Noël', she said, 'you know I am a grandmother. I know I am a grandmother. If he plays for me, everybody will know I am a grandmother!'

By now a generously rounded Greenwell might almost pass for a grandmother himself. He has done a brilliant setting of the ship's concert from Coward's narrative poem, 'P & O'. I wish he'd set the whole thing as a concert piece for piano, orchestra, and narrator.

The only wrong decision was to include a speech from *Pont Valaine* of doubtful relevance. When I saw Peter afterwards I said it was all wonderful – 'But you won't be doing *Pont Valaine* again.' He hooted with laughter and is wisely going to cut it.

I drove down with his agent, Michael Ladkin, who sent out 50 invitations to theatrical managers. Only five replied and none turned up. George Biggs of Mayfair Theatre had told me he would come but didn't. When I compare the sheer joy of the evening with the depression which settled on me a few nights earlier as I watched a lacklustre *Threepenny Opera* in his Donmar Warehouse it beggars belief.

I took Glen Roven with us. For him it was a revelation both of material (Coward's) and finesse in performance (Greenwell's).

Tuesday 14ᵗʰ February

Valentine's Day – none.

A day for talking to apprentices. One Richard Selwyn Barret is trying to make a documentary film about Marty Feldman: 'None of my generation seem to have heard of him.' Marty died a couple of days before Caryl Brahms in December 1982. I gave Barret David Nathan's book *The Laughtermakers*.

Just after he left, a boy called Sholto from the Peterborough column called. When Juliet Stevenson died last night in *The Duchess of Malfi* at Greenwich she had a posthumous fit of coughing. Could I suggest other rib-tickling post-death distractions? Unwisely I gave him the apocryphal story of Donald Wolfit encouraging an actor who was due to slay him and had forgotten to bring on the weapon hissing, 'Kick me,' and then expiring crying, 'The boot was poisoned!'

After he had rung off, I got down Gyles Brandreth's *Theatrical Disasters*. In my *Theatrical Anecdotes* I tried to avoid stories of 'The scenery fell down – oh how we laughed!' order. But Gyles has Gielgud touring *Hamlet* in India during the war in a military chapel in Rangoon. Gertrude's train sent clouds of dust flying. The corpse sneezed. Reproached, Gertrude protested, 'I don't really feel like a queen unless I can fling my train.'

Another actor's body was racked by sneezes when he played the corpse in Agatha Christie's *Who Killed Roger Ackroyd?*, an effect emphasised by the rise and fall of a dagger sticking conspicuously out of his back.

In 1926 on the third night of *The Constant Nymph* Edna Best died and Noël Coward (as per script) lifted her body on to a bed and threw up the window to say, 'Tessa's got away; she's safe; she's dead.' He was then due to burst into tears as the curtain fell. On the third night the sash cord broke so Coward got as far as 'Tessa's got away; she's safe; she's *ow!*' as the frame smashed down on his hand. She sat up and laughed and so did the audience.

I'll bet 'Sholto' uses the apocryphal Wolfit.

To the Theatre Royal, Stratford in the evening for *Zorro*. Poor Ken Hill, author and director of the show, died during rehearsals. Gaye Brown drove me down with her son Charlie, and Juan, a Spanish school mate from the Oratory. Toni Palmer, Ken's widow, had returned to rehearsals on the day of his death and the theatre was heavy with emotion – Victor Spinetti, Lionel Bart, Peter Docherty. They were also buzzing with excitement at Joan Littlewood's return to her theatre for the first time in God knows how many years. Gaye's friend Brian Berry had met Joan when she arrived from Paris via the Chunnel.

She was said to be holding court in the gallery and was threatening to make a curtain speech. It didn't happen; but she told Spinetti, after she had been confronted by the riot of crimson plush redecoration, 'At one time I was the only red thing in this theatre.'

I read that it is the hundredth anniversary of the first night of *The Importance of Being Earnest*. A new biography of Lord Salisbury (the Prime Minister) by Frances Stewart explores the undertones of homosexuality in the play. It is suggested that Wilde was attacking the grandee Tory family of Cecil (Salisbury) whose family motto is 'Late but in Earnest'. The word 'earnest' was Victorian slang for homosexual. Also, one of the girls is called Cecily, and both young men in the play lead *double lives*.

The release of the latest State Papers includes an account of the wartime internment of Sir Oswald and Lady Mosley. Julian Critchley once made a visit to Birch Grove to lunch with Harold Macmillan which he records in his autobiography *A Bag of Boiled Sweets*. Asked about Mosley, Macmillan said: 'He came to see me once and said, "Harold, I'm thinking of putting my people into black shirts." "Tom," I replied, "you must be mad. Whenever the British people feel strongly about anything they wear grey flannels and tweed jackets." '

There have also been revelations in the papers about the painting done by the Brontë sisters. The great-grandfather of my friend Michael Hill was a farmer at Hawarth. He knew the family well and (according to Michael's father who as a young boy heard it from him) often gave the Brontë girls a ride in his trap. On one occasion great-grandfather was dining at the Rectory when Patrick Brontë (the girls' dad) suddenly got up from the table and fired a shotgun out of the window with no explanation. Perhaps the wayward Branwell was up to something?

Wednesday 15th February

I was right about Sholto and the Wolfit story.

Dinner chez Irving Davies with two other choreographers, Lindsay Dolan and David Toguri. Heavy with reminiscence. Lindsay and Irving have staged many musicals for me and Toguri was our leading dancer on *Not so Much a Programme* – Alan Bennett christened them 'The VietCong dancers' and when David left and was replaced by René Sartoris, handsome French/Swiss, they became 'the Pompidou Dancers'.

On to a Lebanese restaurant in Shaftesbury Avenue for a farewell supper for John Berger, the company manager for *A Passionate Woman*, who is leaving to join the *Oliver!* company. Noisy.

The Mile High club became respectable today. (My only opportunity was on Pan Am from Washington in the sixties.) The breakthrough came when an American couple were married in a Boeing 747 at 35,000 feet. The priest said, 'I've never held a wedding so close to God.' According to British law a marriage ceremony can only be performed in 'a place that is stationary'. Since an Act of 1837 the idea of marriage by ship's captains has been a myth for novelists and scriptwriters.

Thursday 16th February

A very ambitious workshop of *The Three Musketeers* by George Styles (music), Paul Leigh (lyrics) and Peter Ralny (book). It was long, but full of invention. A charming D'Artagnan, singing splendidly (Hal Fowler) and a first-class clown playing Planchet in Nick Holder.

I sat with Wendy Toye and we were both impressed. But will it find a stage, I wonder. It would have to be expensive.

Met Glen Roven at the Groucho to go to the first night of Simon Gray's *Cell Mates* at the Albery. Big turnout of Alternative Comedy

Establishment. I am told the play has been doing the rounds of managements for some time and that Gray finally badgered Stephen Fry (as George Blake) and Rik Mayall (the Irishman who sprang him) to star in it. It started promisingly in prison but got thinner as the evening wore on. Not helped by Gray's determination to direct and the long unwieldy scene changes. Stephen was a touch tentative but Mayall excellent with great energy. Small parts well played.

There is a headline clanger in *The Times*. '*Child Ryhmes* [*sic*] help to Sort the Sexes.' Apart from the misspelling the answer was given by the witty late Paul Dehn when he wrote:

Hey, diddle diddle, my son John
Went to bed with his trousers on.
So much better than my son Bert
Who went to bed in his sister's skirt.

Friday 17th February

First notices for *Cell Mates*. Lukewarm for play and Stephen. Lunch at Bibendum with Greenwell, Ian Keil, his long-time friend, and Michael Ladkin, his agent. Much talk of plans for perpetuating the one-man show. What he needs is a manager.

In the evening to the NFT with David Warbeck to hear the near soft-porn kitsch movie director Russ Meyer's *Guardian* interview with Jonathan Ross – after a screening of his ghastly black-and-white melodrama *Faster, Pussycat, Kill Kill Kill*. Meyer is on *Loose Ends* tomorrow. Warbeck starred in his slave movie *Blacksnake* with Anouska Hempel. Meyer was ribald about Miss Hempel's lack of 'cantilevering'; but, skilfully interviewed by Jonathan, he was very funny, especially about losing his virginity. He was in the army when France was retaken and met Ernest Hemingway who insisted on taking his platoon to the local brothel. Ignorant of the procedure, Meyer asked a fellow soldier, a Southern hick, how old he had been when he lost his. 'Fourteen,' said the boy. 'How old was the girl?' Meyer asked. 'Hell, no! It was a chicken,' was the reply.

Saturday 18ᵗʰ February

Birthday. Sixty-four. Listed in *The Times*, *Telegraph* and *Independent*. Shunned by the communist *Guardian*!

Howard Brenton on *Loose Ends* was much more charming and amusing than I had imagined from the rather dour press he gets or gives. He was perceptive about John Dexter rehearsing his fine translation of Brecht's *The Life of Galileo* at the National. He and Dexter were suspicious of each other – key figures from two different generations of Royal Courtiers. 'John, I learnt later when we got to know each other, told me that for most of the rehearsals he was convinced I was going off each evening to a committee of "comrades in leather jackets" from whom I received my orders for what I would say in next day's rehearsal.'

Russ Meyer trod a very skilful tightrope, managing to project his raunchy image in acceptable broadcasting language. We did not get the virginity story. He likes his artists to refrain from sex during shoots. He developed bosomania at the age he started looking at the gigantic breasts in Al Capp's *Li'l Abner* strip, and his latest discovery is called Pandora Peaks. He was funny about being summoned before British Equity and asked by council member Miriam Karlin, 'to tell us what he means by fully cantilevered and gorgeous'.

The monologue opened with Eric Cantona, who very sensibly violently threatened an ITN reporter who interrupted his family holiday in Guadeloupe. 'ITN later admitted that Kate Adie was not available.' It was also the week of appalling behaviour by rioting English soccer fans in Dublin. As Neil Shand wrote, 'where was Eric Cantona when we needed him?'

I had a mad taxi driver to take me home after my weekly Waitrose visit. He has an obsession about criminals who impersonate policemen. 'That Colin Stagg,' (the man acquitted of murdering the girl, Rachel Nickell, on Wimbledon Common), ''e wears high heels under his uniform. It's a disguise. You can't tell his height. An' there was another one – look at this,' he handed me a form, ''E nicked me for goin' the wrong way up a one-way street.' There was a spelling mistake, 'buisness' but the second suggestion, that 'Cort travening a no entry sign' was a nonsense, didn't hold up. The copper had plainly written, or nearly written 'Contravening'. The taxi driver wasn't having any of it. 'There's false policemen everywhere. They're not real. They're all over the M25.'

There is a new biography by Jane Ridley, *The Young Disraeli*. 'Bisexuality came as naturally to Disraeli as Tory Radicalism.' It calls to mind one of de Gaulle's rare jokes. 'Marshal Lyantey [Governor of Morocco] is our only marshal with any balls on him. What a pity they are not always his own.'

Sunday 19th February

There is a legal battle going on between a chap who bought some land from Harrods and formed a school there called Harrodian. Harrods don't want him to use the name. There was once an equally opportunist bloke called Albert Hall who started up an orchestra. He was legally restrained.

Lots of odd bits of news are trickling out of Italy alongside the major scandals. Father Reginald Foster, the Pope's Latin Secretary, a jocular fellow, has unearthed a bit of ancient graffiti in Rome. It is a more radical version of 'An apple a day keeps the doctor away': it reads, '*Caca et declina medicus*' – 'Shit well and avoid doctors.'

Back in Italy Prince Carlo Ruspoli, who runs a charm school in Rome, is reported as saying, 'It is all very well knowing where your four forks go on the dinner table but it's no good if you then stick one of them in your neighbour's eye when you don't agree with something he says.' Browsing through the Sunday papers also reveals that yet another Kennedy is running for political office – which triggers a recollection of Macmillan's quip when the Kennedys first moved into Washington in 1960: 'It was rather like watching the Borgia brothers take over a respectable north Italian town.'

Still on an international note, the most useful phrase in a new Greek phrasebook for tourists is: 'Wait, I am looking for the phrase in this book.' The late James Cameron, a journalist much given to globe-trotting, was required, when visiting a newly independent African state, to answer the question on a form: 'Sex of wife?'

Monday 20ᵗʰ February

A meeting of the Development Committee of the Theatre Museum in Covent Garden. We meet occasionally to see how we can back up the Director's efforts to mount exhibitions, rebuild and redesign, raise money, claim from the lottery and from the millennium fund.

First night of Sean Mathias's transferred production of *Design for Living* at the Gielgud. It is much improved by the recasting. Rupert Graves and Marcus D'Amico are a huge plus – both with some sense of style and fun, and they also lift the girl, Rachel Weisz. She has had rave notices and is undoubtedly very sexy; but she is also gauche and inexperienced and the new boys have given her a nodding acquaintance with jokes. When I saw the play at the Donmar I admired Sean's detailed exploration of the shifting sexual liaisons and deplored the lack of humour. He needed another week of rehearsal to put back the jokes. Some, at least, are restored by the new actors. Perhaps Sean's absence in New York for a lot of rehearsals helped. The evening still features the worst performance in London for many years from Ms de Villeneuve, a beanpole ex-model in a party scene in Act III.

Odd fact: today is the anniversary of Whitcombe L. Judson's decision to patent the zip fastener. Nowadays the Japanese firm YKK produces millions of them daily. Zips have been held to be a prime aid to the 'sexual revolution'. Certainly they speed up the sexual permutations in *Design for Living*.

The designer of the Spitfire, R.T. Mitchell (played by Leslie Howard in *The First of the Few*) is to be honoured by a Royal Mint Medallion and a postage stamp. Bang in the middle of the 'Not Many People Know That' records is the fact that Supermarine (the company for whom he designed the Spitfire) only survived in the early thirties when they had no aircraft orders by making lavatory seats. So, no loo seats, no Spitfires, no Battle of Britain triumph ... such are the slender threads of history.

Wholly bizarre is the double life of Buster Keaton's widow, Eleanor. She has just turned up at the Berlin Film Festival as Keaton's representative and was also revealed as the dog trainer who coached a St Bernard for his appearance in the new movie, *Beethoven*.

61

Tuesday 21st February

Haircut at the Park Lane hotel. For once no jokes, respectable or not, from Jack Lee, the veteran barber who has, at some time or another, trimmed everyone. His heyday was the fifties when he visited the Palladium each Sunday in case a bob was needed for *Sunday Night At* . . . He was a bit miffed at not being on my *This Is Your Life* – he has appeared on several. However, he did accept that I had not drawn up the guest list.

I have been reading about the founding of a Wodehouse Society to celebrate the twentieth anniversary of his death. According to Christopher Sykes in his biography of Evelyn Waugh there was once a memorable exchange between Waugh and Graham Greene. Greene expressed his hope that, after writing *The End of the Affair*, 'It will be fun to write about politics for a change and not always about God.'

'Oh,' remarked Waugh, 'I wouldn't give up writing about God at this stage if I was you. It would be like P.G. Wodehouse dropping Jeeves halfway through the Wooster series.'

Nicholas Fairbairn, the eccentric, flamboyant Scottish Tory MP, is dead. At one time he ploughed a busy furrow through the beds of the ladies in the BBC's current affairs department. He didn't enjoy one busy presenter, 'because she was a screamer'!

Wednesday 22nd February

It's the week of the great disappearance. Writing this up a couple of days later I had better lump all the Stephen Fry stories into one. Stephen disappeared on Monday. He left notes for his parents, sister, co-star and author-director. Apparently he thinks he is 'letting them all down' by his performance in *Cell Mates*. He did a church charity on Sunday night in Islington, narrating *Peter and the Wolf*, excused himself from the cast party and has not been seen since. I missed the first excitements. Alarm bells started ringing after he was absent from Monday's performance and the understudy played. I heard nothing yesterday or today, when I took a three o'clock train to Manchester to record a television show.

The Mrs Merton Show – the programme – is another of those semi-fictional TV interview shows. Daughter of Dame Edna, a cross between Clive Anderson and Alan Partridge. Caroline Hook, a bright young stand-up comic, appears as a mumsy, nosey, cosy North Country matron asking very rude questions under the excuse of apparent innocence. Her most famous question was to a presenter called Debbie McGee whom she asked innocently, 'Tell me, Debbie, what first attracted you to the millionaire, Paul Daniels?'

OUP pressured me to appear on the show to plug the new *Dictionary of Humorous Quotations*, which has arrived and looks very handsome. I doubt if the plug will remain after editing. She kept pumping for anecdotes and her sharpest shaft was when I talked about buses pulling up outside *A Passionate Woman*. 'Yes, Ned, but is there anyone in them?' The only answer was 'Not during the performance, dear, they're all inside the theatre.'

God knows what the final programme will be like. She had two of the arch bores of all time on the show – Mr Motivator (a black keep-fit fiend) and Terry Major-Ball (the Prime Minister's brother) – a sweet man but unstoppable once started. To see them intrigued by each other in the Green Room was to witness a marriage of true minds. The other guest was Nick Owen of the mid-morning plug-hole – *Good Morning with Anne and Nick* – and he doesn't exactly set the table on a roar.

Thursday 23rd February

It was today that I became aware of Stephen's flight. One's first thought is always 'has something terrible happened to him?' Though it seemed highly unlikely in Stephen's case. However, his colleagues Mayall and Gray were expressing genuine concern. Suggestions of stage fright, overwork and criticism were bandied about. It was a relief to hear that a fellow traveller had seen him on a cross-Channel ferry.

I got back from Manchester to find the usual 20-odd calls that a theatre crisis always spawns – John Sessions's 'stage fright'; Peter Cook's death. Now Stephen's disappearance. The *Standard* and the *Mail* both wanted pieces. The *Standard*'s brief, a light-hearted look at it in defence of Stephen to make up for some of their recent sniping at him, was the more congenial. They gave it the emotive title, 'We should all go on strike for Stephen'.

Recently Stephen has gone aggressively public on his distaste for the popular press. He has come in for more than his fair share of sniping. I doubt if it is the measured criticism that has upset him.

He has been enormously successful, and recognised as such, over the past ten years as a playwright, as the adapter of the book of a hit musical, as a novelist, as a television and theatre comedian, as an actor and as a screenwriter. No wonder he has attracted the attention of the more envious, aspiring hacks. They are required to provide a page of squibs, arbitrarily turning on its head the view which the most sensible hold on any subject. They provide a 'provocative' point of view. That is the brief of the ever-increasing breed of Johnny-come-lately columnists.

What better target for them than a man who is good at almost everything? Even better a man who chooses to opt out of their particular skill, preferring celibacy. The meanest, cheapest stone was thrown by a journalist who advocated something like a 'kick-a-Stephen-Fry-day'. Yob culture rules in the best papers.

Perhaps we should take a lead from Lysistrata, who encouraged her Greek colleagues to absent themselves from the felicity of sex with their husbands until the men abandoned war. 'Theatricals' could decline to receive the press for six months. The border between Fleet Street and Shaftesbury Avenue would be closed, diplomatic and all other relations broken off: a publicity strike called.

Happy in the knowledge that *A Passionate Woman* is running at the Comedy Theatre through the summer, I quite like the idea. Keith Waterhouse's new play is unlikely to be launched until the autumn when the ban could be lifted. The prospect appears doubly attractive.

Of course the strike will lead to some unemployment. The leading show-business writers, Michael Owen, Baz Bamigboye, Robin Stringer, etc. will have time to sit down and write the novels they have been putting off for years. I'm not sure about the critics. I doubt if Stephen's quarrel is really with them. But, then again, if the critics were suddenly banned, the Irving Wardles, the Jeremy Kingstons and the Nicholas de Jonghs who have already toyed with playwriting could be joined by Benedict Nightingale of *The Times* and other ambitious colleagues with time on their hands . . .

Perhaps we could arrange a playwriting course at the Royal Court for critics at a loose end. Michael Billington of the *Guardian* could fulfil his cherished ambition to be a stand-up comic.

Of course Stephen Fry brought a great deal of attention to himself by disappearing. As with Lord Lucan, in more melodramatic circumstances, and Judge Crater in America in the thirties, disappearance breeds legend. So it did with Agatha Christie, and subsequently that spawned a movie too.

There have been less sensational exits from the stage. David Langton, who went on to become the master of the house in *Upstairs, Downstairs*, disappeared from the West End hit *Seagulls Over Sorrento* in the forties and turned up much later in Canada. A star Irish actor left a stage in Dublin, wandering up the aisle and out of the building during a performance of *HMS Pinafore* in the eighties. Alcohol was blamed. But the trusting management still brought him to the Old Vic a couple of years later, adding a frisson of excitement to a dull production.

The earlier actress, Maude Gill, once revived a costume drama and engaged an actor who felt more comfortable in modern clothes. So unhappy was he on the first night that the prospect of playing a love scene in fancy dress with Miss Gill threw him into a panic. When the time came for them to embrace he lost his nerve, forgot his lines and blurted out: 'I fain must leave thee.' Then he walked off the stage and was never seen again.

When Noël Coward had his first hit the pace was different.

> With this success came . . . an extravagant amount of publicity.
> I was photographed and interviewed and photographed again.
> In the street. In the park. In my dressing-room. At my piano.
> With my dear old mother. And on one occasion, sitting up
> in an over-elaborate bed looking like a heavily-doped Chinese
> illusionist.

But Coward had no television series to do in tandem. No radio to speak of. No screenplay deadline. No flights to America to co-star with Walter Matthau all at the same time.

'And if you lose hope, take dope, and lock yourself in the john,' he chorused. 'Why must the show go on?'

Even Coward used to set off around the world after a three-month run in a play to recharge his batteries. Stephen appears to have taken the ferry to Dunkirk. I wish him a safe journey and a reasonably speedy return, the sooner to delight us – and not too much press attention when he gets back.

He must have been under some pressure which he thought was intolerable: but surely could have buckled to. My impression on the first night was that it was Gray's most mediocre play and likely to peter out in a few weeks anyway.

In the evening I went to *Killer Joe* at the Vaudeville; a violent, much-praised American play about 'po' white trash', which I hated. A patina of pretension was applied to B-picture squalor. It was the first night of a transfer from the Bush. I assumed that the curtain would rise at seven and so hurried to arrive in time. In fact it went up at eight, so I was an hour early . . . So was my guest Rick Kerwin (Rick is an ex-dancer – 'Younger Generation', etc. who now has a busy and lucrative career arranging fashion shows). The bonus was that we went across to the Savoy and had delicious native oysters and a bottle of Chablis which should have made the play seem better but didn't.

We ate afterwards at the new Bar Central in the King's Road which was packed. Why do some new restaurants instantly attract a crowd while others languish unloved? Adventurous food, a good location and willing waiters don't always ensure a turn-out. Whatever it is it has worked for Bar Central, SW3 as quickly as it did for Bar Central, Waterloo, our favourite luncheon place when we were rehearsing *Woman* at the Old Vic.

Friday 24th February

Off to Hull for an OB *Loose Ends* with an audience. First a visit to Mr Bashaarat – who is going to mastermind my implants. Much X-raying and many explanations of how many implants would support how many crowns and give me back my back teeth. I was also given a child's guide to *Tooth Replacement* with a huge picture of a great green tree standing in a field of buttercups, backed by a clear blue sky and subtitled 'How nature intended it'.

I finished reading Jean Hartley's excellent memoir *Philip Larkin, the Marvell Press and Me* on the train. She is on the programme tomorrow. The cover recommendation from Bron Waugh says, 'I must confess that I found the book completely fascinating.' Couldn't agree more. She casts a very clear eye on her poor background, growing up in Hull; and tells an extraordinary story of provincial poetasters producing a magazine and publishing early Larkin, Amis, Davie, Thwaite, etc. from a back street cottage. She draws a very convincing picture of the unlikely squalor from which she and her husband brought it off and is sharp without being spiteful about the break-up of the marriage. There is a wonderfully funny vignette of her husband thrusting a long romantic poem which he had addressed to her under Larkin's nose. At the time Larkin was sitting squashed between them on a small sofa. He had no alternative but to read it. When he got to the bottom of the page he struggled to find something to say, 'After what seemed like an eternity, George said encouragingly: "It goes on over the page." Larkin later commented, "It did too!"' I must get her to tell it on air.

I discovered a perfect BR lunch – two starters, potato and leek soup and pickled herring in sour cream, with a salad and cheese. Arrived at Hull with Graham Norton who is to interview Hull's female World Judo Champion. *The Good Food Guide* doesn't list any restaurant in Hull but Egon Ronay came to our salvation with Cerutti's, where we had a convivial time. Monkfish and scallops wrapped in bacon in my case. Long ago we established a tradition that the BBC pays for the food on these occasions and the regulars stand the wine. This worked well with our more established contributors but it now means that with the fledgling comics and reporters I have to do the lot. A black mark for Emma Freud who should have paid half at the Castle, Taunton, six months ago and has still forgotten!

Saturday 25ᵗʰ February

Neil Shand's *Loose Ends* monologue a joy. We were in the Gulbenkian Theatre at Hull University. Audience about 400. People always complain that in the studio the jokes are delivered to 'sycophantic sniggers'. When you have 400 souls baying with laughter it's harder to uphold the charge. I liked Neil's suggestions that Larkin was the victim of a famous misprint and actually wrote, 'They tuck you up, your mum and dad'. The *Sunday Times* has been advancing an absurd idea that Michael Foot was a KGB agent of influence and his codename in

Moscow is Boot – 'a sort of double-O-seven and a half, wide-fitting presumably'.

Best of all was the suggestion that 'Buckingham Palace announced today that any watercolours by the heir to the throne will henceforth be signed "Mr Wales – the artist formerly known as Prince".'

John Godber, the playwright-director of Hull Truck was the first guest. He is going up the playwriting charts. In 1992 he was listed as the fourth most performed playwright in Britain – after Shakespeare, Ayckbourn and Arthur Miller. In 1993 he was acclaimed as the second most popular *living* playwright. In 1994 he was placed first after Shakespeare. He was remarkably level-headed and engaging and even finds Michael Winner, who hopes to film his very funny *On the Piste*, 'amusing'. It was funny in the theatre; but then, so was Alan Ayckbourn's *Chorus of Disapproval* before Winner gave it his light touch.

I didn't take greatly to Hull, although, as Hermione Gingold used to sing, 'The people were nice.' (In the last verse she got to a cannibal island where she couldn't stand the vegetables . . . 'but the people were nice!') With a declining fish industry Hull's main claim to fame is owning its own telephone system. Andrew Marvell, William Wilberforce and Amy Johnson are its notable children. I asked my friend Michael Hill, an ex-sailor who has been to every port, if he had visited it. 'Yes,' he said, 'on my only visit, many years ago, I wore a false moustache to cheer myself up. It didn't.'

Monday 27ᵗʰ February

To Julian Slade's basement in Beaufort Street. Edward Snape (an extremely young producer) and Charles Stephen (his partner) are sending out Julian's *Salad Days*. In the summer and autumn. It will feature Kit and the Widow. It was a great surprise to be asked to direct it. I think it will be fun, with Lindsay Dolan to stage the musical numbers and Tim Goodchild to do the sets. His third time – he's done a rep production and a West End revival at the Duke of York's – and he muttered, 'Third time lucky.'

I remember so vividly the innocence and charm of the original in 1954. I can't wait to see if we can achieve a similar freshness. Any attempt at bringing it up to date will sink it.

We talked about what Kit would play – he, of course, wants to play everything. How we can make the Widow's mute role more involving. We can probably do it with a double magic piano so that he can play it on stage.

In the evening *Indian Ink* – Tom Stoppard's re-jigging of his radio play *In a Native State* for Felicity Kendal and Art Malik – opened at the Aldwych, with Margaret Tyzack excellent in the old Peggy Ashcroft role. In *The Times* John Tydeman, who produced the radio version, told an engaging story of the horror with which he and Tom realised that Dame Peggy wanted to play her very young self in a flashback. Tom volunteered to disillusion her. Lovely though the voice was it was no longer 'young-young'. She wept and stormed and said, 'I only accepted the part because of that scene' and then pulled herself together, said, 'Oh well, it was worth a try,' and beautifully got on with it.

Ms Kendal's celebrated nude scene is over in a jiffy – indeed I was still waiting for it to happen after it had finished! *Indian Ink* is beautifully, lavishly staged by Peter Wood. It should do well.

Coincidentally there is a very odd series, largely about the subcontinent, going out on BBC2 on Mondays. It is called *Ruling Passions: Sex, Race and Empire*. It struck me as licensed prurience. So far we have not got as far as the witnesses Austin Gill quotes in his BBC book. In 1902 General Sir Hector MacDonald, Commander-in-Chief, Ceylon, was found '*in flagrante delicto* with no fewer than four Sinhalese boys in a railway carriage at Kandy'. A bit further down the scale a junior army officer at some lonely outpost of the Empire admitted, 'I prefer to satisfy myself with a lady of my own class but in the absence of the best I gladly take ... prostitutes of all classes and colour, men, boys and animals, melons and masturbation.'

To Elena's L'Etoile for supper. Elena mothered generations at Bianchi's in Frith Street and then carried on the torch at L'Escargot in Greek Street. She is indefatigable. I haven't been since her opening party but she seems to have settled in well and is proud of her success inside the Ackerman group. Moving on from L'Escargot, she helped out at the Gay Hussar for a bit and felt out of place. Now she is glowing and talks of opening a round-table luncheon club upstairs.

Tuesday 28ᵗʰ February

I did a voiceover for the London Underground at a buy-out fee in Gresse Street. About a dozen words for two radio commercials. Richard Griffiths, a comforting presence, was another voice.

To Hickstead for dinner on the eve of Douglas (Bunn's) birthday. The girls are bearing up. Chloë was home from school: she has stopped boarding and is going as a day-pupil for a bit. It is near Charlie's birthday so I took him a *Dumbo* video which I should have sent him on mine. It's the easy way of remembering – a trick I got from Edith Evans. That is how I remember godsons' anniversaries. He said, rather grandly, 'You don't have to give me videos always, Ned. I like CDs now,' and showed me his new CD player.

Wonderful *foie gras* which Tracy (Brook) had brought back from her visit to France to close up her house there, and a melting fillet steak. It was good to see that stricken household picking up the threads together. As Douglas is a leap year baby I think he is due to be about fourteen next year.

March

Wednesday 1st March

VISITED *A PASSSIONATE Woman*. The cast are in great shape and the figures continue to climb. A jolly supper at Giovanni's next door with Steph and Mulrooney.

Thursday 2nd March

Trying to find out how Michael Redington's revival of Coward's *Peace In Our Time* is going. It has just opened in Woking – (Neville Chamberlain's actual words, of course, were 'I believe it is peace *for* our time . . .') 'Just think of the people we'd be seen dead with,' Rebecca West wrote to Coward when she discovered they were both on a Nazi list for immediate execution had they occupied Britain in 1940. The general feeling is that it will tour but not make town. The director, who did a disastrous job on *The Winslow Boy*, apparently added an apocalyptic ending at the expense of rehearsing the play proper. That has now gone so maybe he will have time to give it some pace. He is *so* politically correct that he asked the cast playing patriotic Britishers under the Nazi jackboot if they 'minded' wearing Union Jack armbands, 'You know, National Front and all that!' I wish Redington could forget it and concentrate on Keith's *Bing Bong*.

I see a 'pushy 44-year-old blonde' called Joy Johnson has left the BBC where she was a news editor, to become campaign director for Tony Blair. Bernard Ingham nicknamed her 'the shouter' because of her noisy picketing of 10 Downing Street. More mildly John Major asked, 'Who is that woman who makes me feel like a criminal every time I enter Downing Street?'

With any luck she might shout away the next election for Blair.

To Wimbledon in the evening. A filthy, snowy-wet night; but two one-act plays by Geraldine Aron are being presented in the tiny studio theatre. I did her lovely, heartbreaking piece *Ba and Ger* twice for actors looking for a showcase, and her *Same Old Moon* at Southampton a few years ago. It went extremely well; but when Stoll Moss offered us the Garrick, the fledgling producer confessed that he hadn't raised any money. Enterprising Geraldine sent it to Prince Edward, who had just joined up with Biddy Hayward – sent it to Buckingham Palace, natch. Biddy put it on at Oxford, and then the Globe, directed by a humourless girl from the National. Disaster. When I bumped into Biddy she said breathlessly, 'I should have called you: but the moment I read it I knew it had to be directed by a woman . . .' and then, seeing my raised eyebrow, she added, ' . . . and it had to be directed by someone *young*!' I said I wouldn't mind the operation but I didn't think I could afford the goats' glands.

These two plays are brilliant and deserve more than the local press they've had. *The Stanley Parkers* is about two male lovers. It is moored around a bed. Although they interact they never speak directly to each other. All their remarks are addressed to us. It is a device Geraldine has used before – notably in *Ba and Ger*. She is *very* skilful with it. The play is funny and at the end very moving – its perfect length is about 35 minutes. The second play – *The Sisters Donoghue* is only a little longer. Three Irish sisters who have lived wildly different lives meet for a reunion and relive a violent incident in their childhood. Again it is witty and funny but this time it escalates with great skill, almost into Grand Guignol. Well worth the cold, rainy trip. Brian Rix and Elspeth were there to see two friends in the cast. They were equally impressed.

Friday 3rd March

Big anti-hunting debate in the Commons and on *Today* this morning. Can't understand the fuss. Most people who grew up in the country can't. Anne Mallalieu QC the Labour peer, is – like Penny Mortimer – a leading light in the fight against the bill. I wonder if she knows Surtees's famous horsy novel, *Mr Sponge's Sporting Tour*, in which he writes, 'Women never look so well, as when one comes in wet and dirty from hunting.'

Some backlash against the Stoppard play. A very sniffy Indian in *The Times* calls it 'Pastiche to India'.

We are having a very happy correspondence in the *Spectator*. It was triggered by Keith Waterhouse's 'Diary' a few weeks ago. He is writing part two of his memoir, following *City Lights* with *Streets Ahead*. He complained that he had kept neither letters nor diaries – then he came upon some old account books which enabled him to tie down certain dates and jogged his memory. What on earth, he asked, was a revue called *The Night is for Delight*, for which he earned £15 15s at Guildford in the sixties? I quickly faxed in this reply:

> Sir: The reason Keith Waterhouse contributed to a revue at Guildford called *Night is for Delight* (Diary, 11 February) is because I asked him to. As he had already been paid for use of the material on *TW3* he did rather well to collect another £15 15s. When you consider that his collaborator, Willis Hall, got £15 15s as well, you might consider that he was overpaid.

It was printed on 18 February. The next week Keith wrote that this was not the case – he and Willis shared the money. Not to be left out, Willis wrote this week complaining that there was also 10 per cent to be deducted for the agent. I have sent the following:

> Sir: Messrs Hall and Waterhouse protest too much. Their arrangement with their agent is no concern of mine. Furthermore I have checked with my bank (not Barings) and I learn that the sum of 15 guineas in the mid-sixties is the equivalent of some £120 nowadays in (I think the phrase is) real terms. An ample reward for a skit which is being given a second life.
>
> May I usurp your prerogative and suggest that this correspondence is now closed?

Craig Charles has been cleared on his rape charge. The jury were only out for an hour and a half. He paints a horrid picture of his time in jail when he was refused bail – threats from other prisoners and having to defecate in a bucket in front of other cell mates.

It was impossible to escape one irony. Craig was supported in court by his policeman brother and his father. The father's appearance was miraculous. Not once but *twice* when Craig failed to make the *Loose*

Ends studio he rang in tearfully to say that his father had died. He even invented a funeral at which the old boy's first wife, never divorced, arrived from Africa. Craig piously thanked God that his mother had died earlier and been spared this humiliation.

To the National Theatre for *What the Butler Saw*. A wonderful, full-blooded helter-skelter production by Phyllida Lloyd. As fulfilling as her *Threepenny Opera* was disappointing. The bloody shootings at the end were played with full gore and only threw the audience for a second. Two very good youngsters. Debra Gillett as Geraldine and a beanpole called David Tennant as the boy, who looked quite extraordinary in drag.

Richard Wilson, who is on *Loose Ends* tomorrow, played Dr Rance with magnificent madness.

Saturday 4th March

Rather a turgid *Loose Ends* once Neil Shand's monologue was over. Nice joke about the Queen being asked to produce identification at Barings and offering a stamp. Also, in the aftermath of Chelsea football yobs rioting in Brussels, a good phrase to define the Belgian police: 'Walloons with attitude'. Chris Armstrong, the Crystal Palace footballer, has been banned having tested positive for cannabis. Said one manager: 'After the recent weather he's lucky to find enough grass to play on – never mind smoke.'

Richard Wilson is a charming, intelligent chap but getting him to expand in an interview is daunting. Give him an audience and he flowers, but one to one it's like pulling teeth. Judd Hirsch (star of *Conversations With My Father*), another excellent actor, is a thundering bore who *knows* he's interesting – lethal.

In the George afterwards I could not get Richard Wilson to confirm that John Alderton had tried, in rehearsal for *What the Butler Saw*, to cut some of Richard's lines on the pretext that 'Joe never wrote that. It must be Kenneth Halliwell.' The most Richard would concede was that Alderton had taken up a lot of rehearsal time. He wouldn't budge on another story either. According to rumour, at the Groucho party after the first night Mrs Alderton (Pauline Collins) sidled up to Richard in the early hours and hissed, 'Was he a cunt?' Rather shocked, Richard agreed, 'Well, to tell the truth he was.' 'He always is!' said the loyal wife. Who can say whether or not there is a word of truth in this improbable tale?

Monday 6ᵗʰ March

Scratch an Actor MS to Sinclair-Stevenson. A sigh of relief. Now a tense wait for a verdict.

Trevor Cookson, a glass-walking-stick enthusiast, came to view the little collection I inherited from Caryl (Brahms). He had heard them mentioned on the 400th edition of *Loose Ends*, broadcast from the flat. As he has hundreds he wasn't overly impressed but there was one fat-drum-majorette-cloudy-white-with-red-and-blue-stick which he said he hadn't seen before.

To London University to the Senate House to judge – with Tony Banks and Jeffrey Archer – a national debating contest. Jeffrey and I thought Oxford won but we were outvoted by Banks, the University rep and a man from the sponsors, Melitta, the coffee company. The whole thing was highly organised, the other finalists were two teams from LSE and one from Southampton, who triumphed. Jeffrey got in his favourite joke in his summing-up speech – third time I've heard it. 'I've just been to Scotland talking to Conservatives in the constituencies – so it's nice to see an audience.'

On another campus (Leeds) there was a good quote from Caspar Weinberger, the former US Secretary for Defense.
When he was hassled by students he said, 'Don't worry, I have found that when they shout they generally don't shoot.'

Tuesday 7ᵗʰ March

The President of South Korea, Kim Young Sam, is practising a 'royal wave' for his visit to London. The one he uses back home is too like a Fascist salute. He should heed the Queen Mother's advice to the Prince of Wales: 'This is how you do it. It is like opening a huge jar of sweets.'

Saints and Sinners private members' lunch. Jimmy Tarbuck very enthusiastic about Neil's monologue last week. Michael Medwin told me a charming story of the late Julian Belfrage to whose memorial service most of us were going – Julian had negotiated a year's contract for Michael at the National. A few weeks later they met at the Turf Club. Julian asked Michael if he'd like a drink. 'Better not,' said Michael, 'I'm going to the theatre.' 'Oh,' asked Julian, 'what are you seeing?'

The service was very moving. All Julian's star clients turned out – plus crowds from Ireland and the Turf. The readers were Judi Dench, Ian Holm, Alan Howard, Rupert and Crispian Belfrage, Ann Bell, Brian Kenny, Penelope Wilton and Robert Lang. Judi read Canon Henry Holland's 'Death is Nothing At All'. I've never seen her so moved or stronger in exerting iron control between each sentence to get through. Ronan Browne played a lovely lament and a warming jig on the Irish pipes. Dan Day-Lewis, dressed in his usual undertaker's aspect, claimed that inspiration from beyond told him not to read Edward Thomas's 'Lights Out' but to sing a song, *a capella*.

First he told how he had gone to Doncaster with Julian to see a faith healer. Julian had insisted they take second-class tickets but go straight to the first-class dining car and eke out the meal until they got to their destination. For someone with such a tortured reputation Dan managed to bring a joyous, coltish sense of celebration to the service.

Conversations With My Father at the Old Vic with David Kernan. Judd Hirsch terrific in a terrific part. First-generation Jew in America denies Jewishness – becomes rootless. Wonderful set. The rhythm of the Alan Ayckbourn production didn't seem quite right; but I enjoyed it hugely. An attractive brunette crossed us just before the curtain rose, entering the row from the wrong side. 'Where's your escort?' I asked, thinking I'd have to get up again seconds later. 'I don't need an escort,' she smiled. 'I'm the wife of the star.'

To Bar Central (King's Road) for supper. It is becoming an invaluable new hang-out.

Wednesday 8th March

Joe Harmston who was my co-director in Athens two Christmases ago for *Our Song* has at last sent his diary account of our adventures. It is riveting and funny. He writes with a very clear eye. It is also very libellous! I haven't had time to read it properly but dipping in is a delight.

To Southwark Cathedral for Bishop Mervyn Stockwood's memorial. I only knew about it because Robert Runcie wrote to ask if I knew any Mervyn stories he could use. I wasn't much help. I got there half an hour early to find the Cathedral very full and an officious woman usher demanding to know the colour of my ticket. As I did not have one she commanded me to the outer darkness pointing to some black seats in a corner at the back. I chose to join some anoraked priests, also at the back but with a marginally better view.

It was a stately service much lifted by a remarkable sermon by Runcie (who used one reference to Zsa Zsa Gabor which I had given him). He took his text from Ecclesiastes, 'the most mysterious and cynical book in the Bible': 'Cast your bread upon the waters,' to emphasise the generosity and extravagance with which Mervyn threw himself into his ministry. 'Meals are made for laughter. Wine gives joy'. He emphasised the Bishop's talent for spotting quality like David Sheppard and John Robinson – 'he was centre-stage; but what a supporting cast'. He referred to Mervyn's 'touching and hilarious struggle to practise what he preached'. He highlighted his hatred of committees, synods and working parties, 'Paralysis by Analysis'; and recalled Mervyn dodging an entire Lambeth Conference by applying for duty in the House of Lords.

On his psychic investigations, 'He was the first New Ager.' On the charismatics, 'He swayed and clapped with the best of them.' When he felt he was drained, 'He taught bishops how to retire', finding fresh strength in the retirement. Finally Lord Runcie plainly could not resist the last Mervyn anecdote. During the 'outing' of bishops by Peter Tatchell and his 'thought police' at the last Lambeth Conference Mervyn was on the list. The Bishop of Bath and Wells, in whose diocese he lived, thought he should warn him, so he telephoned. As soon as he got the gist Mervyn cut him short. 'Jim,' he said, 'I couldn't care tuppence. And if the press get on to you – tell them I've had a lot of women too.'

Laughter rang through the church and when the sermon was over there was prolonged applause – obviously spontaneous in what had been a very formal service.

Great excitement at the Comedy. I dropped in to see a matinée on the way back from the funeral and found Gordon Alcock, Alfie Lynch's understudy, on. BR had let Alfie down on his journey from Brighton.

Gordon was excellent. He will certainly be given the part when Alfie departs in April. It will be his first big West End role. He is an ex-amateur from the Potteries.

Thursday 9th March

A very lively *Evening Standard* Literary Lunch at the Dorchester. Andrew Wilson manages these affairs very engagingly – although on this occasion one of his book reviewers, Frances Fyfield, a lawyer, was alarmed to find that he had placed her next to Joan Smith, a novelist whose latest book she had rubbished as 'Mrs Dale's Diary but not as interesting'. However, a few moments later I saw Andrew bringing them together and in no time at all they were getting along famously.

Ms Fyfield also asked loudly, 'Who is John Bayley?' while standing back to back with him and his wife, Iris Murdoch. Wendy Cope read her poems happily. Michael Dobbs snappy on his relations with the BBC over his new novel – their attitude can be summed up in the words 'Dobbs has gone bonkers!'

I sat next to Simon Callow who had rushed from filming Tony Palmer's Purcell film in which he plays Charles II. Filming at Greenwich, in the Painted Hall of the Naval College. As he left the set in full costume, he told me, he was confronted by an American matron. Surprised by this royal apparition she blushed, dropped a half-curtsey and got stuck in it. He was very eloquent about Orson Welles – his new biography. In writing about Charles Laughton he found his initial doubts about his subject turned to respect. With Welles his enthusiasm moved into scepticism as he proceeded. At the lunch table he sounded a little doubtful about the prospect for Glen Roven's musical which he is slated to direct. I hope his doubts are groundless.

I was back in the same room in the evening to do a charity speech for the Royal Academy of Arts international dinner – a fund raiser. I was hijacked by Rose Hepworth and Peter Boizot of Pizza on the Park. Sat next to the wife of the Dutch Ambassador – a cottage loaf wreathed in smiles – and a little American woman whose husband is a major benefactor. Not my finest speechifying hour. The French Ambassador, proposing 'The Academy' had the right idea. He just stood up, said, 'The Academy,' and sat down again.

Friday 10th March

To Croydon to see a touring *Underneath the Arches*. Almost all the cast in their early twenties, trying gamely to represent those bald, paunchy, ageing clowns. Sweet but sad!

Great relief. Christopher Sinclair-Stevenson rang just before I left to say he likes *Scratch an Actor* – 'page-turner'. I imagine this means 'of no literary merit – possible commercial prospects'. I queried his enthusiasm. He said I mustn't question his honesty. I said I wasn't questioning that but his judgement. He said that was worse! It was good of him to phone so promptly. I had anticipated that he would read it this weekend.

Saturday 11th March

A very lively *Loose Ends* in contrast to last week's pudding. Ariel Dorfman – *Death and the Maiden* – also on for his new novel *Konfiding* – much in the same manner. He caught the mood of the programme instantly and managed to be clear and literate, amused and amusing. He fell immediately into conversation with Art Malik (another charmer) about Tom Stoppard's play which he much admired. Two good musical items: Drayton Underground, a fine *a capella* quintet, sang one of their own songs, about sixties movies, and Terry Neason, who is at the Lyric Hammersmith, tore into *Lover Man*. We finished with George Melly who was in rumbustious form. Everyone came on to the George afterwards – my first round came to £50, the highest yet! George in compulsive joke-telling mood. 'Have you heard about the new male morning-after contraceptive? It changes your blood group.' 'When Old Mother Riley [Arthur Lucan] died on stage in Hull they phoned his estranged wife, Kitty McShane. "Arthur's died." "Where?" "Hull." "Typical!"'

And finally a desert island joke. An unpreposessing little man finds himself shipwrecked on a desert island with Michelle Pfeiffer. She doesn't fancy him but as the days go by he is so kind and courteous to her that they make love. She enjoys it and they continue to do so. She is so grateful that eventually she thanks him for giving her so much pleasure and asks if there is anything she can do for him to repay him. He said, 'Well, yes, there is,' and asks her to put on a pair of his trousers and a shirt and hat and smear a bit of mud on her cheeks to look like a stubble. Then he asks her to go and lean against a palm tree. When she's wondering what on earth is going on he goes across to her and leans on the other side of the palm. Then he bends towards her and says, 'You'll never guess who I'm fucking!'

Monday 13th March

Lunch at Bar Central – funny to see it empty when their evening and weekend business is so good. We talked about plans for a TV show. Michael Lander had suggested a sort of 'Listings' and review for 30- and 40-somethings, Ivan Rendall and his director from Zenith favour a variation on a chat show – not a million miles from a televised *Loose Ends*. They plan to come to Birmingham to watch the live one we're due to do at the end of May. A promising lunch – not as kite-flying as so many of these affairs are. We shall see. I have my doubts.

Wrote speech for Foyle's Lunch – *Quotations* not as much fun to sell as *Anecdotes*!

Tuesday 14th March

A lively lunch at the Grosvenor House – more people there than I expected. Peter Boizot from Pizza on the Park brought all his Pizza Express managers in what looked like a works outing. They all bought books. All in all I signed about 30 and a few 'for stock'. On the way in there were crowds in Park Lane – only they were turning up for a Radio and TV Awards lunch in the Great Room. We were in the Ballroom. I was reminded of an evening when Keith Waterhouse and I turned up at the Ashcroft Theatre, Croydon to see the touring production of *Jeffrey Bernard is Unwell*. Hundreds of excited women were making their way along with us. Keith himself got very excited. When we arrived we found that the Chippendales were appearing in the neighbouring Fairfield Hall!

Christina seemed very frail. She still finds the occasional shocking question: 'Did you know Aleister Crowley?' she asked me. 'No,' I said. 'He was called the Beast,' she confided, 'and he asked me if I knew any rich people he could blackmail. He said he'd see me all right if I found any.'

It was a good top-table. Alicia Markova, very sprightly. Gerald Kaufman chaired. Elaine Paige, Stephanie Cole, Pat Hodge, Duke Hussey, Roy Hattersley, Keith, Dennis Waterman, Victoria Mather. Alan Clark arrived halfway through the meal but enjoyed himself chatting up Elaine, Hodge and Victoria in the bar upstairs afterwards (a bottle of Pol Roger champagne in the Red Bar cost £42! I bought one. Keith, who got there first, bought two). Alan left with Victoria but I'm not sure if we should read too much into this. Jill Arlon said he did not stop scribbling notes during my speech. Roy did the thanks and as always reminded me that long ago I had rejected him for *TW3* Actually, I think it was *Not So Much a Programme*.

To dinner at Andrew and Sonia Sinclair's in Tite Street. Ted Heath, the Melvyn Braggs, Victoria Glendinning and Wilf Stevenson from the NFT. Talked to Ted Heath about his appearance last weekend on *Any Questions* with Roy Jenkins, Gerald Kaufman and an American woman from the *Spectator* (Anne Applebaum) who was hopelessly outgunned. I remembered my first *Any Questions* with Freddie Grisewood in the chair and Edith Summerskill and Alan Melville. When a question about marriage came up Freddie bellowed, 'A question about marriage and two bachelors on the panel! How queer!' Edith Summerskill then compounded it by turning to me and yelling, 'Did he say *queer*?' Delicious food. A light seafoody salad, chicken in a perfect sauce with baked potatoes and a melting pudding. Home by eleven.

Wednesday 15th March

The Stephen Fry aftermath rolls on. The closing notice for the play has gone up. Duncan Weldon expects to lose £300,000. *The Times's* Dr Thomas Stuttaford, who claims to be a Fry family friend, diagnoses cyclothymia or 'bi-polar affective disorder'. To an ignorant lay person it sounds like manic-depression.

Two gossip column mentions of the Foyle's lunch – *Times* and *Standard*. 'Lord Archer of Weston-super-Mare – the only seaside pier on which Danny la Rue has not played' given another airing. Better coverage than average. Quentin Letts (*Telegraph*, 'Peterborough'), though accorded a top-table seat, failed to report. Black mark the next time *he* rings for a quote.

To *Caprice* for lunch with David Pugh and his partner, Billy Russo, to talk *Passionate Woman*. Australian possibilities with Ruth Cracknell, the Edith Evans of Oz, look good. Also, we need to get on with re-casting it for London. Stephanie, tired and overworked (together with her house move) must be accommodated. Will Neil Morrissey stay on?

There are bright prospects for Broadway if we can take advantage of a new union agreement. Possible tour – with whom? Possible second tour then going off to New Zealand. Maybe a need to simplify the set. Gwen Taylor? Lynda Baron? Jean Boht? I gave him as much gossip as possible. There is a possibility that Dennis Waterman and Robert Powell might play Keith's *Bing Bong*. David appears interested in an experimental tour with them to see if it would work. I sent him a script.

A script came in from Jeremy Burnham who has adapted *Vice Versa* as a musical – with Jonathan Cohen, a talented accompanist, arranger and ex *Playschool* TV star. I must find a day soon to catch up on scripts. The pile is too high.

Dennis Waterman reports that Robert Powell is *very* keen on *Bing Bong*. Keith is going to lunch us at L'Epicure before I do the Lloyds Private Banking Awards on Tuesday. I must read it again. There's Alistair McAlpine's very sharp book to finish before Saturday when he and Rupert Everett are on *Loose Ends*. I've read Rupert's new novel, *The Hairdresser of San Tropez*; but I must also get through the fascinating 1,000 pages of Asa Briggs's latest volume in his history of the BBC – *Competition (1953–74)*. I am to review it for the *Telegraph*.

Thursday 16th March

Oh dear. The dentist again. I feel yet more in harmony with Anthony Powell. Two bits had fallen off – attacked by nothing more violent than oat flakes and soft toast. David Croser keeps showing me X-rays which he assumes I will understand and then takes more which fascinate *him*, but not *me*. However, he has stopped the jagged edge of what, I think, is a 'canine' and I'm only going to get an 'ordinary' bridge on the right top and the two implants down below. Then two days off after the implants (i.e. reading and writing and no drinking) and a six-week – or was it a six-month? – wait before they can hang teeth on them.

To Hackney with Joe Harmston whose account of *Our Song* in Greece I keep dipping into; it is still accurate, ribald, libellous and wonderful. Joe is committed to Chichester. I wish I could persuade him to come to help on *A Passionate Woman*. There are so many burgeoning productions I must find an assistant.

At Hackney we saw *Hamlet*. Jonathan Kent has done the best *staging* I have ever seen. Set – Peter J. Davison. Lighting – Mark Henderson. It's the Merchant-Ivory, Edwardian *Hamlet*. But it's very fast, very exciting and if no one, not even the Dane stands out, no one lets you down. Ralph Fiennes, Francesca Annis (Gertrude), Tara Fitzgerald (Ophelia), Peter Eyre (Polonius) all good – but it's the production, fast and furious, which stands out – and a splendid carrot-red Laertes. An ingenious tripling of the Ghost, the Player King and the Gravedigger, 'the Digger' – as Wolfit used to call him. They are all father figures for Hamlet. It's a very good idea. Terence Rigby, who took them on, sounds a little too like Robert Hardy playing Churchill in the first two incarnations and isn't quite humorous enough – even in gallows humour terms – for 'the Digger'; but it's a great, significant triple.

Happy meal (spinach soup) at Bar Central. Joe demolished an enormous bowl of mussels before driving north. He is a joy and very clever.

Friday 17ᵗʰ March

Usual routine. *Loose Ends* reading and notes. Interrupted (an hour late – the fault of the domestic airline) by a pleasant, comely Scots journalist, Gillian Glover, en route for Japan. She was doing a piece on the *Dictionary of Humorous Quotations*. Journalists don't always confess; but after three amontillados she admitted that she had never forgiven her mother for telling her that she was conceived in a lay-by after her parents had consumed a Melton Mowbray pie.

Much excitement about Peter Tatchell and Outrage 'outing' gay bishops. The Bishop of London (known when he was clearing up the mess at the Oxford Theological college as 'Ena the Terrible') declared his sexual life a celibate 'grey area'. According to John Mortimer, the late Lord Camoys had the best euphemism. When asked why a relative had his training at a priest's seminary cut short, he said, 'I believe he was aiming too low at the leap-frog!'

Saturday 18th March

A very odd fan letter from Brighton from a '28-year-old professional sportsman' who wants 'to meet and play and laugh and sing'. I am reminded of Graham Greene's religious fan who wrote from Switzerland suggesting he join her 'where the snow can be our coverlet' – a prospect he found even less attractive than martyrdom. Must go carefully on this one, I think. I have to speak in Brighton in May. Perhaps a quick drink then would be best.

A happy *Loose Ends*. Alistair McAlpine faintly insisting that his new book, *Letters to a Young Politician from his Uncle* is fiction in spite of it being a blatant attack an Major. In the pub he was very jolly over his usual drink (triple scotch regularly topped up with water) about his timing and the maximum publicity it afforded the book – PM's Question Time, etc.

Quiet weekend. Read Jeremy Burnham's conscientious musical version of *Vice Versa*. It didn't excite me, I'm afraid.

Monday 20th March

London Book Fair at Olympia. To promote my *Oxford Dictionary of Humorous Quotations*, OUP have been running a competition to identify five allegedly obscure quotes. Drew the winner out of a bag and was photographed posing against a huge photo blow-up of the cover which was perched on an ivy-clad plinth. I wandered about a bit. The only interesting bit in a corner at the far end was a louche area where remaindered books were on display amongst beer cans and wine glasses and half-empty bottles of plonk.

I remembered stories of publicity stunts in the past. A publisher told me that he once hired a 'dolly-bird' (what an evocative period description) to wear a dress made up of reviews of the book he was promoting. It caused a mild sensation. Nothing looked like causing a mild sensation this year. Didn't stay long.

Tuesday 21st March

Riotous lunch with Keith W., Dennis Waterman and Robert Powell at L'Epicure. Steak and kidney pie and discussion of *Bing Bong*, Keith's play. They have both now read it several times and are keen to do it. They would play two jealous, failing sitcom writers. It's a black and bitter contemporary comedy. Strange that its genesis was my suggestion to Keith that he read Laurence Irving's biography of his grandfather, Henry, to see if there was a part there for O'Toole. Although he loved the book he couldn't see a play in it but in some odd way it triggered this vastly different result.

Michael Redington has definitely decided that he can't mount it ('I'll take one unit'), so we all decided to have a go at Duncan Weldon with it.

On to a rehearsal for the Lloyds Private Banking Playwright of the Year Awards at the Marriott in Duke Street. They have planned a very elaborate cabaret with a fifteen-piece orchestra culled from the London Philharmonic, under Kenny Clayton. Sacha Distel, Ron Moody, Liz Robertson, Rosemary Ford and three young singers, Paulette Ivory, Katrina Murphy, and Jay Marcus who is about to take over from John Barrowman in *Sunset Boulevard*. The theme – if it can be called that – was songs from shows derived from books and plays. That let in almost anything, including *HMS Pinafore* which wasn't derived from a book or a play!

I changed there in a room I was supposed to be sharing with Melvyn Bragg. They had forgotten to book one for me. Then Melvyn arrived and created a fuss because he expected one all to himself. I'm not sure if he wanted to collect his thoughts or whether he had some other, more mysterious motive. Anyway I moved out and sulked in the band room.

Dined next to a very pleasant Australian, Joe Penhall, who was nominated for his play *Some Voices* upstairs at the Royal Court. As judges, we didn't know the actual winner, only the three most likely: David Edgar's *Pentecost*, Jonathan Harvey's *My Night With Reg* and Terry Johnson's *Dead Funny*. I didn't disillusion Joe as his proud parents had come all the way from Melbourne for the event.

Much to-ing and fro-ing about the extracts from the three leading contenders which were read by Neil Pearson, Jan Francis and another good actor under the direction of James Roose Evans. Apparently Lloyds went cold on some of the language in *My Night With Reg* and emasculated the excerpt. James nearly walking out in protest. It went smoothly on the night and *Dead Funny* was a popular winner, netting the author £25,000. The others got certificates.

Wednesday 22nd March

Auditioned a very bright young pianist/musical director, David Shrubsole, at Julian Slade's for *Salad Days*. Had the impression he was also auditioning us. We would be delighted to have him. Suspect that he will say 'no' – tempted by offers to do something inside the Cameron Mackintosh empire – probably *Miss Saigon*.

Magic evening. To the Donmar with Glen Roven to see *La Sylphide*, the Adventures in Motion Pictures Company's 'Wee Scottish Ballet'. Matthew Bourne, the choreographer, is Britain's answer to Mark Morris. It was wonderfully light and infectious, the story set in a Gorbals tenement. Glen could hardly believe that this was the same choreographer who had served up such leaden work in *Oliver!* at the Palladium. On to the Comedy to catch the second act of *A Passionate Woman*. A very good house in fine form, as was the cast. Glen most impressed. He had enjoyed the first night but found it twice as good with a relaxed audience. We took Stephanie on to Elena's L'Etoile which proved a very happy choice. It was full of 'faces'. David Puttnam, Malcolm McLaren, Simon Ward, and George Fenton who was on a break from working on the score of the new Julia Roberts movie. Elena is now really enjoying her new premises. Lunches are always full and evenings are obviously picking up. It was new to Glen and Stephanie and the combination of ancient premises and modern cuisine is settling down splendidly.

Thursday 23rd March

To Broadcasting House for a cocktail party to launch Asa Briggs's latest volume in his history of the Corporation. I didn't like to talk to Asa as I still don't know if I'll be talking to him or to Ray Davies (Kinks) on Saturday morning. An odd alternative. I'd had to read the book quickly as my review was for the coming Saturday's *Telegraph*.

If the rest of Asa's book is as on the ball as those sections of which I have direct knowledge – particularly *TW3* – it is a remarkable achievement. However, since he calls my own account in my autobiography, 'the most perceptive history', I can hardly say less.

I went on to the King's Head, Islington, to see *Burning Blue*, a play by an ex Top Gun about gay naval airman. I have to interview the author, D.M.W. Greer on Saturday morning. Not surprisingly there's a strong autobiographical feel to it and its shifts between past and present are often ungainly. There is a very funny performance by Martin McDougall as a hayseedy pilot to whom Greer has given a very good line. The pilot is asked by the investigating officer whether he has ever been involved in sex with other men or little animals. His answer is a quizzical 'How little?'

Friday 24th March

I have started a new life as the voice of the *Independent*. Not particularly lucrative as this is only for a radio ad and each recording is a buy-out. However, one can't complain about an hour or so spent reading 50 or less words of copy in a faintly amused voice.

Pleasant people from the new Saatchi agency. We record in the Saunders and Gordon studios in Gresse Street. They are always late. The copy is always in a state of flux. I am shut in a small room behind a glass panel. Through it I can see them conferring anxiously after each take.

I've been reading Alan Clark's *Diaries* again with a view to dramatising them for the Birmingham Rep at Bill Alexander's suggestion. There is so much open lechery there that I wonder if I should not introduce a little here. Except that my life is quite the reverse of lecherous at the moment. I experimented a little by flirting with Ben, the technician. Handsome, mid-twenties, six-foot-two or three, black jeans and sneakers. Huge shoulders under a stiff white denim shirt. My efforts totally unnoticed although two of his entirely innocent lines about editing the tape were susceptible of infinite *double entendre*: 'I might just let my computers tamper with you'; and, 'I don't think I can insert anything into you there.'

Interview with *The Mrs Merton Show* went out, much cut, including my reason for doing it which was to plug *Humorous Quotations*.

One glancing reference survived and a solid plug for *A Passionate Woman*. However, the *Anecdotes* came out strongly.

It is, I see in *The Times*, the anniversary of the death of Queen Mary in 1953. She had one rather endearing regret in her life. She told her daughter-in-law, now the Queen Mother, 'Do you know there is one thing I never did and I wish I had done: climb a fence.'

She did achieve one curious ambition, though. When she was evacuated to Badminton during the war she surprised the Duchess of Beaufort by saying, 'So *that's* what hay looks like!'

Saturday 25th March

The Bank of England Bonk dominated the *Loose Ends* monologue. Rupert Pennant-Rae, his American mistress and poor Helen P-R, who used to be an assistant at the BBC in 1970 when we did *Quiz of the Week*, make up the triangle. There is a limit to the number of jokes that can be made about 'quick withdrawals', 'flexible friends' and 'closed positions'.

Amiable guests. Ray (Kinks) Davies, a very sharp Scots woman novelist, M.C. Beaton, who was quite caustic about the BBC's adaptations of her Hamish McGregor novels, a thoroughly boring American woman astronaut, Marsha Ivens, and David Greer. Sandi Toksvig interviewed an amiably barmy punk-rocker, John Otway. Mark Bunyan unveiled his new anti-vegetarian song – about the delights of eating Bambi, or Ferdinand the Bull, or Donald Duck.

To Nottingham to see Alistair Beaton's adaptation of Gogol's *The Nose*. Highly enjoyable and lavishly staged, it is the start of a new regime at the Playhouse. It is perhaps a little long and the end isn't right but it's a good start. Alistair very nervous and visibly relieved at the enthusiastic reception. I didn't wait for the party, having an early call.

Monday 27th March

To Sadler's Wells with Glen Roven to see, or rather hear, Alistair Beaton's new translation of *Die Fledermaus*. Same production and design team as for *The Nose* – almost as disastrous as the other was successful. It looked awful, the singers – with one exception – couldn't act; but mercifully John Owen Edwards in the pit was getting some lovely playing out of his 25-piece orchestra. Alistair had been ruthless with the spoken text but the singers all brayed as if Welsh persons trying to gain entry to an eisteddfod. Only the Australian Adey Grummet, who had sung the audition song on *Loose Ends*, managed an approximation to acceptable acting. Alistair has invented a very funny Frosch, the jailer. Instead of the usual lurching, paunchy, middle-aged drunken comic he came up with a perky errand-boy type, his entrance on a unicycle. We went to the Thai place around the corner from Sadler's Wells. *Two* starters proved far too much for me.

I read in the *Standard* that Lauren Bacall has got herself into a spot of bother in Paris where she is promoting her autobiography. She found herself sitting next to a man from Oxford. 'In that case you must know my friend, Isaiah Berlin,' she said brightly. 'I am he,' came the embarrassing reply.

Tuesday 28th March

Early to Manchester for a literary lunch to plug *Humorous Quotations*. I travelled up with Keith Waterhouse. We both had hearty breakfasts which was just as well as the lamb steak at the Ramada Renaissance lunch was inedible. There was the usual agreement between the speakers that we would not exceed ten minutes. Dear old John Cole led off – charming and amusing but pushing twenty minutes. Keith asked me to tug his coat-tail when he passed ten but sat down at nine so I didn't have to. John Simpson (*Oxford Book of Exiles*) did a stately twelve but I managed to sit down at exactly 2.30, well in my limit. Signed about twenty copies.

Wednesday 29th March

Mich Raper's funeral at Putney Vale Crematorium. He was my first London landlord on Chelsea Embankment – No. 6 – from 1954 until 1963. On second thoughts, those are the dates when I lived there. Mich moved on earlier, leaving the flat with Ken Fortescue who had been his lover. Mich was at Oxford just before me. He worked variously in radio and television for Luxembourg, the BBC and commercial TV. I last saw him some eight or nine years ago when he was producing the mid-morning short story at Broadcasting House. I hadn't realised how important his poetry was to him. John Benson read his last poem 'Sid'. A light and playful piece using advertising phrases.

Apparently he had the beginning and end for some time and woke up one night not long before he died to find that the middle had arrived in his head. He sent it, as always, to his sister Prue to type up. I could only note the last two lines.

Till Angels lose their maidenheads
And all the stars are tight.

Anna Sharkey read a lovely and appropriate poem by Emily Dickinson – a poet to whom Mich had introduced Anna and her husband, Jonathan Cecil.

Because I could not stop for Death.
He kindly stopped for me –
The carriage held but just Ourselves –
And Immortality . . .

So I've now buried both my first London landlords – Kenneth died in the early eighties.

Thursday 30th March

Dr Acalay did his first root canal job. It was quite painless apart from the little jab of injection. My mind wandered to the House of Commons where, in 1945, Clement Davies, Liberal leader in Churchill's caretaker government once got up to speak. He was a tedious orator and Churchill let *his* attention wander too – only to be surprised by Davies's unexpectedly abrupt return to the benches. He asked what had happened and got a strangely mumbled reply. Clement Davies had shot both sets of his teeth across the floor of the House.

I am trying to get to see *The Madness of King George*, but something always seems the change the plans. I wonder if 'opening it out' cinematically has encouraged Alan Bennett to open it out historically? There was a ludicrous incident at his coronation which would have amused AB. A retiring chamber including a loo had been prepared for the Queen. During the ceremony she fled to it in urgent need of relief only to find that most absentminded of prime ministers, the Duke of Newcastle, seated upon it.

News of the great success of *Vita and Virginia* on Broadway with Vanessa Redgrave and Eileen Atkins. This is also Alan Bennett territory. Reviewing a book about the Bloomsbury set for the *Late Night Line-Up* in the sixties he ended with the suggestion that should someone ever be casting Virginia Woolf, 'Don't forget Dusty Springfield.'

To the Berkeley for dinner with Nadia Nerina and Charles Gordon. A jolly party including John Julius Norwich and wife; John Plender, the financial journalist, and his wife, who produces midnight chat shows for radio on Five Alive. She rather irritated me by saying what a pity it was that *Loose Ends* had become safe. In *l'esprit d'escalier* I might have said that the only one of hers I had heard was quite shapeless – not to say pointless: but thought it better to keep quiet.

This Saturday is April Fool's Day so we'll have to see how unsafe we can be.

Friday 31st March

Some auditions for *Passionate Woman*. We haven't cast the new men yet. More radio voiceovers for the *Independent* and some prerecording for *Loose Ends*. The April Fool joke is to pretend that the BBC is so keen on 'multi-skilling' that I'm going to have to be heard hosting programmes of Radios 1, 2 and 3 as well as the 10 o'clock show on Radio 4. Judi Spiers (Radio 2), very Miss Showbiz, came in to introduce Ben Waterman, piano-playing prodigy from Chard in Somerset who has now moved to London, and I taped myself panting along the tunnel which leads from BH to Radio 1 across the road where I am to invade Danny Baker's studio just before eleven.

April

~~~>||<~~~

Saturday 1st April

THE *LOOSE ENDS* joke worked quite well. It can't have fooled
anybody but it was fun. The first April Fool I heard was on
waking up – *Farming Today* of all places! It went on for nearly 20
minutes with Germanic thoroughness. The conceit was that Europe
was laying down colour-coordinated fields, green strips balanced
against strips of that bright rape-yellow and, I dare say, some purple
clover and vetch in between.

There was a small embarrassment when the excellent actress, Rosemary Leach, appeared not to understand Beatrix Von Watzdorf, a girl
who has appeared as a man pretending to be a girl at Madame Jo Jo's
drag club. She mentioned drag queens in the communal dressing-room
complaining of 'fish' and Rosemary pursued the reference with the
puzzled diligence of a performing seal.

Monday 3rd April

I met another potential musical director, Stuart Hutchinson, at Julian
Slade's flat. (Mr Shrubsole has gone to the Mackintosh camp.) He is
keen to do *Salad Days*, loves touring and is currently MD for *The
Sound of Music* in Hornchurch. Quite a cutting tongue.

In the evening I hosted *The Campaign* National Newspaper Advertising Awards at Grosvenor House. Just a question of getting them on
and off. No jokes required. Rory Bremner provided those very
efficiently before and Ray and Dave Davies and the Kinks did a highly
popular hour-long set afterwards. I have never seen them live before
despite nearly 30 years of friendship. In spite of all the reports of their

on-stage feuding they seemed to have a remarkable rapport and it was fascinating to watch them playing off one another.

Tuesday 4th April

To Roberto Devereaux's launch for Christian Lacroix at 29 Old Bond Street. It was crowded with B-list celebs, many of whom were unable even to get in. I elbowed my way along with Nickolas Grace, first to a glass of champagne, then on to say hello to Roberto and shake the great man's hand. I then fled as I heard Roberto piloting him across whispering, 'They say Snowdon's arrived.'

I went on to the Comedy where David Conolly was 'on' for *Craze*. He did a very professional job. Stephanie and I went on to L'Etoile where she was to feed our producers, David Pugh and Billy Russo.

A thoroughly good gossip.

Saturday 8th April

A relaxed *Loose Ends*. It must have been passable as Ian Gardhouse rang to say well done afterwards.

Beryl Bainbridge was funny about her early career on Variety bill. She and a friend, on the way home from the Cone Ripman school at Tring, entered a talent contest in Nottingham and were booked for a week in music hall. We played her 'Hang on the Bell, Nellie', their opening number, and she happily recited 'The Bloke from Birkenhead' – her dramatic monologue. They were following Dave King and preceded some acrobats! That was the end of Beryl's vaudeville career.

Haydn Gwynne came to talk eloquently about *Twelfth Night* and we played her the *Ziegfeld* recording in which she sang 'More Than You Know' beautifully. It was the limited edition memento of the most expensive musical flop ever in the West End. Alistair Beaton and I did the book. I think we lost poor Harold Fielding £4 million. They only made 250 copies, then 'the tapes were destroyed'. They charged £200 apiece. I got number 205. I think I did a deal for £150 for Alistair and me as we had written the book and at least one of the lyrics.

Miles Kington has sent me his very odd first play, *Waiting for Stoppard*. He manages to send up Stoppard, Lynn Barber, arts-programmes researchers and the police. It reads very well. I cannot gauge how stageworthy it is. I shall watch for reviews. His wife is directing a week's try-out at the New Vic studio at Bristol so we may soon know. Finally there was a sprightly 83-year-old Frith Banbury, about whose career in the theatre Charles Duff has written a book – *The Lost Summer: the Heyday of the West End Theatre*. Coincidentally my review of it in the *Independent* appeared this morning.

Frith greatly helped to nurture and reveal the talents of Wynyard Browne, N.C. Hunter, Rodney Ackland, John Whiting and Robert Bolt. He also sensitively realised middle-period Rattigan in *The Deep Blue Sea*, and in the book he disposes of the rumour that a gay version ever existed.

Duff is very funny about Frith's reaction to being studied. From a noncommittal 'Well, I won't stop you,' it

> suddenly became far too over-excited. I was bombarded with suggestions: who to see; what to focus on, even what opinions to hold . . . I took to switching on my answer machine to monitor all calls. Then after one Banbury message – the longest I have ever received from anyone – I disconnected the telephone. Then the letters started . . .

It was a very different era from ours. After Wynyard Browne's first play *Dark Summer*, Frith's mother, satisfied that at 35 her boy had settled in his career, gave him £10,000. Immediately he paid Browne £1,000 – one half non-returnable, the other in advance of royalties for his next four plays.

Only a few months ago, watching Wendy Wasserstein's play, *The Sisters Rosensweig*, I was happily reminded of a well-heeled, star-studded, fifties Tennent production at the Haymarket. Gentle, gracious, elegant and comfortable, it had many of the hallmarks of a Banbury production from his heyday.

No book constructed round the career of Frith Banbury could be devoid of anecdotes. There are the classic encounters of Dame Sybil and Dame Edith during Hunter's *Waters of the Moon*. Edith in tears about Sybil's over-acting; Edith pacified, after six months, with a new Balmain gown ('and do give Sybil a new cardigan'). Binkie Beaumont removed a snowman from the set because it upset Dame Edith. That reduced the designer to tears: 'The Dame's tears,' came the steely response, 'are more important than the designer's tears. Get rid of it.'

On Gladys Cooper's entrance on the first night of *The Holly and the Ivy* she had forgotten to take out a Polo mint she was sucking. On her first line she spat it across the stage, past a bemused Paul Scofield. At the dress rehearsal, she had been fascinated by Act One – not being in it, she had not bothered to read it.

Best perhaps is the gentle N.C. Hunter's widow who turned to spiritualism after her husband's death. In the grave his determination appeared to stiffen. When, during a revival of *The Waters of the Moon* in 1977, the management asked Mrs Hunter to accept a smaller author's royalty to keep down costs, she consulted her dead spouse. Norman said no.

Frith got through quite a few of the stories on the air.

At the George the three members of the visiting band, The Rocking Birds, turned up. Three strapping 30-somethings (country rock) who once had a deal with Sony who dropped them when the Sony corporate structure changed. Now they've bravely called their new album *Whatever Happened to the Rocking Birds?*

I did a quick Waitrose, demolished a large fillet of smoked haddock, and went to 76 Oxford Street – my first visit to Talk Radio. Quite a large studio and office space it seemed, since they appear to have no listeners. A pleasant youth talked about the *Humorous Quotations* and introduced another man who professed to be an expert on memory. I have my doubts. I got back to miss the Grand National but in time to see Jenny Pitman the winning trainer in happy tears and her young first National jockey very chirpy.

Magdalena brought bread. She thinks her mother is dying and plans to fly to Bucharest. She is terrified of the airbus since the recent accident. We must arrange for her to fly BA. To the Caprice to feed Millicent Martin and her husband (almost my longest-known friend in America), Marc Alexander. Both looked fine. Millie is on a break touring *Noises Off*. We are offering her the take-over in *A Passionate Woman*. I hope she likes it. The Caprice smooth as ever. I walked them to the theatre and came home to an early night.

I read of Labour Party rumblings to reform the House of Lords. Lord Redesdale, father of all the Mitfords, would not have approved. In a memorable speech in the House of Lords he once defended the hereditary principle as 'the very foundation of the Christian faith'. According to Jessica in *Hons and Rebels* he 'patiently explained that just as Jesus became God because he was the Son of God, so the oldest son of a Lord should inherit his father's titles'!

Sunday 9ᵗʰ April

David Thacker's production of Arthur Miller's *A View from the Bridge* has started the new fashion for theatres opening on Sundays – long a commonplace in New York, it has only just got round union objections here. It's good for actors. Having had to work late on Saturday they play their Sunday matinée, have the evening, all Monday and Tuesday until curtain-up, to rest or frolic. Of course Monday nights are notoriously slow.

It was a spare reading of the play with some very good acting; but the text has some difficulty surviving the 40 years since it was first done. I find it hard to sympathise with Eddie Carbone whom I wanted to commit into care almost as soon as the play started. This in spite of a fine performance by Bernard Hill and another immensely sympathetic one from Joseph Fiennes – to add to the excellent tutor with which he partnered Helen Mirren in her wonderful *A Month in the Country* last year.

I went with Glen Roven, who is off to Gozo to celebrate signing on with Brian Brolly, the manager for his Dr Seuss musical. We bumped into Toby Robertson who has finally got round to raising the subject of my introduction to *Theatrical Anecdotes*. My 'American friend, David Yakir,' I wrote, 'bumped into the inspired provincial and touring director, Toby Robertson, in New York and dragged the conversation around to me without mentioning that we knew each other. "A funny thing about Ned Sherrin," said Toby. "Everybody in England thinks he must be well-known in America. Everybody in America thinks he must be well-known in England. In fact, nobody knows who he is anywhere."'

'I wrote to you at the BBC,' he said. 'Did you get the letter?' I didn't and said so. Toby attempted amiably to deny what he said, but did not protest too much when I elaborated on the veracity and told him I was particularly proud of riposting with the 'provincial and touring' tag.

The Quote of the Week is from the Prime Minister addressing the Surrey Cricket Club's 150th Anniversary dinner. 'The game is uncertain. The career is chancy. But they both have their charm. Politics is often about nightmares. Cricket is mainly about dreams.'

Millie rang to say she loved *A Passionate Woman*. I hope it works out.

Monday 10ᵗʰ April

I lunched at Bar Central with Bill Alexander, artistic director of the Birmingham Rep and his producer John Stalker (no relation). They have the rights – or they have an understanding, due to run out, with Alan Clark – to make a play out of his *Diaries*.

By a magic chance both sides suggested I should do it – I have co-opted Alistair Beaton. The rights still have to be negotiated. Mark Berlin represents Alistair (as well as Keith W). He will probably handle it for us as we could best use the formula he devised for *Jeffrey Bernard*.

We instanced various approaches:

1. Find some device of incarceration as for *Bernard* – so that he can review his past with the small supporting cast nipping in and out to evoke special incidents.

2. Some bigger-scale Brechtian scheme, possibly with a Clark character and a detractor.

3. A Foyle's lunch for Alan. He begins his speech and the assembled worthies slip into the various characters as required. Possibly a hint of Saltwood Castle upstage, also evoking the Palace of Westminster.

4. No single Alan Clark but a dinner party at which he is expected. The others talk about him and take turns in appearing as him as their anecdotes are acted out.

I liked Bill Alexander. He is enjoying Birmingham and is still bitter about his exit from Stratford. He appreciates the idea of a woolly, well-meaning leftie like him being fascinated by the politically incorrect Alan Clark.

Very funny tenants' meeting in my block at 7.30. I had forgotten and was going to make a telephone call and try to behave badly when I opened my little pocket diary and saw the entry. Apparently the building must be seen to and we must subscribe thousands of pounds. Two Ealing Studios estate managers addressed us in Boultingese satirical language and a few of my neighbours asked tentative questions with which they dealt easily. Just as the rather efficient chairman was closing it, someone – could it have been me? – asked a frivolous supplementary and a barney started between the men in suits and a foreign person about his drains. We fled.

Tuesday 11th April

Auditions for *Salad Days*. We are looking not for a piano but for a young hero and heroine. They need to be nice, fresh and young. The girl must sing particularly well. The boy must act, sing a bit, leap about as if dancing, and act charmingly. The girls, with one exception, were hell. Mrs Worthington is obviously alive and well and sending her daughter to auditions. The men were much better. At least two genuine possibilities, including Simon Connolly, the boy who scored a success as the errand boy in *She Loves Me*, which despite all its notices and awards appears, as ever over 30 years, not to be drawing the town.

Wednesday 12th April

To Birmingham, crack of dawn, to do *Good Morning with Anne and Nick*. Anne is still 'bonding' with her new fifth son. Nick and a blonde girl from Slough were hosting. Others included a flower arranger, Caroline Blackwood, whom I managed to miss on Intercity breakfast, a psychiatrist who looked like Starsky (of *S. & Hutch*), whom I wouldn't trust my psyche with, a transvestite and his happily married wife and Britain's first man in space, a wonderfully professional interviewee. I stuck to sports quotes which pleased Nick Owen and the camera crew.

Before catching the train back I did a local radio show with an obvious local character, Malcolm Boyden – very waggish Black Country. The perfect local radio host – plainly he hadn't had time or inclination to read the book and sensibly he was quite unworried.

He gave me a bottle of his home-brewed stout ('Boing Boing Stout – best before a Baggies Match') which the limo driver to the station said was an accolade.

Did a signing at Waterstone's in Kingston in the evening – about

30 people and a very enthusiastic young staff. Apparently 60-odd had asked for tickets and they couldn't understand why more had not turned up. I suggested that Crystal Palace and Manchester matched on TV might be a contributing factor.

14th April – Good Friday

I picked up a half a dozen beautifully fresh hot cross buns in the King's Road and took them to the office for the *Loose Ends* team before going down to a studio to do fifteen interviews for *Humorous Quotations*. Good Friday was a good day to choose. I had to stay in London anyway and local radio stations probably found it hard to get interviewees.

Mainly the same questions were asked, but there was an amusing man on holiday in the Shetlands with his two children pretending he was in the Inverness studio on his own. He had great difficulty keeping the kids quiet and worried away at the shortage of Scottish quotes.

Saturday 15th April

Loose Ends. I talked to Christopher Martin Jenkins about the paperback of his very comprehensive cricket anthology. I'm not sure he had read it again recently – he got very mixed up over one or two of the entries and didn't jump with enthusiasm when I defined Peter Roebuck as the best contemporary cricket writer. Alexandra Bastedo was easily on top of her new book *Beware Dobermanns Donkeys and Ducks*, about her ever-growing collection of animals near Chichester. Mickey Hutton, a Newcastle comedian new to me, was funny and open.

The Neil Bensons picked me up at the George and we drove to Hickstead. Charlie has been given some cricket gear. He is not yet master of the game and tends to run off the field and sulk if given out. The Ross Bensons and the Nicky Kermans are also here and a lot more dogs as Tracy Brook's have come back from France and are out of quarantine. Much excitement as Charlie's new hamster has bitten through everyone's gloves and fingers and had to be returned to the pet shop and exchanged.

We played baby cricket on the lawn – no runs to be scored behind the wicket as it encourages damage to the dining-room windows and the conservatory. Young Douglas Brook and I opposed Charlie Bunn, Neil Benson and Sonny Mallet, Laura Levy's son. Charlie scored none, I think, but bore up manfully. Sonny did rather better and Neil scored 40-odd. I hadn't batted since a charity game in Greenwich, Connecticut, in 1977 – Gentlemen of England *v.* Rank Xerox – or bowled since three overs in a showbiz game near Beaconsfield in the late eighties. This was followed by several weeks of arthritis. Douglas Brook got 20 or 30 and I nudged in past the opposition total. With luck the child-standard of the game will not have set up any more aches and pains.

Sunday 16ᵗʰ April

Consumed with aches and pains! Peter Ryan, doctor, counselled two extra Panadol. I went to church at Albourne with Ross and Inge Benson and Arabella, their tiny, exquisite daughter. The Bishop of Horsham was making a guest appearance. A perky little Australian, he looked rather like Tony Robinson, the actor who plays Baldrick in *Blackadder*, in bright robes and electric mitre. He made great play of leaning on his crook in off-duty moments. I found the eccentric order of the Sung Eucharist hard to follow; we seemed to miss confession, the prayer of Humble Access and the Bidding, in favour of a reaffirmation of our baptismal vows, including the Bishop's advance on the font at the back of the church whence he sprayed the faithful with water propelled over us by a branch of yew.

Ross and I found his sermon a bit too much like a warm-up for a TV variety show but Inge was enchanted by its extroversion. Arabella behaved well throughout. The Bish had a 'visual aid' – a pair of spectacles painted black with a white cross on each lens. He made the point that without these glasses all he saw was a roomful of people 'in varying stages of decay'; if he put on the glasses he could hear the word of Jesus and he became concerned and responsible not only for himself but also for those around him. This and a great deal of gesticulation held the congregation. I can't take all the turn-round-and-shake-hands-with-your-neighbour business which we were encouraged to do. The Bishop traipsed round the lovely little church during collection and shook hands with everyone fixing us with his piercing blue eyes. Too happy-clappy for me but the church was very full and the sacrament was administered three-handed with great speed and efficiency.

The tenderest Easter lamb for lunch with beautifully roast potatoes and a delicious ratatouille. And some wonderful Cheddar cheese called Dorset Dump, brought by the Kermans.

I read a pedestrian biography of Billy Rose which I've been meaning to get round to, until dinner – immediately preceded by the last episode of Joanna Trollope's *The Choir* direly adapted by her ultra-pedestrian writer husband Ian Curteis. The pace was leaden and there seemed to be a choice of endings, each one featuring a more exotic sunset and ambitiously swelling music.

Salad-and-omelette supper, enlivened by a phone call from the *Daily Express* asking Douglas for information on one of Prince Philip's grooms who has been shot in America. Douglas didn't know anything about him so we propelled Inge Benson to the phone as editor of the Royal mag, *Majesty*. She had driving lessons with him. She talked for a long time and we await her quotes in the morning. Bed at 12.30, a very early night for Hickstead.

I forgot the conversational highlight of the weekend. Jodie Kidd, sixteen-year-old great-granddaughter of the first Lord Beaverbrook, was in four pages of the *Telegraph*'s Saturday supplement – as a model. All girls want to be super-models now. She may, it is said, earn a million pounds this year.

Recently she was modelling adjacent to Naomi Campbell, another over-priced and undercantilevered beauty. Ms Campbell, as big star, had dropped a tight or a stocking or some woman's thing.

'Pick it up,' she commanded Jodie.

'Get a life,' said Ms Kidd stalking off on her flamingo legs.

Monday 17ᵗʰ April

Much about the royal groom on page 2 of the *Express* but no mention of Inge! Cricketing aches and pains almost gone.

The good weather has gone too. Grey and windy from my bedroom window overlooking Douglas's magnificent cellar which is housed in the ruin of a thirteenth-century monastery in the grounds. I shall get out and go for a walk around the show ground. The slopes leading down to it are still an ocean of pale daffodils and narcissus. But all are too far gone to be plundered for my sideboard.

The Bensons drove me back after we had feasted with our hosts at the Shanghai Brasserie – late Castle Inn. Douglas's daughters, Chloë and Daisy, returned from a horse show. They eat, sleep, wash and fax in the huge horsebox. The girls are fifteen and twelve and look a wonderful, stylish, natural nineteen and sixteen. Lorna would be proud, but sad at Charlie's confused confidence to a little friend late at night.

'Sometimes I worry that Mummy might die.'

'But . . .'

'Oh yes, of course, Mummy is dead . . .'

At home I did the correspondence and had an early night.

Tuesday 18th April

First day of rehearsal with the men who are taking over the roles in A Passionate Woman. Stephanie will stay until July. Wisely, but generously, she came in to read the play with the new boys. Gordon Alcock who understudies Alfie Lynch and did so well the day BR let Alfie down has been promoted. One of the new two is Ian Puleston-Davies, a friend of Mulrooney's. He and Neil were at the Guildhall School together. Ian is two years the senior. Neil, whose grant never seemed to come through, spent some time sleeping on the floor of a flat Ian had assumed control of after his ex-girlfriend left. Unfortunately her father was the landlord and he soon had them both out. Ian's an engaging, inventive Welsh farm boy and had mastered a lot of the text – though when we got him on stage, of course the moves threw it to buggery. Gary Webster is playing James Gaddas's role – the ghost of Stephanie's lover. Described as Welsh, James played it Geordie, and Gary, after one tentative line as Welsh is happy to play cockney. He had an honourable success doing Minder following Dennis Waterman.

I had not heard – Stephanie couldn't wait to tell it – the story of the previous Thursday. An old lady – maybe an octogenarian – in a wheelchair had a commanding view of stage and audience from her vantage point in a box. When Steph entered the old girl turned to the stalls and said, ''Ere she comes, that's Stephanie, give her a clap!' and proceeded to lead the applause and add comments. When Alfie Lynch made his entrance in Act Two, she yelled, 'Here's another fine actor!' and led another round. As the set revolved and Stephanie appeared on the roof she waved and shouted, 'Hello, Stephanie!' Somehow both cast and audience loved it. At the end those on stage gave her a round and bowed to her. David Conolly, the boys' understudy, saw her son/minder pushing her chair across Leicester Square afterwards and heard her announcing in stentorian tones, 'Next, I want to see *Oliver!*'

We should warn Cameron Mackintosh.

A good day on stage and a jolly coming-together luncheon at Giovanni's, nearly next door.

Wednesday 19th April

A party in Flood Street for Alexandra Bastedo's book *Beware Dobermanns, Donkeys and Ducks*. She brought two ferrets but refused to put them down her trousers. I talked mainly to Lucy Fleming and Simon Williams. Patrick Garland introduced his wife – eloquently as always. And she, Alexandra, *sans* notes, remembered everyone she had to thank. Her publisher, Jeremy Robson, looked genuinely pleased that someone else appeared to be paying for the party.

As I was about to go I was introduced to the American playwright Bernard Slade (*Same Time Next Year*) and his wife. They were charming, interesting and interested – fans of *Side By Side*. We compared notes on John Alderton who is a friend and, more especially, on Michael Crawford who had a non-success with Bernard's comedy ages ago at the Prince of Wales. On another occasion when they met, Crawford kept referring to himself in the third person. 'Michael would do this,' 'Michael wouldn't do that.' Finally Bernard enquired, 'Who's Michael?' Crawford looked amazed. 'Me,' he said.

Thursday 20th April

To the Waterside Inn after early rehearsal. I am chairman of a curious foodie club called The Tabasco Club because it is to some extent backed by Paul McIlhenny of Tabasco ilk. We met at Patrick Gwynne Jones's restaurant Pomegranate in the Grosvenor Road, and about 60 food writers, restaurateurs, etc. bussed to Michel Roux's Waterside

Inn at Bray. It was a jovial journey, much oiled by champagne. Simon Hopkinson and Brian Turner were a little the worse for their celebration the night before at the Glenfiddich awards. Simon had won best cookbook. There was general tut-tutting about Jonathan Meade who had apparently been rude about Richard Griffiths who was compering the occasion. Simon took him off to Bibendum for dinner afterwards and had to borrow a chair from Daphne's. Richard does not fit cosily into chairs with arms.

I had not realised that Simon had relinquished his hands-on cheffing at Bibendum and is concentrating on his books and his *Independent* column. The bus passed the Lyndsey House on Cheyne Walk where he used to cook for Christopher Selmes and Geoffrey Roberts. He recalled the famous night when Alan Clark tasted some New World wines there and went on to screw up his ministerial speech in the Commons and was challenged by Clare Short.

Mr McIlhenny looks straight out of Faulkner or Tennessee Williams – apparently he looks even more so in white suits on the island whence Tabasco comes. I had better list the menu:

Bavarois de Tomates, Parfum de Tabasco

Asperges Sauce Hollandaise à l'Emince de Truffes

(Here arrived the Château de Chamirey, Blanc, Antonin Rocket 1992)

Choucroûte de Fruits de Mer

Tranche de Boeuf en Brioche, Petit Primeurs Jus au Basilic with Château de Rully, Rouge Rully, 1989

Assiette de Trois Desserts with Tokay Aszu Puttonys, 1990

The river sparkled, the food was special, the Fruits de Mer came in the loveliest light broth. I sat between Simon and a pleasant McIlhenny relative who is doing research at Cambridge, and could not have had a better time.

Friday 21st April

Voiceover for the *Independent*.

Rehearsal – Stephanie has joined us late afternoons and the process of getting to grips with their roles is becoming more real for the boys. Harder for her to adjust to different characterisations when we spent so much time and care on working out the original show – and she and her colleagues have found so much to add since then. It's always a difficult process for the inhabitant and the newcomer. She is being magnificently patient and flexible.

Then to Broadcasting House to look at the new 'Radio Theatre' – late concert hall. Looks all right . . .

Saturday 22nd April

A lovely *Loose Ends* audience in the new hall, filling both stalls and the small balcony.

A rather lacklustre monologue – it's usually such *fun* to do it for an audience and not be accused of getting sniggers from a small clique. Today's sagged. Rue McClanahan, on *The Golden Girls*, a TV series, whom I have hardly seen and who is to play the Josephine Hull role in *Harvey* in the West End, was charming. Ms Hull said one of my favourite things about playing Shakespeare: 'Unless you're a king you never get to sit down.'

Rue was very sharp about poor Raquel Welch and her disastrous tour of Shaw's *The Millionairess* which won't come to London – 'So much energy in such a wrong role.'

Nick Broomfield – always labelled 'Pretty Boy' Broomfield by his rivals – was on to celebrate his three video documentaries. His trailing-Maggie-Thatcher-show – he never really got to her – had two revealing passages which didn't make it. One was a story about her singing 'Baby, it's Cold Outside' in some unbelievable contest at a plastics factory outside Colchester in her youth. The other was about Robert Runcie – a friend of hers at Oxford – who made the point that she was very strong on the Old Testament, an eye for an eye, etc. but couldn't grasp the New and all that compassion.

Sunday 23rd April

The first reviews for the *Oxford Dictionary of Humorous Quotations* are coming in. A very sniffy one in the *Independent*. Two raves: Claire Colvin in the *Sunday Express* and Peter Grosvenor in the *Daily Ditto*. A large one from Bevis Hillier in the *Spectator* – some criticism but *quite* good. Best was a huge extract from the Introduction on the cover of the *Telegraph*'s Arts and Books section, illustrated by a big cartoon of famous quotees.

That's the right sort of criticism.

Monday 24th April

I rehearsed the newcomers again. Vast steps in learning – and characterisation. Poor Ian Puleston-Davis racked by flu but carried bravely on.

To Manchester at four (by OUP car) to do a Lit. dinner and signing for *Humorous Quotations*. It was a happy gathering organised by Dillons in their office bistro and wine bar, oddly named Ganders Go South. I failed to find out why. Their young staff were cheerfully welcoming and recovering from all the internal schisms inside Dillons. One young man, Nick Lewis, who had been an undergraduate at Warwick University, was proud of his correspondence with the late Kenneth Williams. Russell Davies printed several of Kenneth's replies. Nick told me that he had written to him sensing a kindred spirit when he read of Kenneth's penchant for being alone in his *Autobiography*. I checked it when I got home just after two in the morning (Mr Baldwin is a very efficient Jehu). I like Kenneth's words to him on the subject of friendship. 'There are no rules. The friends are those who take the chaff and grain together, keep what's worth keeping and with a breath of kindness blow the rest away.' The letters are helpful to a younger person, but not patronising. They also point up how much Kenneth was worrying about his own pains. He still had time to write ' . . . Yes, I know what you mean about adolescence and the turbulent nature of burgeoning sex-urges. Just remember everyone else experiences much the same but few of 'em are articulate about it. You're both sophisticated and self-aware, so of course you feel it much more.' There is also a very Kenneth lewd joke in the last line of the last letter printed. He is talking of the BBC's (now lamented) Paris studio. 'Oh! I know that studio like the back of hand. And I've looked at *that* quite a few times.'

Collectively they were very chirpy about other writer/speakers who have addressed them. Maya Angelou, very star conscious – furious no one met her at the station. Jeffrey Archer – never been: 'We hear he's difficult.' Alan Bennett – 'He went to Waterstones – Faber are very snobby.' I enjoyed it and them and their audience.

Tuesday 25ᵗʰ April

We rehearsed with Stephanie. She is marvellously good at adapting herself to the new actors. Where Mulrooney was an endearing giraffe as her son, Ian is a little terrier. Where James Gaddas as her ghostly lover was strong and silent, Gary Webster is a cocky, sexy wideboy. Ian's flu has ascended into a head cold. Stephanie was majestically able to put a disappointment about a BBC series out of her head – or gives a very good impression of doing so – and played with them in total concentration.

I'm looking forward to my trip to South Africa. I haven't mentioned it, have I? I'll fill in tomorrow.

Friday 28ᵗʰ April

David Yakir arrived on the overnight flight from New York. He's an old friend from my time there when we were doing *Side By Side By Sondheim* on Broadway in 1977, and we have established a sort of same-time-next-year pattern of shared holidays. Well, not exactly shared and not exactly at the same time because it usually depends on someone asking me to go somewhere and talk to someone (e.g. QEII), or write about it on my return, and paying for most of it. A few years back we did the Orient Express and Venice; last year we went to Morocco. This year I wanted to see South Africa for the *Mail on Sunday* so we plan to do Cape Town, Johannesburg, the Mount Grace Country Hotel and then finish up in Sun City. Yakir has been getting very excited over the phone – first of all about the Palace at Sun City, to which we were going anyway, and then about the Blue Train from Cape Town to Johannesburg. This I had not heard about but the travel agents managed to get us on for about 500 quid. It means leaving Cape Town a day earlier but it seems worth it for a lazy, luxurious look at the countryside which promises to be spectacular.

Friday has become a crowded day. I have to do a voice over for the *Independent*; a dress rehearsal for the new cast of *A Passionate Woman*; preparation for *Loose Ends*; and an award ceremony and after-dinner speech at *The Lawyer's* prizegiving. And there is an annoying glitch in that Wendy Driver of the *Mail on Sunday* rang to say the flight was so full no one could get us up-graded for the twelve-hour journey to Cape Town. Not the best way to start a holiday. I'm tempted to review the flight rather than the visit.

David went to see *Pash Woman* at the Comedy (with Robert Farrant) and I joined them at Joe Allen after the lawyers' do, which was uneventful. They had enjoyed Stephanie and Neil Morrissey particularly but Yakir couldn't see it as a Broadway or off-Broadway prospect – in contrast to most Americans who visit.

Saturday 29ᵗʰ April

A smooth *Loose Ends* with Dale Winton, son of Sheree Winton, a busty blonde whom I used a couple of times for small parts in *TW3*. She committed suicide – traumatically for Dale – when he was in his very early twenties. Now he is a very popular, Larry Grayson-style, camp compere for a morning shopping quiz. The others were Kim Criswell, who is opening at the Pizza in the Park with a wonderful Mermanesque voice; she probably sang the wrong song, a point number, not quite clever enough. But she talked well. Rudolph Walker and Keith Allen, the comic and entrepreneur who has a reputation for being difficult but behaved beautifully.

To Heathrow in time for the six o'clock flight. South Africa Airlines staff still very apologetic about the full flight but at least they found us two seats upstairs with plenty of leg room and a pass to the executive lounge.

Imagine our surprise as we came on board and went up to the top level to find that the economy, business and first-class sections were all half empty. I can't see the point of lying when we were bound to view the evidence for ourselves. If it's against company policy why not just tell us? After dinner Jayne Morgan – *Loose Ends* producer – materialised beside us. We are doing the show from Johannesburg this next week. I thought she would be on a later flight but she hopped onto this one at the last moment as more convenient. She confirmed the wide open spaces downstairs. I took a sleeping pill and had a reasonable night.

Sunday 30th April

'You must try the ostrich egg omelette for breakfast,' my friend Benson
had said, when he heard that I was starting the trip at the dignified
Mount Nelson Hotel in Cape Town. 'Do I have to eat the whole
egg?' I asked in some dismay. Benson thought not; but his expression
indicated that a trencherman of his capacity would think nothing of
dispatching one, or even two.

Nevertheless, the dream omelette buoyed me up on that long overnight flight from Heathrow – six in the evening to six in the morning
as near as dammit; and it heartened me as we drove on against a
delicate rose-pink sunrise from the airport towards Cape Town. We
gave Jayne a lift from the airport and we got more pink sunrise than
we had bargained for as my map-reading first sent us some thirty
kilometres away from Cape Town, past heartbreaking rows of squatter
lean-tos – acres of rickety wardrobe-sized dwellings. Each hovel
housed a family not yet awake. We repassed them as we realised our
mistake and traced our way back towards the massive Table Mountain
– uncapped by its 'table cloth' of cloud on this clear morning. Finally
we drove confidently through the stately Doric columns at the entrance
to the Mount Nelson, installed in 1924 along with sixty palms from
the Canaries, to make a suitable approach avenue for the visiting
Prince of Wales the next year.

The room was not ready – it was, after all, still only just after eight
o'clock, so we found our way through gardens laden with hibiscus
blossoms to the Oasis restaurant where breakfast beckoned. A Buck's
Fizz shook off the travel weariness. A buffet of exotic fruits was a
perfect prelude to my encounter with the vast egg and among the
chafing dishes I could see a burly chef who looked remarkably like
Graham Gooch and a huge bowl of egg-coloured stuff which I assumed
to be my ostrich grail.

The fruits despatched, I approached the chef. 'I hear you are justly
famous for your ostrich egg omelettes,' I said, sucking up. This did
not go down well. 'No,' he replied, 'people didn't like 'em.' (It was
only last Christmas when Benson returned with his glowing report).
'We had to take 'em off.'

Never mind, I had picked up a brochure advertising an ostrich
farm before I left the airport. There was hope yet. Jayne went off after

breakfast with an ex-boyfriend with whom she was staying until she flies to Johannesburg. He is very good-looking, involved in some sort of good works and devoted also to having a good time. Yakir very susceptible to his charm.

The Mount Nelson overlooks Cape Town and stands pinkly and proudly immediately beneath Table Mountain, which is eerily floodlit at night. It is a perfect place from which to explore the Cape. Settled and bathed, we investigated the newish Waterfront development for lunch. The Victoria and Albert Basins are now crammed with malls, bistros and boutiques resembling their bustling counterparts in Sydney, San Francisco and, in drier surroundings, Covent Garden. Once a no-go area patrolled by aggressive customs police, the Waterfront owes its new freedom to a prostitute who protested her harassment by officials, took her case to the High Court and won. Her legacy is a thriving food, entertainment and shopping Mecca. The promotional magazine *The Waterfront* beckoned us to the Dock Road Restaurant with a fine photograph of its chef Barak Hirschowitz, knee-deep in surf, clutching a fat, struggling crayfish: lunching on two of its close relatives (3½-pounders), slurping a Bloody Mary in the sun, listening to an *a cappella* black choir on one side of us and a guitar-led fifties acoustic group on the other, we did our sums and realised that if the cocktails came to 6.80 rand each, and you can buy more than 5 rand for a pound, we were in for ten days in which every hour was Happy Hour.

In the afternoon we toured the tip of the Cape – a wonderful drive along the rocky, most southerly edge of the Atlantic Ocean, easy to accomplish in a long afternoon. Spectacular mountain ranges rise steeply from the narrow, cliff-hugging road. First after Table Mountain you follow a route dictated by twelve enormous peaks, The Apostles. Then you are nearly crowded into the sea by the breathtaking Chapman's Peak Drive. David, who was negotiating this perilous course, still had time to compare it to the most arresting views of Southern California and indeed, as our trip progressed, everything we saw began to mirror for him some outstanding piece of American scenery. Cape Town he equated with San Francisco.

Sadly, we could not compare our evening target, the rich winelands of Constanzia, with his homeland. By now it was dark and our target was Cape Town's most famous restaurant, Constanzia Uitsig, the showplace of a wine farm, slap bang in the middle of its own vineyards and only some twenty minutes' drive from the Mount Nelson.

By day we would have had the famous 360-degree views of mountains and sea, a trademark of South Africa's oldest vineyards, first established in the seventeenth century. Constanzia Uitsig boasts lawned gardens, a watermeadow and a Victorian cricket pavilion.

The carpaccio di pesce, wafer-thin slices of raw fish dressed in soya sauce, red vinegar, sesame oil, ginger and seaweed, is the most memorable dish I ate in South Africa. I enjoyed my braised tripe; Yakir thought his duck tough enough to lead to suspicions that it might have had a disturbed childhood – basking though it was in a tempting honey and lemon sauce. Odd if it was a local duck – they raise them amongst the vines at Constanzia Uitsig to control the snail and slug population. All over the Cape you see signs saying KWAKERIE. I refused to ask what it meant in case it did not translate as 'Duck Farm'. We were guided to two young Constanzia wines, a frisky Sauvignon Blanc '94 and a mellow Shiraz; and once again marvelled at a total tab (with two dry sherrys) of R182.50 – which at my rule of 5 comes out at just over £35 the entire meal for two.

May

~~~~~~~~~~◦||◦~~~~~~~~~~

Monday 1st May

A DAY TO explore the Stellenbosch, rolling green countryside over-looked by impressive rocky outcrops – the home of the largest selection of South African wines and the site of the first 'wine route', established in 1971. The vines were turning to autumn reds and golds, their boundaries marked at the end of each row by a solitary red or white rose bush. 'New England in the fall' was Yakir's comparison. We ignored the temptation to go mad tasting in the cool cellars, and found the delightful Devon Valley Hotel billed correctly as 'a rare find in the heart of the winelands', where we sat on a sun-kissed terrace looking down across the valley, safe in the knowledge that wine, soup, charcuterie and a ploughman's would knock us back less than twenty quid.

I had wondered if there would be any theatre to catch in South Africa. I knew English music-hall acts had gone out with the Gold Rush in the 1880s and that Gwen Ffrangcon-Davies and Marda Vanne ran a successful company in the forties; and of course there is Athol Fugard's work, but after all this *is* the country where 25 or so years ago Anne Ziegler and Webster Booth played *Who's Afraid of Virginia Woolf!* And where my friend Michael Hill was introduced to an actor in 1946 who was described as the 'Gielgud of South Africa'. Michael asked him what he was in at the moment and he said 'Panto'.

If Cape Town is the gateway to the country then Pieter Dirk Uys is a satirist who can lead the visitor expertly and amusingly into the new South African political situation. Having given the new regime a twelve-month honeymoon period he returns to the Dock Road Theatre with an entirely new one-man/woman show *You ANC Nothing Yet*. His targets range from our Queen to Winnie, Queen of Africa. In

June he's coming to the Tricycle in Kilburn as part of LIFT (London International Festival of Theatre). After the show he was very funny about South Africa's prospects of snaring the Olympics in 2004. As the airports are run at the moment he reckons it will take eight months to get the athletes into the country and another eight months to get them all out. We went with Jayne and her host.

Yakir snores like an enraged elephant. Otherwise a peaceful night.

Tuesday 2nd May

I was still hoping for a taste of ostrich. I consulted the flyer I picked up at the airport advertising the 'West Coast Ostrich Ranch . . . open daily . . . restaurant serving authentic ostrich steak and eggs'. We found it half an hour's drive due north. I am now an expert on ostriches. Their huge eyes allow space for only tiny brains. They mate six times a day. One cock is usually allocated three hens. Each egg-laying season the hen first produces a small infertile egg, about the size of a goose egg, to prove that she can do it. They feed on hay, vitamins and their own droppings and are very susceptible to tapeworm. They fight a lot and have huge protective breastplates. They have to be mature before you can identify their sex – then the males are much showier and develop red legs. The gestation period for an ostrich egg is six weeks.

We got to sit astride a corralled ostrich to be photographed with Table Mountain in the distant background. There are some 150 birds of all ages on the farm, tended largely by teenage girls. We were shown round by a world-wandering Taiwanese who had been there six weeks. Having majored in ostrich I wanted to eat some.

'An omelette, perhaps?'

'Sorry, eggs are out of season.'

'A steak?'

'Sorry, in the deep freeze.'

'What about this smoked ostrich toasted sandwich?'

Diligent enquiry elicited that it was 'off'.

On the other hand, the souvenir shop was bulging with ostrich curios. There were eggs to commemorate the World Rugby Cup, decorated with the badges of all rugby playing nations; half-eggs with stuffed baby ostriches peering out; cartooned eggs with fluffy cartoon characters inside; ostrich fans, ostrich-feather dusters; ostrich egg candles swimming in wax; single, gaudily dyed ostrich feathers and ostrich-foot lamp stands.

I was 'ostriched-out' by the time we got to dine in the stately red plush Grill Room at the Mount Nelson and rejected Ostrich and wild mushroom consommé, Ostrich carpaccio with a soufflé of prunes and parmesan shavings, and Ostrich *filet* marinated in Bulgarian yoghurt. We drank a very pleasant Merlot, oddly called 'Meer-lust'!

Conversation on these expeditions often descends into comparing intestinal notes. I am having no trouble, quite the reverse. Yakir is complaining a great deal.

Wednesday 3rd May

The second leg of the trip was the Blue Train, the most luxurious in the world. It has been in some sort of service since the twenties and so it is a comfortably developed and developing institution, not a beautiful anachronistic, deco museum-piece like the Orient Express. However, it is just as cosseting and the twin cabin is twice as spacious. It included a roomy shower room with a jet of steaming high-pressure water. No need for recourse to eau de cologne, so essential on the Orient by the time you reach the Tyrol. We had handed in the car to Avis, and a sweet local driver, very proud of the Blue Train, took us down to the station.

The journey is a bumpless, no-rattle joy. For twenty-four hours it is not even 'happy hour' – all drinks are free. As you leave the station punctually at 11 a.m., Torro Seegers, the train manager, bounds into your sitting room as you open your complimentary bottle of champagne and briefs you about the journey. The train glides imperceptibly through dreary industrial suburbs – but only for a few minutes. Then plains line the route with acres of vines and orchards broken by fields of ripening squash and florid peppers.

When you feel like an apéritif you pass smoothly to the observation lounge. You are greeted by 'biltong bites', weathered meat which looks like candied fruit but is much tougher. OK for a trek, perhaps, but better olives with a dry sherry. Of course they have these too. You move on through the high ranges of the Elandskloof mountains, sheltering more orchards and vineyards and fields of sunflowers and maize. As the anniversary of VE Day was coming up, all South Africa was phoning in about it on the radio channels. I sampled snoek pâté and, after soup and yellowtail fish, did battle with roast crocodile tail in a seeded mustard sauce. I ignored the skin (hard), left the centre (tough); but enjoyed the gelatinous layer in between.

By now we had slid through Wolseley and Worcester and curved among the dramatic Drakensberg Mountains. It was not only my New York companion who could envisage Native Americans cutting us off at the pass, leaping along the tops of our carriages and being foiled only just in time by John Wayne at the head of the US Cavalry.

At teatime the north-bound Blue Train stops for one hour at Matjiesfontein to play a great joke on its passengers. It certainly puzzled the parties of Japanese and the elderly American ladies whose faces and eyes had been lifted so drastically that only their colouring distinguished them from their Asian fellow travellers. After the Touws River – at the summit of the great Hex River Mountain Pass – the track crosses the Karoo, a desert, its name derived from the Hottentot word for 'thirstland'. Matjiesfontein, founded as a health resort 150 years ago became a military centre during the last Boer War. Dismounting, we were encouraged to take a bus tour. A red double-decker bus carried us along a Victorian main street still boasting a post office, bar and hotel. We turned a corner, passed a few more trim white villas and a tiny church and then turned again. A piece of dirtland was pointed out. Once, in the nineteenth century, a Test match was played on it. Then we were back at the station. A three-minute tour! The effect was only spoilt by the jokey tickets carrying regulations like 'standard condition of touring – the throwing of bones from the upper deck is strictly forbidden'. The two of us had a beer in the period bar – flaunting an advertisement for Old Ned aftershave and framed turn-of-the-century menus of innumerable courses invariably starting with turtle or mulligatawny soup and featuring game and a 'haunch of mutton'.

Thursday 4th May

We pulled into Johannesburg punctually at 11.30 and were presented with a certificate confirming that we had indeed travelled on the Blue Train. Elderly Americans were shunted into shooting brakes to go off on safari. The train was to take on some new arrivals – and the remnants of our group on to Pretoria. I recalled someone's – was it Harold Evans's? – vignette of Harold Macmillan in Pretoria during the Wind of Change tour: 'found the Prime Minister in his gayest mood ... he even gets up from the table to give a personal demonstration of a Morris dance in evidence that the English also have tribal dances.'

His mood must have deteriorated by the time he came to the actual speech. According to Alistair Horne's biog, 'one of his entourage recalled him having to be led to the lavatory to be physically sick'.

Johannesburg is a work-stop for me, doing *Loose Ends* live from SAB studios on the Saturday. Continuing the American parallel, the city combines Detroit – glum industrial; Chicago – big business skyscrapers; and Beverly Hills – lavish, high-walled, protected homes. It also offers one of the world's great theatre centres – the Market, where we caught a thrilling *Titus Andronicus*, led by Antony Sher, surrounded by a superb cast of local actors who all come to the National with it in the autumn. The tragedy *here* is that it was sparsely attended. It was depressing to hear that the artistic boycott is held locally to have destroyed South Africa's long habit of theatre-going. It was directed by Greg Doran, a brilliant bit of pacing and unobtrusive modernising, or rather fitting into the local landscape. Doran is very good-looking. Yakir has flipped again. Again to no purpose!

Ever adventurous on the reader's behalf, in the handsome high-walled restaurant at the Market I sampled masonja (mopani worms) with peri peri sauce. The peri peri part (very hot) was all right but the worm itself was like eating shrimp shells. The waiter said he preferred the way he fried them at home! Everything else was fine. I didn't notice 'Malamagogu – traditional black African tripe' on the menu until I got back to the hotel so I cannot report on it.

Oh, yes; and we had lunch with Jayne at a fancy French restaurant which 'catered for the Queen' on her recent visit. Very good.

Friday 5th May

A day spent setting up the programme and doing book interviews for *Humorous Quotations*. We dined Chinese with Jayne. She and Yakir are getting on very well. I went to bed early. He explored Champions, a gay disco. He arrived back quite early, having found it full of alarming young yuppie-ish South Africans – some one or two thousand he estimated – largely in the open air, with only one black face on view.

I recalled Stanley Baker's comment when he was making the movie *Zulu*, and read the law that the punishment for sex between whites and blacks (in 1963) was twelve strokes with a whip. According to Michael Caine he asked rather loudly, 'If I get caught, can I have the twelve lashes while I'm still doing it?'

Saturday 6th May

We did *Loose Ends* from a big music studio at South Africa Broadcasting in Auckland Park, Guateng. Just as well, as we had two groups, one a white *a capella* team who call themselves Not the Midnight Mass – because they made their début slung on at midnight in a Johannesburg club by a club owner who had no confidence in them. They were an instant success and are now very big all over South Africa. They have still to come to Edinburgh where they would be very popular – 'so expensive', they say. They reminded me of the old South African revue group Wait a Minim which played successfully for a couple of years at the Fortune Theatre in London and went on to Broadway. The other, black, group have had a success in Edinburgh and their old, grizzled pianist had been at the Shaftesbury Theatre back in the fifties with *King Kong* – a huge hit then, full of massed, stomping dances in Wellington boots. The late Oliver Tambo's son Daly – now a chat-show host and fashion designer – was the first guest. Extravagantly dressed in his own designs he was quick and camp.

Jayne Morgan pressed Yakir into service as a floor assistant to ferry guests from reception through the labyrinthine passages which make finding one's way around Broadcasting House in London a doddle in comparison. As he is now impossibly grand, heading his own company in New York with God knows how many fetching and carrying for him, he couldn't wait to get home and tell them how hard he had been worked. One white ANC woman politician and folk singer, who flew up from Cape Town that morning, only just made it on time. She talked with great intensity. She has just been banned from singing a speech in Parliament. Foolishly she took her guitar into the chamber and the Speaker refused to let her use it. She should have sung *a capella* as she did for us, then she would have been launched before they could stop her. Sadly the line to London went down towards the end of the programme when she was in mid-song. She has a lovely voice and is hunting a new recording contract. The breakdown was infuriating. The BBC had booked the line through Mercury apparently. Cheaper than BT but *no backup*! The result was that we lost about eight or nine minutes.

Thank goodness we got in Sello Mako Ka Ncube before the disaster. This most charismatic actor is playing Aaron the Moor in the Market *Titus*. He has enormous presence, keen intelligence and a wonderfully attractive and musical voice. He was about to take on Othello for another company when this offer came along. There will be time hereafter. He'll be a terrific Othello. Meanwhile he is an electrifying Aaron. I got him to speak the lines which follow soon after his 'is black so base a hue?'

Coal-black is better than another hue,
In that it scorns to bear another hue:
For all the water in the ocean
Can never turn a swan's black legs to white,
Although she lave them hourly in the flood.

They had a powerful effect on the tiny audience in the theatre and he delivered them thrillingly into the microphone. I hope they had as huge an impact at home as in the studio.

Sello is a disarming mixture of modesty and awareness of his worth. I prised a story out of him about playing Mark Antony last year. He is a TV soap star here. When he appeared, the theatreful of kids went mad. He had to quieten them and explain that this was a play, they must not cheer every time he entered. Then he smiled in an endearing sort of pride – 'it was like the Beatles!' he said simply. He should have a huge success in London – at the Tricycle in a local classic, *The Suit*; and at the Cottesloe with *Titus*.

The play sits famously on the recent history of bloodshed. One little boy who had lost his father watched it and all the slaughter intently but unmoved until the curtain calls. Then he burst into tears. Asked why, he wanted to know if his father too might rise up again.

The radio programme over, we hired a taxi to lead us out of

Johannesburg which is eccentrically mapped and defeated my readings. Some twenty kilometres out the driver pointed us in the direction of Mount Grace – the fourth leg of the resumed holiday.

Sunday 7th May

Mount Grace is an idyll set on a substantial hillside. A collection of thatched cottages are sprinkled around a grassy park, a swimming pool, two dining rooms and a lounge with a breathtaking view across rolling country. Lazily we did not avail ourselves of the walking trails, riding, tennis courts, pool room or the nearby Koi farm, trout farm, Wonder Caves and rhino reserves. We closed our eyes to the 123 species of birds listed in *Newman's Birds of Southern Africa* – from the Bar-throated Apalis to the Red-Throated Wryneck.

Summer sun smiled across the pool and in through the windows of Hartley's Bar – named after a famous Victorian White Hunter. According to Stuart Brand, the young John Travolta look-alike who co-owns the hotel, his father embroiders the legend of Hartley vigorously. Did he really frighten off a lion who was ruining his chances of stalking a herd of elephant by roaring at the beast through a beard of Tennysonian proportions?

Yakir frustrated yet again. Young Mrs Brand is an expert watercolourist.

The star waiter was one Pat'son, a Malawian who plays keyboard and guitar in the nearby town of Magaliesburg some afternoons and dreams of following a friend to perform in New York. Two others – two brothers – were equally charming, curious about England, proud of the standard of education in Malawi, which is obviously high, and delighted to discuss the theory of how a good mud-hut is constructed.

Mount Grace was an enchanted spot to gird our loins ready for the assault on the capital of Kitsch – The Palace of the Lost City. We had 'done' San Francisco, Southern California, New England, The Wild West, Detroit, Chicago and Beverly Hills. Mount Grace was a corner of the Napa Valley. Now we were ready for Las Vegas.

Monday 8th May

I had been expecting the Sun City complex to be a monument to vulgarity. In fact, the correct word is 'ostentatious'. No one could accuse the Palace of understatement; but the sort of extravagance it calls to mind is more like Henry Randolph Hearst's spectacular folly, San Simeon.

The Palace is the centrepiece of a vast leisure complex. Every palm, jungle tree, and piece of tropical foliage, every rock, rough-hewn or sculptured, is imported. Water is pumped up and down its pools and thundering waterfalls. There is a man-made beach with man-imported non-stick sand. A man-made machine produced waves in the 'Roaring Lagoon' big enough to support surfers. A man-made bridge is rocked every half an hour by a man-made earthquake. There are two golf courses. One is designed by Gary Player. On the other, one hole requires a drive on to the green over a crocodile pool. Unlucky golfers retrieve their balls at their peril. You can picnic in a hundred-acre game park or drift over it in a hot-air balloon.

Inside the hotel, sumptuous suites can go for as much as 12,000 rand a night. One of the two vast restaurants, The Crystal Court, with its giant sculpted columns, is on a scale that Cecil B. De Mille would have enjoyed toppling. Four nearly life-size, raging elephants form its centrepiece. The great crystal chandelier is hung with curving glass droplets evoking wispy, white ostrich feathers.

Everywhere the jungle motif is repeated. From carpets, curtains, murals, mosaics and the backs of chairs, the faces of monkeys, lions, rhinos, hippos and elephants stare out. Tusk shapes decorate the roofs. Bronze impala flee from bronze big cats by the entrance. In the Shawie Court a bronze cast of the biggest elephant in the Kruger National Park (Shawie) rears skywards in front of camera clickers – one a minute. Of course you can gamble at the sparsely attended tables or the busy slot machines and there is a tacky floor show. But the abiding memory of the Palace is opulence and comfort, surprisingly good cooking and impeccable service.

Wednesday 10th May

We flew back to Johannesburg from the only thatched-roof airport I have seen – 240 happy hours were over. We decided to have a go at upgrading for the return flight – caused a great fuss – and got the last two seats in club class. It was well worth it for the comfort and the splendid night's sleep.

Thursday 11th May

Yakir is staying until Saturday. He has been an ideal companion. We seem to pick up where we left off. There is always a wealth of information to convey – about his mother, the death of his father (last year), his performance at the funeral, his brother Scottie. Mama is hustling for a condo in Florida, where all her friends go. David has a very intense Jewish family loyalty, stiffened by deathbed promises to his father.

Then there is the vast off-stage cast of his office. When I met him he was feckless and 30-ish with an obsession for a glossy-model-driven clique in Manhattan, refusing to mature although there was a very definite theatrical talent as a director which he never really pursued. When we split up he eventually found a niche in a big advertising firm in New York, Grey, and showed a remarkable flair for organising their computer systems. Some wonderful equation balancing his emotional immaturity with his mid-30s social experience made him perfect to lead the way in the agency in the most rapidly expanding field. Now he has his own company inside the parent firm, called Blue Marble (the astronauts' first description of how the earth appeared to them from the moon). I have a very clear picture of the entire staff and all their squabbles and pretensions. It will be twelve months before I catch up on this everyday story of advertising folk.

I flew to Edinburgh in the evening to talk and sign at Waterstone's in Princes Street. About a hundred turned up. All very pleasant. Just got the shuttle back in time.

Monday 29th May

Since returning from South Africa I have had a curious reluctance to write this diary. Today is a bank holiday and so there is no excuse for not dragging myself to the desk.

It is not as though life has been uneventful. I've been to plug the book at a literary lunch in Brighton. It seemed to go well, although a respectable-looking old woman sidled past me on her way out and said disappointedly, 'I thought you'd be dirtier.' She then proceeded to tell me an appalling joke about what a gay ghost gives another gay ghost for Christmas. (Answer: the willies.) I went on to tea with Brian Brindley who has moved into a perfect Regency house, and stuffed it beautifully with the Victoriana and ecclesiastical furniture he has been collecting all his life. He is no longer a priest, having converted to Rome and had a small heart attack. He has also grown mutton-chop whiskers and a bravura white moustache and looks like some sort of high-camp version of Colonel Sanders.

The book trail has been hotting up. Having flown to Edinburgh the day I got back from South Africa, I did Hatchards in Chester and Dillons in Trafalgar Square. All talks and signing. In between I went down to Taunton to help launch an appeal for funds for the Brewhouse Theatre. I've also talked after dinner to rich Americans conferring at Stapleford Park; gone to Birmingham to talk at Waterstone's the next night; had a couple more bouts of root-canaling with Dr Alcaly; seen *A Passionate Woman* a couple of times. It's in good shape but Stephanie finds it hard to settle down with one of the new actors, having had such a close rapport with his predecessor.

I was back at Birmingham for two broadcasts at the end of last week. We did both from the Old Rep which Neal Foster (actor/producer) now runs. He came on *Loose Ends* years ago to promote his scheme for interviewing celebrities to raise money for his theatre company and credits us with giving him a vital boost. He was rueful about inviting Richard Dreyfuss to direct his Viking *Hamlet* last year, but said the auditions were fun! He does not lack chutzpah. He plans a production of *The Crucible* in the autumn and offered it first to Harrison Ford. Mr Ford said 'No'.

On the Friday we recorded *Counterpoint* with a celebrity panel. Radio 4 are having some sort of music week. John Amis, Richard

Stilgoe and the now sadly deceased Jeremy J. Beadle (no relation to he of *You've Been Framed*) represented roughly Radios 4, 2 and 3. I was worried lest they should fail to match the erudition and generosity which the lay contestants bring to the game but they all behaved beautifully and wittily and Jeremy J., having led at the end of Act One and trailed at the end of Act Two, blasted home to win in the quickfire Act Three.

The *Loose Enders* were up for an audience show the next day and we ate noisily at Birmingham's best bistro, Sloanes. I stayed for the first time at the newish Swallow, an entirely delightful hotel where everyone does their damnedest to be cheerful and helpful.

The programme went well. Not the best monologue but the audience lapped it up. Conversationally we were saved by John Berendt who made an overnight dash from America to promote his splendid book, *Midnight in the Garden of Good and Evil*, a docu-novel set in Savannah and centred around the town's eccentrics and the murder of a 21-year-old hustler Danny Hanford ('the good time that had not yet been had by all') by his protector, an antiques dealer who was reproved because he 'shot the best piece of ass in Savannah'. He was tried four times before getting an acquittal and then dropped dead from a heart attack some few weeks later. It is a riveting book, simply told and 'about to become a major motion picture', with, perhaps, a starring role for Lady Chablis – a real-life Savannah black drag queen.

I think part of my reluctance to get back to this diary stems from a reluctance to deal with a very odd correspondence from the young man in Sussex who wrote to me at the BBC back in early March. He is 'a professional sportsman – 28'. He writes eloquently and clearly, in a neat, educated hand. He expressed diffidence about writing to someone he doesn't know. 'I appeal to the explorer in you . . . rise above physical limitations . . . use a greater awareness and peer through this window of words. Another person there is waiting.' He wants to carry me 'on a journey where we can dance, play, touch, smile and laugh . . . I wish we could dance together, laugh and play . . .' I shall call him 'The Person from Plumpton'.

It was all very odd but there did seem to be an earnest niceness behind it so I waited a few days and then replied explaining that I would be in Brighton for the lit. lunch and perhaps he would care to come. Safety in numbers. He said yes on a card and enquired 'Do you like to be tickled?' I said no, and we finally met that Sunday, chaperoned by a few hundred Brighton ladies. He is terribly nice but I fear he is searching for a relationship of a sort I shall not be able to supply. He has written to ask for another meeting in London, 'Thank you for a wonderful time on Sunday ... I would like to meet again, would you? Perhaps on a more intimate level?' It seems rude not to agree but I have a fateful feeling that it is all going to end in tears.

June

~◊~

Sunday 4th June

YET ANOTHER TEMPORARY root-canalable tooth broke off into a warm croissant, WHEN WILL THIS TORTURE END?!

Ken Follett's forty-sixth birthday brunch – beautifully arranged – he lives about 400 yards away on Cheyne Walk. I had to leave early but the caterers provided a witty array of miniature eggs on toast, miniature smoked salmon bagels, and miniature croissants. Down in the waterlogged back garden there was a more substantial buffet. Happy chat with Des and Claire Rayner.

To the Comedy matinée to see if the new man has settled in. Stephanie has been unsure of her new son. Having, as it were, grown up with Neil Morrissey who 'mothered' her big, naive baby/woman character, she has found it difficult to accommodate a new, small, dark, volatile son. It has always looked good from the front but the chemistry has previously eluded them. I watched it with the producers and Kay Mellor and her thoughtful husband. Small adjustments perhaps; but Stephanie has patiently steered it on course.

I watched the closing minutes of the England/West Samoa game. I don't understand the first move in rugby – but had to watch to make sure we stayed in at best advantage. We did.

Monday 5th June

Time Out Eating and Drinking Awards. At a very curious venue – the Defina Studio Café, Bermondsey Street. Apparently artists who paint in studios upstairs can come down and have lunch for a quid.

There is a democratic air about these awards. Best Bar, Best Budget Meal, Best Vegetarian, Best South American, Best Café. I was presenting Best Modern British Restaurant – one of the nominees – Wide World in Hammersmith – expired between shortlisting and award – so my class was uniquely down to five finalists. The Chiswick in Chiswick won. Although offered a free meal there I was not able to check it out. Among the Modern British dishes offered by the various nominees were pumpkin risotto, confit of duck with white bean puree and grilled Thai chicken with red chilli jam.

An egregious Virgin Radio disc jockey led off the awards – hosted by spiky-haired Gary Rhodes who, I think, can only speak, as he does on television, with tremendous enthusiasm and hand-waving. The female Terry Christian, Dani Behr, was on our table with Frances Barber whom I shall see tomorrow in *Insignificance* at the Donmar. Harry Hill told some very funny surrealist food jokes before giving away the Best Budget Meal Award. I can't be seen writing down jokes and can't easily remember the surrealist sort without transcription. Richard Wilson, enchanting as always, complained because since he became Victor Meldrew he can't be seen complaining in a restaurant. He was depressed because Tony Sher had come to see *What The Butler Saw* on the one half-full, unresponsive matinée.

I got back to a call from Mark Berlin (agent for Alistair Beaton and Keith Waterhouse). Hostilities have commenced with Birmingham and Alan Clark. Duncan Weldon is prevaricating over the casting for Keith's play, *Bing Bong* – well, Betty Bacall can't agree a director for *The Visit* at Chichester and it rehearses in a couple of weeks and the woman in the Ayckbourn musical (a young actress) has died in early pregnancy just before the Chichester season. Who would be an impresario? Why aren't there more impresarios?

Tuesday 6th June

Technical meeting for *A Passionate Woman* touring set. Still no news of a replacement for Stephanie in London. Julie Walters, Pauline Collins and Pru Scales have all said no or aren't available. Millie Martin has taken a tour because she couldn't/wouldn't wait for a decision. She hates to risk being out of work.

Meeting with Stuart Hutchinson (MD for *Salad Days*). He is well ahead with the arrangements and seems very organised. No more casting yet on the senior roles.

To *Insignificance*, Terry Johnson's play at the Donmar, with Rick Kerwin, whose very trendy suit was made out of tea-bag material (the sacks, not 'the little perforations'). He had a suit copied while he was at an ashram in India. The play is a delightful 'imaginary conversation' in an hotel room, between Einstein, Senator McCarthy, Marilyn Monroe and Joe diMaggio (Alun Armstrong, Ian Hogg, Frances Barber and Jack Klaff). There's a bit of Shaw and a bit of Stoppard there but the main thrust is simply to entertain.

A buzzing Ivy. The Michaels of Kent at the next table ('go anywhere for a hot meal'?), Pamela Harlech and Derek Deane came by. Perfect late-night food. Tomato and basil galette with biscuit-thin pastry and a starter-size steak tartare. They provided a tiny egg, quail or plover, to top it. Rick talked earnestly about a mutual friend who is in therapy to make sense of an extraordinary adopted childhood.

Wednesday 7th June

I'm writing this on Thursday, an A4 pad on my knee en route to Bromsgrove in an OUP car. I am to talk to Reed Group Editors. Reed have bought fifty copies of *Humorous Quotations* as presents for the delegates.

To return to Wednesday. Michael De-la-Noy came along at 11.15 – just after my twelve petunias and six trailing carnations arrived to fill out the window boxes. De-la-Noy is writing Mervyn Stockwood's biography for Cassell. He sounded impressed by Mervyn, especially as a talent spotter, and reasonably certain, whatever Stockwood's inclinations and, however much in love he was at various times with young men, that he was celibate. He had visited Jane, Mervyn's sister, to find his *Independent* obit out before her with numerous underlinings and exclamation marks. He thought he had rumbled a lover in Dick Chapman, a schoolboy at Bristol whom Mervyn befriended (and who was at Oxford with me – dazzlingly good-looking), but clearly believed Dick's innocent account. So do I.

To *Measure for Measure* at the Barbican. The play increases in topicality (sleaze, religion, misgovernment, cover-ups) with every viewing. This is the third production I've seen in a couple of years. It has some interesting moments and a magnificent scene-stealing Lucio (Barry Lynch) in that most stealable of roles. Before Laughton's Angelo

(Old Vic, thirties) and Gielgud's for Brook (Stratford, forties), the emphasis was always on the Duke. So it came to be again in this rather operatic production by Stephen Pimlott which, though speedy and gripping, did not have the amazing insight of Declan Donnellan's recent version at the Lyric, Hammersmith. Stella Gonet looked a reluctant nun compared to Anastasia Hille. Alex Jennings, such a fine comedian, lost all personality as Angelo – though he had kept it when he played Richard II. Michael Feast's Duke grew more antic as the play proceeded but brought off some cunning effects.

I took Glen Roven on to St John to eat, in St John Street. Or rather, since he paid, he took me. He devoured his wild rabbit and mash in seconds. I toyed with a bantam egg and a delicious lamb's brains pâté. It was far too late and too rich so I took half home in a doggy bag for lunch today. Just before we finished, a very nice, open, friendly member of the kitchen brigade introduced himself. He turned out to be Ragnar, one of Nemone Lethbridge's two sons. Nemone and I were at Oxford together (two echoes of university in one day) and she has practised as a barrister. Together in 1976 we co-hosted a disastrous magazine programme for Donald Baverstock. Transmitted from Manchester, it was called *Terra Firma*. Her other son, Milo, is doing something legal. Ragnar explained that after university he hadn't known what to do. Nemone took him to St John one night and after several bottles of wine sold him to the restaurant as a kitchen worker. A year later he appears very happy there and is entirely delightful.

At home I read the RSC programme which quotes St Augustine: 'Suppress prostitution and capricious lusts will overthrow society'; and Thomas Aquinas: 'Prostitution in the towns is like the cesspool in the palace: take away the cesspool and the palace will become an unclean and evil-smelling place.'

Couldn't have put it better myself. I have never been reluctant to engage a mature male prostitute. (It occurs to me that I have not mentioned any of my few encounters so far this year. If I am to be honest I must consider that from now on.)

It's certainly a better idea than wooing and exploiting a young actor who might be hoping for work. I don't use the term 'rent boy' – my preference is for the late twenties-early thirties, and 'rent man' isn't a term that's caught on. It's something I've done since my twenties – encounters which have sometimes flowered into friendships. I don't use agencies. I prefer to answer advertisements. I have always hoped to be a considerate host and I can't, over some forty years, remember any disastrous encounters. Naturally some meetings are more satisfactory than others. I admire the skill of those who somehow convince you that they are getting as much pleasure as you are. I suppose it's an admiration for conscientious professionalism. I was pleased a few weeks ago to get a call from New Orleans from an old 'trick' to whom I hadn't spoken for two or three years who just wanted to chat and know what was happening over here.

To go back to Wednesday. The Reed dinner went off all right apart from the main course. For once I tried the vegetarian alternative – an aubergine fritter which was hopelessly undercooked. The dinner chat was the usual provincial-editorial conversation peddling would-be insight into the distant corridors of power. In fact, fifth-hand speculation and gossip:

1. 'The papers have a major sex-scandal with a senior member of the Shadow Cabinet to throw at Labour come election time.'

2. 'A senior Tory grandee "confirms" that Peter Lilley is being "groomed" for leadership of the party!'

I did a generous 30 minutes which was pronounced 'memorable' and got two huge, juicy, bundles of fresh Evesham asparagus as a bonus. I gave one to nice Mr Baldwin who has driven me on most of these late-night forays into Middle England, and look forward to keeping the rest to myself.

Thursday 8th June

Several voiceovers for the *Independent* at Saunders & Gordon – radio and TV. I threw in a free one for some sort of Roundhead and Cavalier charity event in the Midlands.

Tuesday 13th June

A day dictated by the dentist. The cap that Dr Alcaly put on after Friday's root-canaling had to come off at Mr Croser's hands so that a permanent porcelain replacement could be measured – lots of gunge in a mould slapped into my face. Then a plastic replacement cap was cemented in. It broke off the moment I applied some particularly tender tripe to it at lunch. Back yet again to Victoria to have it recemented. This time I am assured it will stay until the porcelain is ready. We shall see.

All this porcelain reminded me of my favourite bad-taste joke (Neil Shand's) when the Duke of Northumberland – a descendant of Harry (Hotspur) Percy – died: 'The last time he'll point Percy at the porcelain.'

An American woman (born in Bath) Meryle Secrest, ex-*Washington Post*, called to talk about Stephen Sondheim. She is writing his biography – with his blessing. She's already done Kenneth Clark (says we should read her new book *re* the second wife to redress the picture portrayed in the diaries), Salvador Dali and Bernard Berenson. She was charming and chatty but there was a puzzling naivety about her questions. I couldn't decide if this was because she is at the beginning of her quest, or because it was a *faux naïveté* and her usual technique for drawing out an interviewee.

Wednesday 14th June

To an hotel near Gatwick for almost the most enjoyable lit. lunch on the book tour, organised by Hammicks. With Lyndsey Davies, who writes about an ancient Roman detective equivalent of Philip Marlowe, and Simon Brett who, apart from all his other ventures, has a series of books about babies 'about to become a major television series'.

Then to *The Times Diary* summer party at the Reform. Stuffed with disappointed and passé politicians. Lamont on the way out as I went in, Kenneth Baker, Alan Clark. I should have asked him about Meryle Secrest after her spluttering over his account of his stepmother in the *Diaries* but told him instead that negotiations for the play were proceeding. He seemed pleased and when I suggested that it will be difficult to find the right actor said grandly, 'One will emerge.'

Talked to Pat Quinn (new Lady Stephens). She is very excited about an LP she and Robert have been recording, including the Falstaff and Hal scene with the Prince of Wales at Sandringham. Also Tom Stoppard. He is full of Tim Currie's new film hit in New York. Apparently it's about monkeys but he is not sure if Tim is playing one or not.

Thursday 15th June

11.00: Visit from Alan Haines, an elderly actor/writer/director, who brought book, lyrics and tapes of a musical he has written based on Stephen Leacock short stories. He's written lots of plays and one musical, *Pretty as Paint*, back in the fifties, which toured. Jimmy Perry was in it. Haines has a production scheduled in Leacock's home town in Canada and wants to mount one here. He 'sold' it with infectious enthusiasm. I must reserve judgement until I've heard it.

13.00. To Army and Navy for a signing. Mini-cab rammed by French bus in Victoria – had to hop a cab to get there on time. Very pleasant hour with the assistant, Colin Usher, recently promoted from long service in the fashion department. Distinctive Army and Navy customers, very civil and chatty – civil servants including an old Sexian (my old school) from the Min. of Ag. and Fish.

14.00. To American church for auditions for the ensemble girl for *Salad Days*. Saw nothing promising before leaving it to Stuart (MD) and Lindsay (choreography).

15.00. Voiceover for *Independent*. Andrew, the other good-looking sound mixer (see Ben earlier) also immune to flirtation through the glass panel. There is a curious ritual at the end of these sessions. The commercial has to be played over the telephone to an off-stage Australian called Amanda, who is apparently very big in the Mirror Group who control the *Independent*. One of our two Sophies, Saatchi girls, holds up the receiver to the loudspeakers and so the result of all that high-tech recording is spewed across the room with a good old-fashioned crackly phone. If Amanda is not too impressed we some-times have to re-record a word. Today she was so pressed that she kept us waiting well into the second hour of studio time (bonus money) and then OK'd it immediately.

17.00. To D. Pugh's office to hear auditionees for the son on the tour of *Passionate Woman*. Only four, but of an excellent standard. Tyler Butterworth, son of Peter and Janet Brown, is the favourite if Neil 'Mulrooney' Morrissey, the original, decides not to tour. Gwen Taylor read opposite them and will, I think, be a joy to work with. Not sure if we can replace in the West End. Stephanie is too stretched to extend until September even if she gets a two-week break.

Pugh told a wonderful Thatcher story. That very day she was on a morning show on TV and so were Pugh's touring attraction, the Blues Brothers. Sarah Greene interviewed her and then said, as a 'neat' link, 'And now from a True Blue to another True Blue – the Blues Brothers' – who launched into their song. Maggie (thinking they must be a young Tory band) refused to be hustled away by her minders and insisted on crossing to the boys after their number and asking, 'Tell me, which Associations are you from?' They hadn't a clue what she meant and stood open-mouthed. The roadie had the sense to say, 'Oh, from all over . . .' and she pottered off happy!

Shock! Horror! Discovered that the Bromsgrove gig for Reed editors was a freebie. I thought it was a regular fee-paying after-dinner. No wonder I got the asparagus and Reed bought 50 books. Oh well! It's just another hazard of after-dinner speaking. I thought my agents had arranged it but it was eager OUP. I've been welshed on in the past – i.e. not been paid afterwards – but never unknowingly sung for free.

Of course that's not the only hazard lying in wait – I meditated with some melancholy on the others.

It is not an uncommon hazard for the after-dinner speaker to face an audience with pens and papers at the ready. Some years ago I was halted in mid-flow by a nearby diner who shouted plaintively, 'Could you go a bit slower? I'm trying to write these down.'

A good, quickfire delivery can defeat all but the most determined joke thieves. Most infuriating is the sight of another speaker getting one of your jokes wrong. I find it very hard to remember other speakers' anecdotes and don't care to be seen scribbling. I think in some 30 years of after-dinnering I have only borrowed two jokes, one from J.J. Warr and one from Denis Compton, plus a passing comment from Stephen Fry who is so prolific he can afford to spare the odd aside. I shall not repeat them here because I am still in illegal possession of said stolen jokes.

Theft is not the big fear for an after-dinner speaker. The possibility of instant disaster always looms. On one occasion I spoke at the Royal Lancaster Hotel. A friend had invited me. It was one of those free speeches that you do on condition that a fee goes to a favourite charity. My old collaborator, Caryl Brahms, had died recently. She had been helping to put a musically talented child through school and £2,000 or so was still needed to complete his education. It seemed the ideal solution. However, by the time I got to my feet it was about half-past eleven – and I was following Barry Cryer. A couple of weeks before, I had preceded Barry at a luncheon which had gone so well from my point of view that he had recourse to his fail-safe opening line in these circumstances. 'Owing to some confusion before lunch Ned Sherrin picked up my speech so I'm speaking from his notes.'

This night was quite different. The all-male audience had heard more than enough talk and thought – incorrectly – that they had had less than enough to drink. I have never ploughed my way through a noisier crew. However, the thought of the boy's education kept me going, and I'm happy to say he is now the highly successful professional soloist musician Caryl prophesied.

It is agonising to hear a preceding speaker losing his audience. Once I saw a toast-master roaming the Lancaster Room at the Savoy trying to hush a crowd who had stopped listening altogether and were talking happily amongst themselves. The speaker, a junior minister, sat down at the end, smiled at the chairman and said, 'That went rather well, I thought.'

Some years ago I followed a similar débâcle. I resolved not to refer to it; but I forgot that my opening words were 'It comes as a great relief . . .' which sounded horribly ungenerous and got a huge, ungenerous and unlooked-for laugh from the beleaguered diners.

Sometimes the rot sets in before you start. I once dined at the hotel next to the Conference Centre at Birmingham. I sat on the right of the President of – let's say – The Shunters and Wheeltappers – who were celebrating their Annual Exhibition next door. Half-way through the meal the Pres. turned to me, 'We 'ad a telly-vision bloke 'ere a few years ago,' he offered, 'turned out to be a 'omosexual. Bloke called Russell Harty. 'E's dead now. Thought 'e was talking to the Wimmin's Institute, I shouldn't wonder. Lads started barracking 'im after five minutes. 'Ad to sit down after ten.'

Not the best way to reassure a guest speaker before he gets up on his feet.

It was OK that night; but I couldn't help remembering my first-ever after-dinner speech. I had just come down from Oxford. After Bar Exams I slipped into television. About five years later, the graduates of my year returned to Exeter College for our first Gaudy – the beano which colleges throw for old members at irregular intervals. As the only person so far to have achieved some notoriety, I had to make 'the speech'. I found myself on High Table sitting between Professor Neville Coghill and Professor Sir Salvador da Madariaga. Within seconds Neville turned to me and said wearily, 'I've heard some terrible speeches in this hall. I don't suppose it will be any better tonight.'

Almost immediately da Madariaga opened brightly, 'I have heard some wonderful speeches in the hall. I don't suppose anything we hear tonight will equal them.'

At least it provided me with an opening anecdote, hot off the press. And now there are so many famous Old Exonians from my year that I shall never have to do it again.

Perhaps the most polished and potent after-dinner speaker currently is Lord Runcie, the former Archbishop of Canterbury. He starts with the advantage that the audience is surprised to come across an Archbishop who is so gracefully and fluently amusing. But Lord Runcie is much better than Dr Johnson's verdict on a woman's preaching – 'Like a dog's walking on his hinder legs. It is not done well; but you are surprised to find it done at all.' Even allowing for the surprise advantage his former position bestows on him, Runcie is in the very front rank. I heard him fifteen years ago at a farewell dinner for Bishop Stockwood when Mervyn retired from Southwark. He proved impossible to follow. The luckless next speaker was poor Frankie Howerd who had not done his homework or tailored his script to the occasion. I retain a vivid image of Francis, sweat pouring down his face as he stuttered to his near silent conclusion.

A couple of years ago I spoke at a Persons of the Year Luncheon – following Lady Thatcher. Most of the lunchers had bought their tickets solely in order to hear the Baroness. She has a wonderfully dismissive ploy in giving way. 'I must close now,' she said, sweetly. 'After all, I am only warming up for the principal speaker.'

Friday 16th June

Technical meeting for *Salad Days*. Tim Goodchild was otherwise engaged. Patrick Connellan has designed a set which I find fun, convenient and attractive and which appears to stay within mean budget bounds. The production manager – Roger Kneale – has an eyrie off Leicester Square which he seems to share with Brian Brolly – among others. It is Brian who is producing Glen's musical. It was a festive meeting. We squeezed one bottle of Italian plonk out of Roger – a gift from Christmas – and Lindsay Dolan approved the false green-grass floor as suitable for dancing – having been shown a couple of inches of various samples.

I did Richard Littlejohn's late-night television show. No chance to plug the book or *Salad Days* but I got *Passionate Woman* in while telling the Maggie/Blues Bros. tale. Matthew Parris flirted shamelessly and gaily with the studio – and TV – audience and I left him in the Green Room surrounded by at least five recently enlisted male fans.

Others on were Nicky Clarke (the crimper), Ted Dexter (ex-cricketer) and King Arthur Pendragon. It didn't finish until 12.45. Taxi at 12.50 leaving Matthew with his 'prospects'. I watched bits of it on tape and then got to sleep too late.

Saturday 17th June

Lay low after Littlejohn viewers stopped me in the King's Road: 'What I want to know is, does it go out live?'

Turned out – on two urgings – for Lily Savage's fortieth birthday at the Playhouse. We were bidden for 7.30. I got there at 7.45. Paul (Lily) arrived at 8.15 so I only had time to wave at him before getting back in my car. An odd group. Mainly middle-aged men, shaved, bald and paunchy. A near-naked waiter with an incredible figure and a curious costume of steel hoops was the star. Paul arrived in a white limo dressed severely. The evening held little promise. Better get home. Said farewell to Helen Montague who is planning to put Lily into a musical version of the Australian woman's prison soap *Cell Block H*. We shall see.

Monday 19th June

I dined at the Herbert Kretzmers', an evening convened for two of Sybil's friends from LA. Beautifully arranged as always, in their downstairs dining room with two tables, Herbie presiding over one, Sybil over the other. The newly married Sheridan Morleys were there and the long-married Patrick Garlands. Patrick was full of stories, many of Rex Harrison – I had not realised that his memorial service at St

Martin-in-the-Fields was only attended by a handful. Ruth Leon-Morley started to tell *my* Coral Browne story (see *Theatrical Anecdotes* – 'Got the trip wires out at Waterloo Station again, 'ave we?') which I thought I'd better reappropriate it quickly as she had started with the pay-off line. Patrick Garland grabbed me at the end to report, *sotto voce*, that the tour of *Billy Liar* with Jason Donovan has just collapsed. Keith Waterhouse will be furious. And Gay Soper, who has just turned us down for *Salad Days*, won't be too pleased either. As Herbie said goodnight he had good news and bad. He'd had an exhilarating session with Declan Donnellan about the lyrics for *Martin Guerre* – the musical he is working on with Boublil & Shonberg for Cameron Mackintosh – but feels that if he can't crack the re-write this time he should abandon it. He obviously reveres Declan.

The bad news is that he goes into Brompton Heart and Lung tomorrow for an examination of his chest, plainly a cause of anxiety.

William Waldegrave in deep doo-doos again over arms to Iran and Iraq. Odd that one so intellectually qualified should be so unlucky. Alan Watkins once wrote of him, 'It would not be unfair to say that he had been educated out of his wits.'

Tuesday 20th June

Christopher S-S came by to collect the corrected MS of 'The Novel'. Very pleasant but still no satisfactory title. Apart from me, no one likes *Scratch an Actor*. I like Glen Roven's *They Smile When They are Low* – or even *When they are Low*. No one else does. I had checked for Wilde quotes: 'Rare, Pure and Never Simple', 'The Good End Happily', 'Mind over Morals' and 'Except Temptation' – as in 'I can resist everything except temptation': but none found favour. We settle (for the moment) on *The Show Goes On*, which I despise but must live with and go on looking for a better. The trouble is that once the wrapper is designed and delivered I'm stymied.

Mike Hill came up from Deal. He had had lunch with Suzanne Amoore – widow of the erratic Derek – an old *Tonight* colleague with a drink problem (Derek not Suzanne). Apparently she confirmed Michael's suspicion that Derek was possibly a double spy. She had established his MI6 connections and a daughter's boyfriend had turned up some KGB evidence in the newly open Moscow. Moreover, after being let go by the BBC he had a more than decent flat in Regent's Park and declined to accept his BBC pension. Very puzzling. He was one of Grace Wyndham Goldie's Golden Boys and would certainly have achieved some more senior position at the BBC but for the alcohol. He was a communist at Cambridge where I suppose he was recruited. Maybe MI6 were running him with knowledge of the KGB connection: but it all sounds impossibly low key. I suppose he might have developed into an 'agent of influence' – but he hardly got far enough.

Mike was his usual mine of gossip. Two girlfriends were off to an unreal-sounding cocktail party for the Pennant-Raes – 'celebrating' their marriage. When the news came on he had his Peter Townsend reminiscences. Townsend – Princess Margaret's great love – has died at 80.

I looked quickly at a new novel Christopher brought for me. *Domino* by Ross King – a young Canadian academic who submitted 50 pages to S-S on spec. Christopher and his reader enthused and met him and asked why he sent it to them. 'Because you publish Rose Tremain and Peter Ackroyd,' he replied. It has now been sold in several countries – £50,000 from Germany – and Mr King is by way of being a rich man. It looks fascinating. An eighteenth-century piece featuring a castrato singer, a great beauty and narrator, who reveals himself early on as an unapprehended murderer.

I put it down when the Person from Plumpton arrived for dinner. We walked to the Canteen in Chelsea Harbour, bumping into Michael Caine on the way, 'Doing Neighbourhood Watch?' I enquired. 'No,' he said unsmiling. The Person is very sweet, single and naive. He had spent the day with his father who is in the Hospice, St Joseph's, in Hackney. I quizzed his entire life history. The food was, as always, light and charming and came to about £100. We returned to my flat and indulged in some friendly hurly-burly on the chaise longue. I lectured him on the need to find younger company but he seems set in his ways.

On a similar subject I see that the England team in the World Angling Championship are to have no sex for a fortnight – the team manager decreed that sex might exhaust his squad. Surely no angler could be complete without the use of his tackle?

Wednesday 21st June

Photographed at the Haymarket with Milton Shulman for some ridiculous *Evening Standard* Christmas supplement. It's a 'Twelve Days of Christmas' photo edition. We are to be Two Luvvies Watching the stage from a box at the Haymarket.

Milton full of his sensational discovery. For six years he has been seeking to prove (for a book) that Martin Boorman was spirited out of Germany towards the end of the war by Ian Fleming – because his signature was the key to getting German money out of Swiss Banks. Sir Archibald McIndoe rearranged his face. Milton was never able to find out what happened to him afterwards. Now he has found a source who knew what happened afterwards but not how he got here in the first place. They are putting their researches together. Source two says he lived until 1989. He was provided with a mistress who is testifying. And he was housed in the Home Counties under an assumed name. Milton is having trouble getting a publisher to swallow the story. Should he call in Trevor-Roper . . .?

I went on to Jack Lee to have my hair cut. He was much excited that I had mentioned him on the Littlejohn show last Friday. He was asleep but friends had told him. I hope it makes up for *This Is Your Life*'s omission.

Thursday 22nd June

A momentous day – or at least a 24-hour wonder. Three voiceovers for three *Independent* ads. I had an hour and a half off for lunch, and since Saunders and Gordon's studios in Greek Street are at the end of Charlotte Street lunched alone at Interlude de Chavot – an old Wheeler's site now reorganised under the old management but with another Marco Pierre White protégé as chef.

Sweet scallops on a vinaigrette of chopped tomatoes, roast chicken breast stuffed with a herb mousse and a vanilla ice with red berries. The largely French staff had no idea of the cricket score but were on tenterhooks for the Rugby International (France *v.* England) in South Africa. They didn't *look* like rugger devotees, but who knows?

Back at Saunders and Gordon, they switched us through to BBC1 to see what was happening. What was happening was Atherton, Stewart and Hick out and a reasonable stand developing between an increasingly confident Robin Smith and Graham Thorpe. Alas, by the time I got home both were out and others were surrendering. In South Africa England were taking a hammering from the French – joy at Interlude?

Then, at about five John Major upstaged the sporting disasters with a dramatic resignation statement as Leader of the Conservative Party, not as Prime Minister. Within minutes the clichés were raining in: 'Lancing the boil', 'Clearing the air'. My favourite cliché-watch will be devoted to left-wingers saying they don't want to 'intrude into private grief'. Ashdown was the first to use it – before six o'clock. It cropped up later on *Newsnight* from a woman called Carolyn Johnson.

It was of course the main topic at Esther Rantzen and Desmond Wilcox's garden cocktail party in Hampstead. Quite a media coven – Rantzen, Rippon, Rice, Su Pollard, Maureen Lipman. Alex Armitage (agent) was just telling me which leading lady was reported to be 'the best blow-job in the West End' when Ann Leslie loomed up to bewail her fate – having to go on *Any Questions* the next day – so I shall never know. Pink champagne, quails' eggs, ambitious canapés and five sorts of asparagus.

On to a party given by Shusha Guppy (journalist and writer of exquisite memoirs of life in Persia and Paris) in her pretty room with two delightful balconies. Tony Smith (President of Magdalen College, Oxford) enthusiastic about a new University Radio Oxbridge due in a year or so. Again Major's move took the mind off the cricket and rugby disasters.

I must not forget a highly amusing film offer which arrived in the shape of a script today. Christopher Milburn (a cousin of my old friend, Gaye Brown) is one of the producers. Mark Greenstreet is the director. It's a sort of 'romp' to be shot in East Anglia in the autumn. I would have quite a long scene with three girls. I play a lovable, bedraggled, 70-year-old music teacher. I told them they should get Freddie Jones, Leslie Phillips or Maurice Denham. I ought to say 'No', not being in any sense an actor, but I am tempted by the amusement of a few odd days on location. There is unlikely to be any money available which is probably why I have been asked. Perhaps the direc-tor will insist on sleeping with me. Or perhaps I should make that a condition of accepting.

Mary I'Anson, who used to 'mind' me and John Drummond and lots of others at the BBC and is now a busy TV movie producer and mother of a musical prodigy, has sent me a copy of yesterday's *Telegraph* crossword. I am a clue, 15 Across to be precise. 'Endorsed by Italian male in front of Mr Sherrin (6)'. And the answer – 'SIGNED'!

POSTSCRIPT
At Ascot there was a more pressing problem than the PM's resignation. Apparently a rugby match was being shown on closed-circuit TV until there was a curt call from Sir Piers Bengough, HM's rep. at Ascot: 'Get the rugger off the TV,' he said, 'Her Majesty wants to watch the racing.'

Friday 23rd June

Signed 30 OUP books for display in Harrods. The previous lot sold before I could get in to sign. I bought *The Jewish Guide to Adultery* as a wedding present for Sheridan Morley and Ruth Leon. Not quite as tasteless as it seems. It's a rabbi's advice on how to keep a marriage together. Difficult people to choose for. Their house is immaculately packed and they have not provided a 'list' at any of the stores.

Lunch at Elena's Etoile with Ned Chaillet who is producing a two-hour *Theatrical Anecdotes* marathon for Radio 2. I am to compère it. He has booked Richard Griffiths, Victor Spinetti, John Moffat, Oliver Cotton and an American actor, William Hootkins, who spends half his time in LA and half here. It sounds a good combination.

John Carlisle, the frightening right-wing Tory MP, has been saying that Major needs to get the 'hearts and minds' of his back benchers. Reminds me of Lyndon Johnson's remark (*à propos* Vietnam): 'If you have them by the balls their hearts and minds will follow.' Emasculating John Carlisle would be a good start.

Sunday 25th June

Very pleasant couple of hours of *Anecdotage* at a funny little sound studio in Delancey Street, off the Parkway, Regent's Park. The five talkers who might easily have been fiercely competitive were wonderfully benign and appreciative of each other. We came away with two hours of tapes which must be sorted for editing by Ned Chaillet so that he can add music and my linking commentary. Inevitably some chestnuts crept in but the two repeating themes were 'Where are the characters now?' and, more interesting, the trail of authentication.

John Gielgud's famous line when Peter Brook asked the cast of Sophocles *Oedipus* to do or say something 'obscene' came up. Oliver Cotton was *there*. After the others had tried rather feebly, Gielgud came forward and said simply, 'We open next Tuesday.' John Moffat – who is both authoritative and encyclopaedic – traced it back to rehearsals for another Brook production, *U.S.*, an anti-Vietnam polemic for the RSC in the sixties, when it was uttered by an elderly character actress. '*But*', he added, 'I was rehearsing for a radio play with Alec Guinness at the time and when the incident was reported everyone had a good laugh. At the end of the rehearsal Alec pulled me aside and said quietly, 'I didn't like to spoil that story, but I first heard that remark when Komisarjevsky was directing in the twenties.'

Sheridan Morley and Ruth Leon celebrated their marriage at the Conrad Hotel in the evening. (They had tied the knot in New York some time before.) A heavily theatrical do. I talked to Graham Payn and Pat Hodge. Frith Banbury said that so many people are ringing him up to ask about his West End past that he thinks he should start charging. Kit Hesketh-Harvey, who is looking forward to *Salad Days* and his wife, Katie Rabbett (who is going to play an incompetent singer in 'my' movie), say we'll probably be staying at their house on location in Norfolk to save money.

John Redwood has caused a stir not coming out openly for Major. Norman Lamont won't commit himself until he hears what Redwood is up to. He looks more self-satisfiedly pleased with himself every time he appears on screen. For the first time it looks as though what was always possible (an upset) might almost be probable. I doubt it.

Tuesday 27th June

Marriott Hotel for a meeting of judges for the Lloyds Private Banking Writer of the Year Award. Last year we gave it to Terry Johnson for *Dead Funny*. This year it looks like being a much more open contest with Marber's *Dealer's Choice*, Stoppard's *Indian Ink*, Sharman Mac-

Donald's *A Winter Guest*, Hare's *Skylight*, Sebastian Barry's *The Steward of Christendom* and a number of out-of-town contenders. And we are still not halfway through the year. Ronnie Harwood's *Taking Sides* was well reviewed at Chichester and comes into the Criterion next week and there will be many more. The prize is £25,000. The others in the top ten get scrolls.

It's a congenial, conscientious group. Melvyn Bragg is a spirited chairman. He advised me before the kick-off that LWT are taking over the *Evening Standard* Awards and want me to host them again. They are to move to a Friday and will be extended to 90 minutes – 10.30–12.00. I am glad – it is my favourite television gig of the year and the Savoy lunch is always such a wonderful annual reunion of theatre people.

The other judges for Lloyds Private include Nanette Newman, Sheridan Morley, Jack Tinker, Clive Hirschhorn, Michael Billington and Paul Allen. Joyce McMillan from a Scottish paper has joined the panel this year. There was some criticism of the preponderance of critics last year but they are about the only people who automatically see most of the plays.

I sat between Jack and Joyce McMillan for the jolly meal that followed the meeting. Jack and I shared forebodings about *Fame: The Musical* which we were both due to see that evening.

Forebodings justified. A dire if energetic evening. I went with Rick Kerwin who had asked me to get the tickets. The people behind the show seem to be largely Scandinavian which may explain its dated look. The choreographer explained in a newspaper a few weeks ago that he was going to revolutionise our ideas of dance in musicals. He hasn't. My near-namesake Scott Sherrin, a tall, young black dancer-singer who was in *Bugsy* as a kid and later in *Five Guys Named Mo* as 'swing', was a lively lead, but the clichéd role 'can't read but can dance' was as little use to him as were the shallow characterisations of the rest of the cast.

I shall be surprised if it lasts a month.

Redwood's campaign is gathering steam; but the awful shower of Gormans, Marlowes, Tebbits, etc. around it looks gruesome – and, thank God, vulnerable.

'Private Grief' watch: A headline – I think in the London *Evening Standard*.

Wednesday 28th June

'*Private Grief*' *watch*: Gordon Brown, Shadow Chancellor, trotted it out again rather lamely, on *World at One*.

Very worried about an apparent dates conflict for the tours of *A Passionate Woman* and *Salad Days*. *Salad Days* has always been fixed but *PW* has swung backwards and forwards between Bristol and Derby, and I've just realised we start rehearsing at Derby Playhouse on the day we move into Norwich to open *Salad Days*. The next morning I'm due in Edinburgh for ten days to host the National Youth Music Theatre's lunchtime fund raisers. Arranged to meet a reluctant David Pugh with Deke on Friday to see if we can find a solution.

Michael Linnett rang to suggest a play by Robin Hawdon (*Don't Dress for Dinner*), a 'comedy farce' called *Perfect Wedding*. He's sending it.

To the American church in Tottenham Court Road for last girlie auditions for *Salad*. Three good girls. One a fall-out from the Jason Donovan *Billy* which appears to be cancelled. It may make Gay Soper available to us. We still lack the two mothers and the tramp. We also 'planned' the 'press conference' to launch *Salad Days* at the Theatre Museum. I'm trying to get Kit and the Widow to run up a special number.

On to the Senate House in Malet Street for a seminar on Satire in the Sixties, only to find it had been cancelled and I hadn't been told. It was a gorgeous hot day and I fulfilled the little dream of going home, pouring a Pimm's and watching Ruzedsksi win at Wimbledon against Forget.

Thursday 29th June

To Glasgow to speak after dinner at a National Association of Health Authorities & Trusts conference. It was at the Hilton, where I stayed. Margaret Beckett had just addressed the delegates – much Tory annoyance that her political speech had only got around to the Nation's Health in the last ten minutes.

I don't think I've been to Glasgow since the 1960s. Oh yes, once, for the first Christmas of Giles Havergal's Glasgow Cits. He produced our non-musical *Nickleby and Me* as his first Christmas show. I remember buckets in the aisles to collect rainwater from the leaking roof. Now his theatre is an international success.

Looking down from the nineteenth floor of my hotel it appears so different. New blocks and new broad highways and underpasses cut through the big old piles of red-brick blocks, the grey gothic towers and the barren fifties high-rises. A glimpse of the empty river is fringed by idle cranes.

At dinner I was near John Humphries who was chairing a mixed debate and question time the next morning. He seemed ebullient in his newfound celebrity as a notoriously challenging interviewer. That morning on *Today* James Naughtie had interviewed John Major: 'I did him on Sunday,' said Humphries. 'They wouldn't let me have him twice in one week.'

On the other side was Jim Calder, an amicable ex-Scots rugger international, now Sales and Customer Services Director of the Royal Mail who are wooing NAHAT and were 'sponsoring' me, i.e. paying the fee.

When I went up to bed I watched a little television. Suddenly around midnight the lights went out. In the morning they were still out – according to a note under the door there was a local power failure. Those who had sought to disco the night away must have had to climb up up to 20 flights – and what about the poor porter who had to deliver all the notices?

I left early, bathed but unshaven, to have a primitive breakfast at the airport.

'*Private Grief*' *watch*: Richard Littlejohn on his late-night show!

Friday 30ᵗʰ June

Crisis meeting about dates with the producer David Pugh and Deke Arlon, my manager. Great relief! It appears I can spend enough time with *Salad Days* and the tour of *A Passionate Woman* to make both realistic. There is a further complication, though. It looks as if Stephanie *may* continue till early September (with holiday) so that Pugh can replace her as the autumn season picks up. A bridge to be crossed when we come to it. Very amicable.

I read the Robin Hawdon play and found four critical pages missing towards the end. They were rapidly sent round. *Perfect Wedding* is a mathematically constructed comedy/farce. I've not done anything like it and so cannot judge it. I am intrigued by the construction – where I usually look for characterisation and language. Both are absent: but it is intriguing and reads as though it could build up a huge head of funny steam. It would be a very interesting challenge.

July

~•~

Sunday 2nd July

GOING FOR THE *News of the World* – Hugh Grant's inamorata 'Divine Brown' 'tells all' – I bumped into Peter Hall pushing his enchanting little daughter (Rosie, I think). The arts pages are full of his return to the RSC – didn't he do *All's Well* there two years ago with Michael Siberry (England's most underrated actor) as Parolles? He was glowing with the irony of opening *Julius Caesar* there the day after the back-stabbing Tory election.

I asked if the rumour was true that he had been at Stratford for the first reading and then shot off to Hollywood, directing the first week from there by fax. 'A good story, but not true,' he said.

Well, he would, wouldn't he?

Monday 3rd July

Afternoon spent with Ned Chaillet editing the *Green Room* pro-gramme of theatrical anecdotes for Radio 2. It goes out on Sunday for two hours. So many good stories from Griffiths, Spinetti, Cotton, Moffat and Hootkins have to go because of the f-word – so many actor stories seem to need it to punch up the punchlines. There was a wonderful new-to-me Gielgud from John Moffat. Sir John was in a classical play in the West End. During the run the director sug-gested a pronounced pause in one of his speeches. Sir John demurred. 'Oh no – I hate to pause in the West End. I paused once in the West End and I clearly heard a man in the gallery say, "Oh you beast, you've come all over my umbrella!"'

Victor Spinetti's tale of O'Toole and Burton on the set of *Becket*. It was early morning and Gielgud, fully made up, was patiently filling in his crossword. (Popular report is that he just fills it in, irrespective of the clues.) The two stars arrived hungover or nearly tanked up and playfully punched and thumped each other and rolled around on the ground. Sir John looked up from his crossword and said wearily to Victor, 'Oh, why don't they fuck and get on with it!'

Hootkins claims to have heard Sir John on *Kaleidoscope* commenting on Olivier's absence from a great theatrical occasion during one of his most challenging illnesses. Rumour had it that he was dying. Asked about this Sir John went into a spin and blurted out, 'Larry . . . he's dead! . . . he's dying! . . . he's getting better!'

Some excellent stuff remains.

Straight on to the Criterion for Ronnie Harwood's impressive new play *Taking Sides*. It examines Furtwängler's 'guilt'. He stayed in Germany under the Nazis – was he a man of principle trying to get Jews out of Germany and keep the healing power of music going during Hitler's hours of darkness, or was he a Fascist who could summon up some eccentric pro-Semitic gestures to clear his conscience or his record? Dan Massey's ravaged, injured, towering bald-eagle performance, was superb but perhaps the play allows him to score too many points while stacking the argument against Michael Pennington's boorish, heckling, philistine American army cross-examiner.

Tuesday 4th July

To Paris by train – 08.23 departure from Waterloo. It was my first experience of the Chunnel. We idled, courtesy of BR, through lovely Kent, hardly noticed the few minutes under the sea and then sped through France and arrived bang on time at 12.30 p.m. Indifferent breakfast but soothing champagne. It was a group visit with lots of friends – rather like a school outing. We transferred to a coach and were taken across the Seine to the *Grande Bretagne* – a luxury river boat – and sailed up and down eating rather good lobster salad and a melting fillet steak. I have never done a boat on the Seine before – this was no ordinary bâteau mouche. My clearest memory is of scanning the banks, which unfolded like the frieze on a Grecian vase, an irregular sequence of figures in relief, a picnicker; a snoozing office worker; a rude part of the tow path, one sunbather on his back, penis erect; loving couples embracing; artisans stretched out in vivid blue jeans and brightly bronzed chests. We reassembled at the Gare du Nord. I had a beer with Michael Parkinson. Together we bewailed the attention span with which today's TV producers invest their audiences. His introductions and interviews on a retrospective series of his old shows are, he suspects, being butchered. We felt happier on radio. We bumped into David Howell on the platform. At 6.30 French time he was able to tell us the result of the Tory leadership election. Major 218 – roughly what I forecast over lunch – John Redwood 89, 10 or 11 abstentions and a couple of 'spoiled' papers. Great jubilation – but, in spite of protests of a new unity, I suspect another split before Christmas may force a general election. Slight delay across France – 'children on line'. It makes a change. At home the talk is all of reshuffles. It would appear that Jonathan Aitken has resigned to fight his libel cases, which leaves even more scope.

Gay Kindersley told me a good story on the return journey. After the war his rather grand grandfather, Lord Kindersley, was told by his wife to get some new shirts. She sent him packing to Turnbull and Asser. The driver waited outside. It was a long time since he had patronised the shop so when the young assistant asked him how he would pay for the six shirts he had ordered he said, 'Account.' Nervously the lad asked what the name was. The old boy looked perplexed. Then he went outside to the car and said to the chauffeur, 'What's my name?' 'It was Lord Kindersley, when you left home this morning.' And he went back happily into the shop to convey the information.

The Times carried the information that today is the anniversary of the birth of Louis Armstrong in 1900. He appeared several times on the old *Tonight* programme – plus wife and trumpet – always more anxious to talk about constipation rather than music. A few weeks after his last visit, Duke Ellington was invited on to the programme. In the hospitality room he was introduced to the formidable (but on this occasion 'tired and emotional') department head, Mrs Grace Wyndham Goldie. She contemplated the elegant pianist for a moment and then enquired jovially, 'Have you brought your trumpet with you again?'

Wednesday 5th July

A brand-new permanent front tooth. Next the implants – late August.

The saga of a title for the novel goes on. 'Sales' don't like *Light the Lights*. I don't think I recorded that idea earlier. They love Christopher's suggestion – unvouchsafed to me before – *Gin and Limelight*, which I can't bear. There isn't a drop of gin in the book. We are back to the drawing board. They're to come up with some more suggestions and I have promised to think again. Why can't we go back to *Scratch an Actor*?

David and Carina Frost's annual garden party. Brilliant weather. The usual huge marquee in Carlyle Square and the usual press of media, politics, social and royal. The three little Frosts have abandoned their duties with the canapé trays. Emma Freud was glowing – having just given birth, rather late, to a daughter, Scarlett. I heard one of the Sloaney contingent screeching, 'Oh my God! Jemima!' as she spotted Mrs Imran Khan with her spouse. As the Royals present were rather minor, fringe ones, the Khans seemed to be the honorary 'Royals for the day'.

Thursday 6th July

Voiceover for *Independent*, after which I met Keith Waterhouse and went with him to the Strand – to Ivor Novello's old flat at the top of the theatre to see Duncan Weldon, whose offices are there, and talk about *Bing Bong*, Keith's play. He likes it and wants to do it, probably in the early part of next year. He thinks a twelve-week tour before London, which would suit Keith and me. Will it suit Robert Powell and Dennis Waterman, who are the preferred leads? That would mean a London opening around Easter.

On to the Theatre Museum for a very jovial launch party for *Salad Days*. Only provincial press as far as I could see, but then we are only playing the provinces. Kit and the Widow sang a special ode for Julian: 'Nobody writes a tune like Julian Slade'. Julian sang 'We Said We Wouldn't Look Back' with much charm and more emotion. He was joined by Simon Connolly and Nicola Fulljames, our two enchanting juveniles, in 'It's Easy to Sing'. I wore the Elvis tie given to me by a Chinese lady journalist in Singapore before Christmas and convinced a few (a very few) of the more gullible, that Elvis had been a big Slade fan and had tried to get Colonel Parker to buy the screen rights to *Salad Days* as his voice was going and he wanted to play Troppo the mute. Unfortunately he died too soon.

To the *Spectator* party in Doughty Street. It was more packed than ever. I armed myself with two large vodka-and tonics and drank one as I forced myself to the end of the garden and the other as I fought my way back. On my way out I briefly explained this excellent technique to Robin Day who said it was the most boring idea he had ever heard. Congratulated Nigella Lawson on Nigel's loss of weight. 'Yes,' she pouted, 'But he's too mean to buy new clothes – so the old ones hang around him and he looks awful.' I missed Nigel himself. The photographs make him look ill, but I gather in the flesh he looks fine – right back to his shape in the OUDS pantomime when he was kicking his legs in the chorus of *Dick Whittington*.

Friday 7ᵗʰ July

To the BBC to record final links for the Radio 2 theatrical anecdotes show, *Tales from the Green Room*, which airs on Sunday. Radio 2 requires so much light music – show songs in this case – that I wonder how many stories will remain.

On to the Ritz for a Magazine Editors' lunch. Keynote speech by young Mr Blair. I was at the *Radio Times* table, invited by one of the many editors, Liz Vercoe. Alan Yentob (BBC1) and Michael Jackson (BBC2) were there. I disappointed Jackson by failing to enthuse over *Saturday Night Armistice*, his new late-night 'satire' show – but there is nothing to enthuse about. Well-produced, reasonable scripts, incompetent performers. Blair was predictable to a degree – especially as his press secretary had cracked it up as a major riposte to all the Tory coverage. Not a sound idea, not even a sound bite on show. Tony Hall, Head of BBC News, sitting next to me shared my dismay – how was his department to get a headline out of it? Blair was a bit more fun when it came to questions – largely because they were so farouche and came from such odd magazines – *Reader's Digest*, the *Lady*, and the *Organ*.

Neil Marcus, a very short and very energetic young would-be director of musicals, came to visit in the evening. He has already got a lot of things on and must now make the decision to leave J. Walter Thompson and take a jump – as an assistant, probably unpaid. I suspect he will make it.

Oh, dear, England heading for ignominious defeat at Edgbaston. Only Robin Smith stood up. Rather glad I didn't do the Taverners gig. (I was asked to talk to the Taverners in Birmingham the night before the first Test by Colin Cowdrey – with the promise of the first day's cricket as a reward. A few weeks ago an embarrassed official called to say 'sorry' – someone else had invited Frank Carson so would I stand down? Of course I could come and hear Carson if I liked. I said no, I'd heard Carson once before.)

Late at night there was an awful episode on the Richard Littlejohn local TV show. He wheeled on a young Australian – Gary somebody – an erstwhile lover of Elton John, who has published his account of their involvement – intense for perhaps two years and off and on over ten. A frail vessel (but with some dignity), Gary obliged as Littlejohn fished the dirt out of him and got his money's worth – the story had been serialised in Littlejohn's paper the *Daily Mail*. Then he turned on him and egged on his guests to subject him to a vulgar verbal mugging. The other two tormentors were Tim Rice, who was at least mild and had I suppose to be loyal to his collaborator, and a ghastly creature called Eric Hall who is, I think, an agent or manager of sportsmen; though I doubt if he knows what sporting means – no disgusting perversion of the words 'man' or 'manly' to heap scorn on a gay witness was left unexplored. Not disposed to sympathise at the outset, my stomach was turned into support by the end when Little-john turned to his audience and snarled, 'You can clap, *or not*, as you please.' Of course no one did. Sadly, his programme was for once recorded and I could not phone or fax a comment. I would have been tempted – for the first time ever.

Monday 10ᵗʰ July

At eleven o'clock recorded *The Tingle Factor*, a Radio 4 programme with roughly the same format as *Desert Island Discs*. Seven or eight pieces of music which have a moment which makes you 'tingle'. I chose Damon Evans's 'It Ain't Necessarily So' from the Glyndebourne *Porgy*. In fact the whole production under Rattle was a tingle, enhanced by driving down to see it with the late Martin Smith and sitting at a table next to Peggy Ashcroft at dinner. She wanted to know if there was a recording. There was not at the time. She wanted it for her granddaughter who was with her. Later, by a happy chance, I was sent two sets of the boxed tapes. I posted one to her and got a wonderfully appreciative letter just before her death. Her spidery writing was all over the place – just like Caryl's immediately before her death.

There was also Nancy Walker's 'I'm Still Here' from Burt Shevelove's seventies tribute to Sondheim, which I flew to New York to see. Cleo's high notes and vocal acrobatics in 'On a Clear Day'; Lis Welch, 'To Keep My Love Alive' – to emphasise perfect diction. 'We Said We Wouldn't Look Back' which I do love, but which was there to plug the *Salad Days* tour. 'Waterloo Sunset' to sum up my feelings about Ray Davies and finally Marion Montgomery's recording of 'Not Funny'.

Jeremy Nicholls was an able and very relaxed interviewer. He endeared himself to me when, hearing 'Not Funny' for the first time, he said, 'What a wonderful song! Who wrote it?' To which I was able to reply, 'I did; with Gerard Kenny.'

To the Groucho for lunch with Glen Roven who brought a new collaborator with him, Jerome Moss. Married to Delia Ephron, Nora's sister, and the book writer for *Ballroom*. They are working on Glen's newest brainwave – a sort of Noah's Flood set in the flood-torn Midwest of America about now, with huge Gospel choirs. They met, of all ways, on the Internet. I don't understand the Internet but Glen and David Yakir are obsessed by it.

I took them on to the stalls bar at the Prince of Wales where Dick Vosburgh and Dennis King are show-casing their new comedy musical *A Saint She Ain't*, freely, very freely, adapted from Molière's *Sganarelle, ou le cocu imaginaire*. The broad outlines of the plot are acted as if by the stars of a forties Hollywood musical featuring W.C. Fields, Mae West, Jimmy Durante, Betty Hutton, Gene Kelly, Rita Hayworth, Bud Abbott and Lou Costello. An immaculate and very funny piece of parody writing, with a brilliant joke: 'I haven't been so happy since *Reader's Digest* lost my address.'

Jerry Moss liked it more, I think, than Glen, who is perhaps too musically minded really to relish this sort of precise, sustained fooling.

I taxied home with Herbie Kretzmer who had enjoyed it as much as me. We both lamented the absence of a venue for it in London. Two months at the King's Head was the best future we could predict. We both thought it could run for years in the right off-Broadway house.

It was so hot that I welshed on a preview of two episodes of the BBC's *Pride and Prejudice* and cooled down over Pimm's and a tomato, basil and buffalo mozzarella salad and asparagus vinaigrette.

Tuesday 11th July

To the 'Chichester Festivities' to do a 75-minute talk (*Theatrical Anecdotes*) in the Bishop's Kitchen. It was a packed house – mind you, it only seated about 100 people – and had been booked out since tickets went on sale. Mrs Kemp (Bishop Eric's wife) introduced me. They were a charming group, mainly elderly, and appeared to enjoy themselves immoderately.

I went on to Little London – now a predominantly French restaurant with an Irish maître d'hotel – they were in some confusion because of a large, noisy party upstairs. Joe Harmston joined me for supper. He co-directed *Our Song* with me in Athens in 1993, bearing the brunt of the eccentricities of the Greek actors' temperaments. At Chichester he is assisting on eight or nine productions and was roundly berated by Richard Cottrell, who has directed what sounds like a lacklustre *School for Scandal*, for not being around enough. There is a good story about Harold Pinter exploding whenever anybody says 'Good morning, how are you?' to him. 'How am I? What sort of question is that? There are people dying in Bosnia and you ask me how am I?'

Two sweet old boys, Frank Middlemass and Geoffrey Toone, came to the next table after theatre. They had been to *Hobson's Choice*, which I shall see on Friday. Frank is playing Old Rawley in *School for Scandal*. Geoffrey Toone reminisced about *The Little Hut*, the André Roussin play translated by Nancy Mitford, in which he played a handsome savage in the late forties. The play is a desert island triangle, which then consisted of Robert Morley, David Tomlinson and Joan Tetzel. There is another little monkey-savage who features in the dénouement. 'Played by Billy Chappell,' I said. 'And when he was off by Ros Chatto,' Toone told me. Apparently she was the ASM and in emergencies had to black up and butch up. Now she is a powerful agent and mother-in-law to Princess Margaret's daughter! By an odd coincidence I was sent the play recently with a view to directing a tour. The dialogue reads remarkably lightly and fluently – but it screams for star personality casting. Which 'star' personality would tour?

Joe talked of his plans. He is still trying to mount his production of *Vortigern*, the Shakespeare forgery (by W.H. Ireland) which hasn't been played since its disastrous first night at Drury Lane at the end of the eighteenth century. The deception was discovered on the morning of the opening and Macready was booed off the stage. Joe may do *The Promise* at Greenwich. He deserves to get on. He is *so* good, exceptionally talented and tactful.

Wednesday 12th July

To Jayne Rayne's house in West Heath Road for dinner. A glittering and friendly gathering. Delicious sole quenelles and wonderfully tender beef, followed by a sumptuous chocolate soufflé. There was no *placement* and I sat between Sonia Sinclair and Susan Crossland. Claus von Bulow was on Sonia's other side – a wicked twinkle. Across the table were Ronnie and Natasha Harwood. Ronnie is rightly glowing over the success of *Taking Sides*. Kenneth Partridge reports that Lis Welch has taken to her bed and is not going out except to the corner shop when she needs something. She switched her telephone off for the whole of Wimbledon and has become so absent-minded that she is apt to write cheques for bills which she has already paid. I have been trying to telephone her for a week without any luck. This, I suppose, is the reason.

Thursday 13th July

I finished reading Ross King's *Domino* and started to read Bernard Padden's play. Bernard is a quaint, camp comic who writes very much his own stuff. This play, oddly in four acts – I suppose two acts each of two scenes, but he calls them acts – reminds me irresistibly of early N.F. Simpson. It opens with an aborted wedding. The bridegroom is a football star. Unfortunately on the eve of the ceremony his right foot metamorphoses into a very large tea cup which reaches nearly to his knee. The play is called *The Tea-Cup*. I must wait to see how he resolves it! Sunday reading.

To Vogue House for Jane Proctor's *Tatler* party celebrating Nigel Williams's new book which they are serialising. Nigel in fine gossiping form. More Pinter stories. He swears that Pinter, running through a play at the Court, heard a rumble during a critical pause.

'What is that noise?'

'It's the Underground, Harold. The Circle Line runs under the theatre.'

'The trains must be stopped.'

He also carried news of Elijah Moshinsky who apparently quarrelled with Ronnie Harwood while producing his last play but one. Then he saw a Harwood novel on sale in a bookshop. A notice said 'Your money back if you're not satisfied'. According to Nigel he bought the book, read half of it and then went back to the shop and took enormous pleasure in asking for a full return of the price.

I walked to the Ivy for Glen Roven's surprise thirty-sixth-birthday party. A wonderful London night; it's not often you can honestly use the word 'balmy'. I crossed Regent Street to the Carnaby area to find it alive with pavement-hugging youngsters in various states of happy undress. The simple circus continued along Broadwick Street and through Soho where the recent pavement restoration by the Westminster authorities was being happily ignored. Alistair Beaton was of the party along with Robin Addison (who had organised it) and Glen's choreographer for his new show and two of her relations. She is obviously bright with a lot of experience in opera choreography. She'll need it if she is to survive on his musical *The 5,000 Fingers of Dr T,* due to open on Broadway next season. His producer is Brian Brolly (late Beatles and Really Useful Company). I dropped Brolly's assistant Peter off at World's End.

Alistair was trapped into telling a story against himself. After years of not being asked for his autograph he thought his moment had arrived when we did *The Ratepayers' Iolanthe* together at the Queen Elizabeth Hall. He saw a woman staring intently at his photograph in her programme. Then she approached him. He practically had his pen out. 'Alistair Beaton?' she enquired.

'Yes,' he said, eagerly.

'Oh, Mr Beaton, could you get me Ned Sherrin's autograph?'

He got his own back at my sixtieth-birthday party which Victoria Mather gave for me at her Battersea home. He had written my *Loose Ends* monologue for the first two years. Called upon to respond to a toast, I said I was unprepared. 'Alistair!' suggested half a dozen voices immediately.

I met Robert Hawdon at Michael Linnett's office over the Prince of Wales to talk about *Perfect Wedding*. He looks just as elegant and nearly as young as he did in small parts in revue in the late fifties. He and Michael are very keen to get the whole *Men Behaving Badly* team to do the show. I suspect that this is why it is being offered to me. Am I the way to Neil Morrissey? I promised to telephone him over the weekend. The play sounds as though it has been hanging around a bit – when I mentioned Carl Toms to design it I got a definite impression that he had already read it and said 'yes' during a different attempt to get it on. Which director?

To Chichester. As a judge on the Lloyds Private Banking panel I am asked to attend some productions to which Lloyds invite 50 or so clients. They feed and wine them. I harangue them for ten minutes about the virtues of the award, which are considerable. We saw Frank Hauser's production of *Hobson's Choice*. It is a play which is 70 years old and shows signs of indestructibility. It was dominated by Nichola McAuliffe as Maggie Hobson. Attack, timing, unsentimentality – all the qualities of a great Maggie were there. I have only seen Brenda de Banzie (film), Plowright, Penny Keith and Julia McKenzie in the role; but this is the one against which I shall measure others. Graham Turner was a splendid, witty Mossop and Leo McKern a sympathetic, if underpowered, Hobson. The regional Lloyds host, who had not seen the play before, asked if it was about 'the Cambridge Hobson'. Apparently he let out horses and you had to take the first in line – unlikely to be the best – hence 'Hobson's choice' as an expression. I wonder if this is accurate?

Saturday 15ᵗʰ July

A wonderful Hickstead day. It was the Royal International, with a huge crowd. Ann and Neil Benson drove me down through hideous traffic. Duchess Fergiana was there to support an Irish riding friend, Robert Splaine, who won the King George V Gold Cup convincingly. She presented the cup. She asked Neil Benson what he did and he said, 'I'm a chartered accountant.' 'What's that, exactly?' she said. Neil blushed and replied, 'A financial adviser.' She laughed and said, 'No, he was never that.'

I had to present the prizes to the women for the Queen Elizabeth II Cup, won by another Irish entrant, Marion Hughes on Flo Jo. I was tempted to apologise: 'The men got a duchess to hand out the awards – you've got to make do with a queen,' but restrained myself. I remembered an early visit to Hickstead when Douglas Bunn asked Caryl Brahms to present the prizes. She was thrilled, but her knicker elastic broke halfway through the ceremony and as the knickers fell she kicked them imperiously into touch.

Ruby Wax was making a documentary series about the Season – Henley, Wimbledon, Polo at Cowdray, etc. They hoisted her on to a horse in an outer ring early in the morning and a county woman was heard to remark, 'Isn't it wonderful what Hickstead will do for the disabled?'

Yet another Pinter tale. When the Bensons' son Mark was thirteen, he was somehow invited to audition for a child's part in a Pinter play at the National – with Peggy Ashcroft, no less. He was a bit late because he insisted on playing his game of cricket or rugger before. However, his father eventually delivered him and waited. He was given the script and read. After one sentence Pinter piped up, 'That's a funny line.'

Mark looked straight at him. 'I don't think so.'

He failed to get the role.

Sunday 16th July

Church advertised as at 12.15. The parsons at Chelsea Old Church are getting very impatient. I arrived at 12.14 and this one had already sped past the Commandments. It happened last month too. There were two sittings for the Sacrament – a good turn-out. Having knelt for my helping I was firmly nudged along the altar rail by the apparently frail nonagenarian (at least) who eventually settled beside me.

On television Brian Walden gave a brilliant, unillustrated, straight-to-camera talk about Clement Attlee. Shades of A.J.P. Taylor. It was not obviously teleprompted but it was remarkably fluent. Walden sat where Taylor stood. He encompassed every Attlee anecdote except, perhaps, the story Peter Vansittart tells of attending an Old Boys reunion at Haileybury at which Attlee was present. A pompous fellow announced, 'Gentlemen, please be upstanding for a toast to the greatest Haileyburian.' Attlee reddened and remained seated. Then, 'Gentlemen, I give you, Field-Marshal Lord Allenby.'

Walden was eloquent about Attlee's terseness in conversation but ignored George VI's nickname for his Prime Minister, 'Clem the Clam'.

Saturday 22nd July

This is a retrospective entry. We started rehearsing *Salad Days* on Monday – at the American Church in the Tottenham Court Road. There are two large rooms and a small one under the church and a pervading smell of soup kitchen – for which downstairs doubles. Huge fridges full of packeted mince for the soupees stand in the corridors.

It has been a good week. I had hoped to run both acts by this morning. With straight plays one can usually do that. However, I had forgotten how much time setting the company musical numbers takes. Lindsay Dolan, who is staging them, is very quick, but with a company this size – fifteen – it takes time. Next week we must work evenings, 10.30–1, 2–5, 6–8. We should have done so this week but I did not wake up to the fact until the last two days.

We started on Monday with a read-through. The show is constructed as a revue with a slight, charming story line on which to hang various sketches. It is hard to remember how freshly it hit London in the early fifties. It emerged from the Bristol Old Vic where Julian Slade and Dorothy Reynolds had devised several 'end of term' entertainments to fit the company. Odd to think that Eric Porter and Alan Dobie were in the original company and Michael Aldridge, James Cairncross, Dorothy and Yvonne Coulette were in the original London company.

Michael Codron 'talent spotted' it for Jack Hylton, who brought it to the Vaudeville where it ran for five years and then toured endlessly. Julian is a sweet, gentle, appreciative collaborator, endlessly supportive. I pressed him to come to rehearsals but he only attended the read-through and Saturday's run-through of Act One.

The featured players are Kit and the Widow, who have been touring for Edward Snape, the manager, and the other experienced players are Rosie Ashe, Gay Soper, Barry James, Sarah Mortimer (who was in the *Sloane Ranger Revue* for me) and Gary Fairhall, a spirited comedian who understudied Michael Williams in *Mr & Mrs Nobody* and was wonderful at Chichester in an Oscar Wilde play. Then there is David Morton who is playing the old tramp. I first saw him as a charismatic juvenile playing the Duke of Dorset in a musical, *Zuleika*, in the fifties. He tells me he has played three times in *Salad Days* – juvenile, parent and now, old tramp. A delightful man, he is infinitely patient and conscientious.

The youngsters are enchanting. *Salad Days* is such a simple, naive, even primitive, work, with an immediately infectious score, that we have been lucky in finding six kids who have lovely voices and can suggest, without parody or pastiche, an innocence which I think we can safely say has largely been lost. Simon Connolly was a big hit in the heart-stopping role of the errand boy in *She Loves Me*, but he is finding the responsibility of playing through this show hard. Of course he will manage it but one dance number has really stretched and depressed him. Opposite him is Nicola Fulljames – who looks equally young and innocent. She has come to her role totally prepared and obviously confident. A wonderfully open South African boy, Edward Baker-Duly, blond as his Swedish mother's complexion would suggest, is very quick and looks equally vulnerable – he is partnered by the 'Fiona' Diane Parrott – a very confident and competent comedienne. Lindsay is funny about her dancing. She does everything with great certainty and it is often only after he has looked very carefully at the result that he sees that it was not what he set!

No matter! They all have the freshness without which, these days, you can't play *Salad Days*; unless you want the usual 30-somethings in the central roles to look retarded.

Only one diversion this week. I took Loretta Feldman, who was over to supervise a 'Marty' retrospective to see Pinter's *Old Times* at Wyndham's. Julie Christie looked fourteen years of age; the play played like an undergraduate revue send-up of Pinter. That view was not shared by Richard Harris ('I adore Pinter') whom we met at Elena's

L'Etoile, where I took Loretta and Stephanie Cole for supper after-wards. It is the last week of the London production of *A Passionate Woman*. A very warm evening, not in temperature (which was extravagant) but in rapport between the two women.

The heat wave has clobbered the last few weeks of the play; and it would be foolish to go through the expensive business of recasting with what looks like another month of high summer to come.

One echo of the Hugh Grant story. Liz Hurley has been quoted as saying, 'How easy it is to fuck someone you don't know.' But not in her own persona. It has emerged that she said it on a 'talking book' tape of Julie Burchill's novel *Ambition*. She recorded it as a give-away tape with the late, unlamented *Modern Review*.

To the last London performance of *A Passionate Woman*. Cast in very good form. A substantial house included Lady Bird Johnson in the front row of the dress circle attended by a gaunt woman who looked like a mummified version of Martha Graham and an elderly man who looked like her too. Lady Bird seemed to enjoy herself. Her stone-faced neighbour only broke into animation when the ex-President's lady turned to her to see if she was sharing the joke. Belatedly she would risk a tight smile.

David Pugh gave a party at Tokyo Joe's, his drinking haunt on Shaftesbury Avenue near his office. I talked to Morrissey about the farce Michael Linnett wants him to read. He will. He was at a table with Mark Rylance and his composer wife? girlfriend? partner? We talked about the Globe. He appears likely to be the first artiste director, having given his *Tempest* there in pouring rain and knee-high mud. He is to open his *Macbeth* in Norwich soon after we are there. A very attractive personality and a good actor, though I did not like his Benedick at the Queens which was almost universally praised. I did not feel that it was necessary to advise him of this!

I have enjoyed the Stephen Spender obituaries. It was fortunate that Evelyn Waugh was long gone and that Bron was not invited to eulogise. 'At his christening,' Waugh père wrote, 'the fairy godparents showered Mr Spender with all the fashionable neuroses but they forgot the gift of literary skill.'

Monday 24ᵗʰ July

A sweet letter from a man, Richard Thomas, who had written beseeching an autographed photograph for two octagenarians whom he meets in his local Waitrose in Marlow. My most unexpected fans. 'I took the precious, signed photograph to give to one of the Waitrose supervisors. But on looking for her found Ted and Ivy, chattering quietly over a neat list – loving budgerigars in Ivy's toque. Ted, spectacles and flat cap.

'Something has come in the post for you. Shall I open it?' They peered and peered like Xmas children. When I gave Ivy the photograph she levitated very slightly. 'Oh! It's Ned!' That was all she could say . . . The supervisor was fetched (with my help) and my wife Georgia was given a vivid account of who you were, etc. etc. And for the next 30 minutes, whenever we passed, Ivy blew us both discreet kisses of joy and gratitude.' He quotes 'an old Victorian saying' – *Chi non mi vuole non mi merita* and translates it for me 'to put your secretary out of her misery', as 'who doesn't want me, doesn't deserve me'.

I must learn how to pronounce it.

Sunday 30ᵗʰ July

Again a week of rehearsals. The mini cab at ten. Rehearsal 10.30. Lunch with Lindsay (choreographer) and Stuart (musical director) at the Spaghetti House. A drink at the pub in Tottenham Street – two halves of lager – between the Equity break from five to six, and two more hours' rehearsal in the Choir Room at the American Church while punk Amazons do aerobics in our main space – a permanent booking two nights a week.

I think I have never eaten pasta – all sorts of varieties – so regularly. A starter portion overfills me but I am developing a taste. Lindsay is doing a terrific job on the company numbers – there are a lot and I have had to scurry with the book scenes where I can find the opportunity. Next week I should be able to pick up some dropped stitches.

I find the innocence, the naivety of the play fascinating. It must be the last innocent showbiz use of the word 'gay'. It crops up all over the place. We are doing a period piece and we must not lose it – equally we must not be knowing about it.

The great encouraging thing has been the application the young people have brought to the play. Simon, Nicola, Diane and Edward have come knowing the songs and learning their lines in the way that professionals are supposed to do but so often don't, saying, 'I prefer to pick it up as I go and learn about my character.' They are a joy and, quite rightly, are now asking for time to explore their lines, their emotions, attitudes, etc. Would that one or two (no more – maybe less) of the older members of the cast had applied themselves in the same way.

Another sweltering hot day. I can't remember being here for so hot a summer since 1976 when we were playing *Side By Side By Sondheim*. I have had to rely on the late-night TV summaries of the 4th, the Old Trafford test. But today, and yesterday afternoon, I was able to watch the ball-by-ball grind of regular, daytime TV. It was fascinating. Cork's hat trick in the first over was one of those moments when we remember where we were at the time. I was running between a cool bath and the sitting room until I abandoned cleanliness for drama. Then I thought it would be over by lunch. However, Lara's 100 was the obstacle and the game lingered on until 5.30-ish. Much fuss had been made of the recall at 42 of John Emburey. A useful but not a significant contribution. How different from the return of Wilfred Rhodes in 1926. At 48 he was called back to face Australia at the Oval. He took 6 for 79 and, to ice the cake, knocked up 28 and 14.

I felt unusually randy and pondered phoning several advertisers in *Gay Times*. I did. They were out – obviously sunning themselves, the better to enchant other clients. Later, I tried again. No luck. The only one to reply wanted £140 plus cab fares and did not sound as though he would enter enthusiastically into the game.

This was a fairly rare impulse this year. Something slowing must be happening to the biological clock. I think I have only called about twice this year – unrecorded here. Both times the same man, described in his advertisement as a 'biker'; he turned out to be Irish, 30-ish, dark, good-looking and amusing. If someone mature chooses this profession it seems fair that he should work at it. In return, apart from the money, one has a duty to make them welcome and at ease. They are invariably anecdotalists who are keen to swap stories (anonymously) of previous clients. I enjoyed Mr Ireland's company and he was very ready to return. He has a motorbike so he gets here in very quick time. Today he must have been among the sun-seekers.

Monday 31st July

Tim West is reading his letters to Pru Scales on Radio 4 before the 9 a.m. news. He came on *Loose Ends* to plug *I'm Here, I Think, Where are You?* and sold 40,000 copies in hardback – we take all the credit! It is an excellent memoir and he reads it with great style and wit. He appeared before the Pope as Thomas à Becket and was mistaken by some Vatican choristers for a real archbishop.

In my head I heard a faint echo of Cardinal Heenan's appearance at Lime Grove long ago. He was dressed in full rig for an appearance on *Panorama*. Returning from the loo he took the wrong turn and was understandably directed to a drama studio where they were recording *The Three Musketeers*.

A new biography of Gracie Fields by David Brett was reviewed over the weekend. Reviews concentrated on her poor choice of men. I only met the last husband, Boris, the Polish odd-job man who came to mend something in her Capri home and stayed.

In the very early days of ATV we did a breakfast show on Saturdays from the old Viking Studios in St Mary Abbot's Place in Kensington. It was a primitive lash-up, not destined to last, but Gracie was the first star guest. She was to appear on the first Palladium show the next night. We paid no fees but gave the guest a present. It was my job to go out and buy it. For later editions I remember getting a Teasmade for Donald Wolfit and a white hearthrug for Dorothy Tutin. Word was passed that Gracie wanted a Parker pen. A pen was procured and presented. She was expressing polite pleasure when Boris butted in: 'We got one already,' he snapped. Much later she appeared on the old *Tonight* show (which I directed) opening the show by walking in on Cliff Michelmore's arm singing 'Sally'.

In his book Brett has a ruder reminiscence of her singing to sailors in the back of beyond south of Manila. Her emergency pianist, another Pole called Buckovsky, was so incompetent that the sailors soon dispatched him with a chant of 'Fuckovsky, Buckovsky' and Gracie happily continued to sing unaccompanied.

August

Friday 4th August

I DID AN after-dinner at Cliveden for some Ford people who had rung up maximum sales or customer appreciation or something – they were very nice, especially a National Hunt owner-jockey who won a race at Aintree before retiring. 'I'm worth six or seven million,' he said encouragingly.

I had to wait a few minutes before dinner while they were being given a pep talk, so I went looking for the famous stick – a relic of the Dukes of Sutherland who owned that splendid house before the Astors. It is said to be Y-shaped and known as the 'Harriet, Duchess of Sutherland Pushing-Up-Hill Stick'. Apparently it was used by footmen to propel Her Grace, a largish lady, from the Thames uphill to the house.

The day started with the Queen Mother's ninety-fifth birthday. I dwelt guiltily on a few of her better quotes which I left out (inadvertently) from my *Anecdotage* book. In her schooldays she sent a telegram to her father, the Earl of Strathmore, asking for more pocket money: 'SOSLSDRSVP'.

About her most convenient form of transport: The chopper has changed my life as conclusively as that of Anne Boleyn.'

To her elder daughter who was drinking wine at lunch at Clarence House: 'Is that wise? You know you have to reign all afternoon.'

In the car on the way back I listened to Mark Steele's very funny new late-night radio series. He advances an outrageously controversial proposition each week. This week he was suggesting that homosexuality should be compulsory. The driver could hardly believe his ears: ' . . . Radio 4?!'

Saturday 5ᵗʰ August

Final run-through of *Salad Days* before leaving for Norwich. Norwich for the company that is. Derby first stop for me to start rehearsals for the *Passionate Woman* tour. The cast in excellent shape. Two worries. Edward Baker-Duly, the South African who plays the young silly-ass parts excellently, has wrecked his knee for the second time. We thought he had recovered from the first crack, which happened in the early days of rehearsals. Today it gave out after the big dance number halfway through Act One. Worrying with only four or five days to opening. He went off to the physio and was going on to Norfolk with Kit Hesketh-Harvey with whom he has struck up a good friendship. Kit's father is a doctor. Fingers crossed.

More worrying, Richard Sisson, 'The Widow', is plainly unhappy with the electric keyboard we have inserted into the 'magic' piano. It arrived a week late. It ceased to function after being inserted into the framework of the little piano and did not come back from repairs until quite recently. He has therefore had no chance to practise with the other musicians to stake out a musical contribution of his own. Now he feels that he will not be able to learn what has been written for him in time for the opening. We may have to use an acoustic upright for the two cabaret numbers which open Act Two, and let him redefine the accompaniment. At the end of the morning he was plainly distressed. He rang me at home in his usual conciliatory fashion and I tried to reassure him. He is always so charming, helpful and reasonable that one has to take his worries seriously.

On the way home I popped into Peter Jones to try to find little first-night presents for the cast and crew. They total about 40 and I hoped to find some modest china with a salad motif. I failed – with some relief as the cheapest saucers were about £5, so £200 and probably more would have been the least. I went down to the gardening section and stumbled on packets of salad seeds. It's the thought that counts!

Julian rang to talk about 'The Widow' problem. 'We've never had a difficulty with the Troppo character before,' he said lugubriously. 'It's usually the two women.'

Sunday 6ᵗʰ August

I set off on this odd odyssey after lunch. In Derby I'm staying in newly built furnished flats, so I packed a carrier bag with what I needed overnight – bread, butter, cereals, lemons, grapefruit juice, Waitrose 'luxury taramasalata', long-life milk, coffee. I harvested what was left of my Waitrose 'living' salad lettuce box and piled into my Redcliffe mini-cab. The local firm have driven me ever since I arrived in World's End. Ten years ago they were a tiny rickety enterprise run by a pleasant Iranian lady. I had one classic encounter back then with an African driver who when I said, 'Piccadilly, please,' pondered it and then, scratching his head, replied, 'Now, let me tink . . . Piccadilly?' Now she runs a fleet of smart cars with much more experienced drivers. This one had a brand-new vehicle and was bitterly disappointed when I tried to open the windows. He wanted to show off his new air-conditioning, so I promptly rolled the window up again.

It's a curious feeling setting off to initiate two tours. One rehearsal period coming to its climax, the other one just starting. I felt a nostalgic pull driving past familiar landmarks. Earls Court advertises the impending arrival of Maurice Cerullo, the ranting preacher, so perhaps it's a good time to get out of London. We sped up from Shepherd's Bush towards the Westway, past the Harrow club where in 1970 I rehearsed an incredible cast to celebrate the centenary of Dickens's death – Tony Hopkins, in one of his earliest TV roles, was Dickens. The other cameos demonstrated how the characters in his life crept into his novels. They included Dame Sybil, Dame Gladys, Stanley Holloway (these three in virtually their last TV roles), Dorothy Reynolds, Mona Washbourne, Dandy Nicholls, Arthur Lowe, Freddy Jones, Patrick Cargill, Joan Greenwood, Michael Wilding, Jenny Agutter, Gordon Jackson. It was a great success, so naturally after two transmissions the BBC wiped it by mistake. Coming off Westway past Paddington Green and Mrs Siddons's statue I got a glimpse of the hospital which took me back even further – to 1955 when I was working for ATV and floor-managing a Christmas transmission from a ward which we thought would be full of children. In fact most had been sent home and we had to move the survivors around the room to give the impression that it was bursting with life.

DERBY

Birchover estates – the furnished flats – were said to be in the Old Kedleston Road but this was a mystery to the cab driver and to the woman in the mini-market where I stopped to get some vodka on the way. We ploughed on up the ordinary Kedleston Road and luckily I spotted one of those signs saying 'leading to Old Kedleston Road' – a tiny cul-de-sac. I was greeted by an effusive blonde, Rachel Watson, like one of those ambitious career women on *The Preston Front*, who has been 'personally responsible for the decoration of all the flats on Birchover estates'. One big snag – no telephone. However, Billy Russo, the assistant director, and the actors, Gwen Taylor, Gary Webster and Nick Conway, are all in the same complex and are all sprouting mobile phones. I can see pros as well as cons in being without a phone but it is irritating for little things like calling a cab.

I watched bits of *Bill and Ted's Excellent Adventure*. A sophomore time-travel romp which I keep hearing about because it helped to start Keanu Reeves's career. It was surprisingly endearing in a light *Doctor Who* sort of way. I imagine it's the source of the constantly reiterated 'Excellent' which is on all young people's lips these days – along with 'No problem'.

Monday 7th August

First reading of *A Passionate Woman*. The usual bonhomie of a cast of actors thrown together with a resident set of technicians. Gwen read beautifully – we must watch the hard side of her character and look for the lovable, vulnerable moments. Stanley Lebor will play the father brilliantly. Nick Conway sounds uncannily like Neil Morrissey as the son and will have no trouble playing mother's boy. Gary Webster as the ghost is not back from his Malaga package holiday so the author, Kay Mellor, read for him.

It's a curious trip going from *A Passionate Woman* – just four players and a tight script – across to *Salad Days* – fourteen youngsters, lovely songs, and rickety, we hope charming, comedy sketches.

The cross-country journey isn't much fun. Taxi to Nottingham and then three hours across the flattest bits of Norfolk in a crowded local puffer. Opposite sat an open-faced young American back-packer who was deep in his *Do Britain on Almost Nothing a Day* or some such title. We slipped into conversation and he seemed to be criss-crossing the country, going from cathedral to cathedral. He had started in Scotland but was making for Norwich, having done Durham and others, zig-zagging on an endless rail ticket. Passing Ely came as a great shock to him as it was not on his itinerary. I pointed out Salisbury and Wells on his map which, since he was already going to Bath, it seemed a pity for him to miss. He was very apologetic about being Californian. Of course he said Norr-wich, so I told him that Diana Cooper always refused to use her husband's title – because it rhymed with 'porridge'.

At the theatre the company had had a happy vocal rehearsal. The company pub – the Little Bethel – is welcoming and Patrick Connellan's huge revolving bandstand looks wonderful.

We checked in at the Sprowston Manor Hotel. It's an old Gurney family home, hugely expanded with extra wings, conference room and a leisure centre including massive pool, beauty section and coffee shop. A good room over gardens, golf course and an open-air chess set which elderly guests can be seen manhandling with some difficulty. Delightful staff, tricky food. The lamb (when the tin cover was removed) had a wonderful pink slice on top, sadly, the pieces underneath were brown and nowhere near as enjoyable.

Tuesday 8th August

A very slow day *just* achieving a full technical rehearsal by the end.

Tragedy struck early. The Widow's magic keyboard failed us again. He was controlled and patient – simply requiring the standby upright so that he could at least play his contributions on that.

It is always the same when you start a 'tech'. You must go slowly and stop and start. The lighting is going to be nowhere near what you hope it will be. The actors who begin to enjoy themselves on a roll must be stopped. Laughs seem a million miles away and only when a soloist floats beautifully into a song where the set doesn't need to be changed or repainted, when no lighting can ruin the moment, when no prop is missing, no costume blemish shows, when no one miscues an effect – only then can one relax and grow in confidence.

It is hell for the actors who have flogged themselves to near-performance pitch and are hungry for an audience.

Of the juvenile leads, Simon Connolly is plainly conscious of the responsibility of leading the show. He never stops practising. In any spare minute you catch him in a corner running over the dance steps he learnt so painfully in the rehearsal room. Because of the nature of the piece – a magic piano turns people into involuntary dancers – Lindsay Dolan has choreographed steps which appear to tug his legs into action, loosening him up until he gives way to joyous abandon. When Simon combines the acting side of the role and the dancing, his face echoing the growing surprise and exhilaration in his feet, the effect is magical.

Opposite him Nicola Fulljames, ex-Footlights and a little older, is the perfect Slade leading lady. She is very pretty and poised, her clear soprano is true and tender and she acts and dances with ease and grace.

They are an ideal couple for the simple fifties never-never land which they inhabit, and they play lines like 'Jane, would it help at all if I married you?' and 'Since we got married I seem to have noticed you more' for simplicity not send-up.

Diane Parrott is straight out of drama school: but she was a late entrant after some work in psychology in Bristol. She is pretty, very confident and plays a brash Sloaney girl with assurance.

Opposite her, as Nigel, the Wodehousean semi-silly ass, is Edward Baker-Duly, who has only been in England three months though he has played leads in *Crazy For You* and *Arcadia* in South Africa. He started dancing at three, and has no trouble with that or his acting and singing. He is very blond, as I said earlier, and pretty-looking – remarkably like Michael Meacham who played his role 40 years ago in the original production. He has been adopted by Kit H-H and they are inseparable, which must be good for Edward in a totally alien environment, a few thousand miles from home.

Andy Norman and Emma Flett are the two ensemble and under-study players. Very young – though Andrew was a child actor in *Bugsy Malone*, and Emma was a dancer (more recently) in *Crazy For You*. They are full of energy and, particularly, dancing skills. Andy is quiet but Emma is an outgoing, friendly extrovert with few inhibitions.

Kit H-H is potentially a fine revue player of the old school. One could imagine him in the Henry Kendall or Wally Crisham or Cyril Ritchard roles opposite Gingold or Baddeley. He is arch, camp and confident and as we see his various outlandish changes of costume and make-up it is plain that he will help to bind the revue side of this entertainment together.

The songs are enchanting, the romantic moments are sweet and touching; but I cannot with my hand on my heart deny that the comedy sketch material is showing signs of advanced old age. We must wait for the audience to see how it survives.

Certainly Gay Soper and Rosie Ashe attack it with energy and experience. Gay was in *Godspell* years ago and more recently played Madame Thenardier in *Les Mis* opposite Barry James for three years. She has a strong, useful soprano and she is a comedienne who worries her way to her effects. This can be infuriating in rehearsal but it usually gets the desired results.

Rosie Ashe's background is in opera. She comes to us straight from the Garsington season; but she has also been doing a lot of straight work in rep at Ipswich. She is a gutsy off-the-top-of-her-head extrovert, a very quick study and altogether a joyous person. She has a passion for pink and was very good years ago as Yum Yum in *The Metropolitan Mikado*.

Barry James turns out to have been in *Night is for Delight*, a revue Caryl Brahms and I put on with Laurier Lister way back in the mid-sixties – embarrassingly I can't remember him from it – though I seem to have seen him scoring in every other West End musical since then. Lindsay, one of whose earliest choreographing jobs it was, cannot remember either. (It was not Lindsay's *first* – that was when he was a tap-dancing champion in Scotland at fifteen. He was on a variety bill and arrived to find that the Scottish vaudeville tradition was for the dance act to choreograph the ensemble numbers, so he got on and did it.) Barry is small, quirky and funny. Patrick Connellan has given him a succession of funny wigs and moustaches, of which he is taking maximum advantage. He plays very well with Gary Fairhall. It has been good to get Gary in. I saw him being very amusing as a 'renter' in an Oscar Wilde trial play at Chichester years ago and he was an invaluable understudy in *Mr & Mrs Nobody* and in *Jeffrey Bernard is Unwell*, but understudying is frustrating stuff and he is thrilled to be back on stage for real. He's great fun, very inventive and gaining in daring as he and Barry work more together. Police Inspector and PC Boot.

Sarah Mortimer, who plays Boot's 'love interest', was in *The Sloane Ranger* revue for me and is a beautifully controlled, versatile comedienne. I gather her father is critically ill but she is being very stoical and loyal to the production.

Finally, David Morton plays the tramp who turns up with the piano and a lot of other vignettes. Very much the senior member of the company. He is infinitely modest, unassuming and hard-working. He has a lucrative line in annual pantomime – he plays Dame and his 6-foot-4 or 5 must be a great comedy asset. He is at Bournemouth this Christmas. I see his programme note says that he has a daughter who is an agent in Australia. So maybe he will end up in *Neighbours*!

James Barber (Yvonne Arnaud Theatre, Guildford, co-producer) arrived for the first night. He has had lunch with Deke and says the deal is set for *Bing Bong*, with Dennis Waterman and Robert Powell. We rehearse in February and open a twelve-week tour in March. Yippee! Now that has to be fitted in with the new tour of *Salad Days* – also due to start in March, in Bath. The amount of rehearsal depends on the number of cast changes after Christmas.

Wednesday 9ᵗʰ August

I spent pre-breakfast packing and addressing my seed packets and took them to the theatre for distribution.

A morning fiddling with and balancing sound. A smooth dress run apart from an appalling stage wait before Act Two, scene one. We had time to re-drill the actors and stage staff afterwards, and crossed fingers.

The first performance – on a super-hot night – went well. Thank God the theatre is air-conditioned! The kids were enchanting and the comedy scenes just about got by. Edward (producer) is very worried about the critic of the *Eastern Daily Press* – one C.V. Roberts, the Tynan of Norfolk. He once reviewed Edward's direction of a student production of *Guys & Dolls* as the worst thing he'd ever seen anywhere!

There were drinks in the bar afterwards – lots of parents starry-eyed at their offsprings' prowess. Then Julian and the producers (thrilled and delighted) hosted a party at the latest Pierre Victoire restaurant to erupt. The cast was suitably relieved and I tried to work out what touring relationships might evolve. Nicola and Simon seemed much more relaxed with one another. The drummer appeared to be moving in on Diane. Emma asked Kit if he thought she had a chance with Edward. Kit noncommittal.

I remembered to order the East Anglian paper to see what savagery C.V. Roberts might spew out.

Thursday 10th August

C.V. Roberts is a critic of great perception and sensitivity! He loves the original and finds the production 'as enchanting, beguiling and adorable as ever'. He nicely points out that it 'lives in a golden age of innocence that never was', and welcomes Nicola and Simon (accurately) as 'glowing to perfection – gently radiating an image of youth unspoiled, and gilding it with personalities and voices that flow over the audience like balm'. He admits that he worried that Kit and Richard might unbalance the show but welcomes them both as totally supportive and brilliant. He suggests the Widow might look up more – a good note – he has very vivid eyes.

'Last night was the first of the tour – frequently it showed, with lagging pace and uncertain continuity. Minor points, however. This is a celebratory revival to be embraced.'

He's right of course: but they will get that together. At breakfast I found that neither Julian nor the others had seen a copy so I went up to get mine. Charles Stephens, Edward's business partner, incurred my heavy (humorous) wrath when, having read the rave, he looked up and only muttered, 'Lagging pace.' He was not allowed to forget it for the rest of breakfast.

I set off for the trek to Derby and arrived just as rehearsals ended and Kay was leaving for her train. They seemed happy with their four days' work.

Friday 11th August

Gwen Taylor is going to be wonderful as Betty, the Passionate Woman. The new note she is striking – irrelevant to Stephanie Cole's splendid incarnation – is a touching return to a teenage personality when she remembers, with her ghostly lover, the trysts which they shared behind the cricket pavilion. Nick Conway (son) and Stanley Lebor (husband) are impeccable and Gary Webster has grown as the sexy ghost; being able to start all over again instead of just taking over.

Patrick Connellan (designer of both *Salad Days* and *PW*) arrived to say that Nicola had bravely conquered food poisoning at the matinée after the first night and gone on! Food poisoning? I think the Pierre Victoire red and white might have played a part.

Back again to Norwich. As I lugged my bags wearily off the train I heard three local lads muttering, 'Better let the old boy get off first.'

Saturday 12th August

A boiling hot day and a thin matinée but the producers say bookings have been brisk. The cast are finding their length. I wish I could spend one morning with them nipping and tucking. The schedule won't allow it until after we open in Derby. I suppose I could then go up and see on Monday, rehearse Tuesday and put the changes in that night – perhaps Bradford or Sunderland. Katie Rabbett (Kit's wife) was there with several broods, including her own. Rather dimmed as she said, 'It has improved, hasn't it?' She meant to be encouraging, I'm sure; but I always interpret that remark as 'Wasn't it ghastly on the first night?'

I had a ploughman's in the local pub, the Coach and Horses, Bethel Street, which has been very hospitable on my odd days here. A buxom blonde approached, diffidently. She was Stephen Fry's sister Jo, lunching, or at least lagering, with her current interest (a chef, according to information later from Hesketh-Harvey), a short, darkly handsome young man in white jeans and desert boots. We joked about Stephen's new hairstyle – 'rent boy bleached' – and the brouhaha over the play and Simon Gray's book. When she heard about it she masterminded a mole operation at the publishers and got a proof copy out in case drastic legal action was required. When she got to the point where Simon prefers his signed copies of the newly published play and Rik Mayall's locally grown dildos as first-night presents over Stephen's Fortnum baskets of Russian delicacies, she decided it could be let go in laughter. Apparently it was some strictures on Duncan Weldon which had to be removed before publication.

I considered Stephen's Fortnum's goodies and compared my packets of seeds unfavourably. The producers have given me a handsomely bound *Salad Days* correspondence set. Kit and the Widow, good solid wooden salad servers.

I asked Jo if she could get him to defect again so that I could earn another £1,000 for a piece on absconding actors for the *Standard* or the *Mail*. Good girl.

A reassuringly quick train home to Liverpool Street. A daring experiment with non-alcoholic apple juice was a thirst-quenching success.

Sunday 13th August

I watched much of the Test match. I have become increasingly frustrated by 'highlights' – all I get to see after rehearsal. It doesn't compare with gradually watching the game unfold and being surprised, delighted or dismayed. Highlights is all plums and no pudding. That said, I could have done without the excitement of seeing poor Knight at silly point put down by a mighty swing from K. Benjamin from a range of two or three yards. He turned with a remarkable reflex and took the ball on the back of the head, not the temple, which would surely have finished him. There followed a distant dumb show in stunned, uneasy silence as a couple of physios and a woman doctor lifted him gently on to a rickety stretcher and wheeled him slowly off to a waiting ambulance.

'Retired hurt' is one thing – but 'Absent huffed' is surely unique in the annals of cricket! This is now in the score book against the name of one Robin Wightman of the North-East Durham League, who left the field apparently in a huff, having taken 7 for 85, when his captain decided to bowl the last over himself. He joined other oddities such as: 'Sick on wicket', 'Ran away scared by bowler', 'Retired hot', 'Shamefully refused to go in', and 'Left to catch train to Continent'.

Monday 14th August

To St Pancras and thence to Derby. Decided against a second breakfast.

We attacked the roof scene in *A Passionate Woman*. It was good for the actors to have some time to clamber around on site. It looks easy from down below but it is daunting up aloft. Gwen is very brave and a trouble-free zone. We got through it twice at quite a lick so now they know the shape of the scene and we can break it up slowly into small sections.

I'll start on that before disappearing to Edinburgh tomorrow at four. You can actually fly from Derby – or at least the East Midlands Airport, 30 minutes away.

I don't think I should enjoy touring. I love being on my own, but on my own terms and in my own home. There is plenty to do to prepare for Edinburgh. We've got Garrison Keillor, Liz Lochhead, lots of comics and musicians on *Loose Ends*, with an audience on Saturday, and I have reams of cuttings to bone up on and at least two books to read – apart from some review copies and some for pleasure. I can cook in this mini-kitchenette – well, Tesco's excellent Caesar salad, cold ham, Tesco's cheddar and a tin of Tesco's tomato soup into which I have infiltrated a beef tomato (well beyond its sell-by date, but juicy), and some chopped spring onions. However, although I love the phone not ringing I regret the *certainty* that it will not ring. Never mind. Tomorrow Balmoral (Hotel, not Castle), and normal service will be resumed.

Tuesday 15th August

A workmanlike day on the roof and a quick spin through Act Two, scene one. Stanley Lebor as Dad and Nick Conway as Mark are off the book and exactly right in intensity. It is a beautifully written scene and a very cunning opening to Act Two.

East Midlands airport busy and efficient. British Midland delivered me bang on time at Edinburgh airport. A sweet little girl sang to herself under her breath all the way and then sat patiently waiting to be collected.

Met by Ros Wolfe who has arranged six guests for the National Youth Music Theatre (NYMT) lunchtime show tomorrow – six in 60 minutes is pushing it. We'll see. A few years ago Jeremy James Taylor had the idea that he could use the lunchtime hour at the George Square Theatre, which the NYMT rents, to mount a sort of chat show – Edinburgh is so full of chattable personalities. The theatre do a play before lunch, a matinée, an evening show and then at ten they let it to a comic act and, if they're lucky, at midnight to a jazz group. It seemed a pity not to maximise the use of the hall – so as President of the NYMT. Friends, I do an informal *Loose Ends*-ish entertainment. I had to miss last year (rehearsing *PW*) – but I committed myself to this year. I checked into the Balmoral, did my homework and went early to bed.

Wednesday 16th August

First lunchtime gig at George Square. A keen NYMT young band. I'd been told they weren't up to it. Plainly they were raring to go. They can have their head tomorrow.

First on was Rich Hall, an American writer and stand-up. Thin, bejeaned. He attacked the audience with grace and enthusiasm, concentrating on Helen Lederer's five-year-old daughter in the front row. She loved the attention. Then two Australians – Lano and Woodley – who won the Perrier Award last year. A perfect, traditional, fresh, young knockabout duo. They were totally different from the usual fringe fare – hence the surprise which greeted their award in 1994. Abbott & Costello time except that Woodley is a beanpole and Lano chunkily good-looking.

John Hegley prowled through two poems – and improvised nicely when a light exploded. He was followed by Will Gaines, the veteran jazz/tap man, incoherent in conversation, but eloquent with his feet. Helen Lederer has a new book, *Living Alone*, about single parents. With all the flak about unmarried mothers I thought she might have thrown in a few quips but perhaps it's too early in her book tour for her to have got her act together.

Finally Bob Downe – joyously extrovert. His stage persona – not *too* far away from himself – is the archetypal Australian daytime chat-show host. The acme of acrylic, Bishop of Beige, Apostle of Airfix hair, saint of shimmering smile, the King of Kitsch. He is appearing at our George Square theatre nightly – but his backing tapes were locked up. Never mind, he wants to come back next week and sing with the band.

A gossipy lager in the Assembly Rooms Bar with a *Loose Ends* regular, Graham Norton, who is up here with his new one-man show. He sounds very excited about the apparently maxi-testosteronous Oz tap group, the Tap Dogs, who tap in construction-worker kit at the Palladium.

I walked back across the top of St Andrew Square and looked down at the gentle pink and yellow sky over the placid water. How good not to be going to sweat on an uncomfortable chair in a hot hall being railed at by an ungracious comedian.

Thursday 17ᵗʰ August

Second lunchtime session. Ros Wolfe, who is booking the guests for the George Square spectacular, is doing an excellent job but this week audiences are disappointingly down on previous years. Today she turned up Richard O'Brien, the Onlie Begetter of *The Rocky Horror Show*, along with the inspired cello clown Jim Tavaré – whose face is the nearest thing to the late Tommy Cooper – and Instant Sunshine, who have been coming to Edinburgh for over twenty years, and are as popular as ever. Sir David Steel, who is a vice-president of NYMT, gave a run down on other fringe shows he has seen. Kate Robbins, an accomplished impressionist who is at the Assembly Rooms was there, and the incredible *Olé*. Paul Morocco is one of my favourite people and performers. A huge, greasy, sweating Levantine American figure, always wrapped in more clothes than you could imagine, especially in this thunderous heat. He and his two companions, Antonio Forcione and Alessandro Russo, are a mad mixture of comedy, juggling and guitar playing. Spitting and juggling table-tennis balls was their main routine this time. Antonio has another act with Neil Stacey. Both are guitar virtuosi and their act Acoustic Mania is coming back to us next week. But as Neil was in the hall I called him up to join the others in a jamming guitar quartet. Being this lot they did no such thing. Just before the show they had discussed a new sort of guitar troilism. Neil sat in the middle and Antonio and Alessandro draped themselves around him improvising at the top and bottom of his guitar. Paul pretended to feel excluded and juggled fruit sadly at the side of the stage. It was the nicest sort of happening and almost completely spontaneous – certainly they had never performed it before.

Antonio had borrowed a costume from the Threepenny Opera wardrobe which David Steel identified as a Privy Councillor's court dress – apparently he has one at home. On Antonio it looked like some Ruritanian robe.

In the evening I had agreed to do a charity after-dinner at the Caledonian Hotel for the Friends of King's Theatre where *Salad Days* and *A Passionate Woman* will tour in the autumn. The oddest part was the determination of Graham, a very handsome 30-something young photographer in dress kilt, who made me pose with every couple at every table for the 'Friends of the King's magazine'. He professed to be studying ballet so I asked him to *Tap Dogs* on Wednesday, but he says his mother is up on Tuesday and Wednesday. I think he thinks quickly.

Friday 18th August

Another good bill. Another disappointing turn-out. Roberto Baggio, a sporting revue group, did a wonderful short bit on footballers' nicknames which always end in Y: 'Giggsy', 'Bigsy', 'Grievsey', etc. carried to virtuoso lengths. They also pointed out that it wouldn't happen in tennis where names had to be long like Navratilova or Ivanisovic. This explains our failure to come up with a decent tennis local champion. Jeremy Bates – a natural for 'Batesy' – should obviously have taken up soccer.

Richard Morton, the Novocastrian *Loose Ends* regular, is supporting Jack Dee at the Playhouse. Morton's been doing a piece in his set about Alison Hargreaves – the woman who climbed Everest without oxygen. A couple of nights ago Jack told him he'd have to cut the gag as she was missing, presumed dead, on K2. At first, he thought Jack was kidding and insisted on performing it. Finally Jack convinced him and he cut it. When I interviewed him at George Square, he started to tell the story – not the joke but the history of the joke – and the audience froze. With immense aplomb he kept at it and by not panicking he came out on the other side with as much sympathy from the audience as if he'd been the victim of a nasty traffic accident. It was a beautiful piece of tight-rope walking to watch.

Dan Freedman, another *Loose Ends* regular, was also a joy, with stories of how he is besieged by two kids aged about seven and nine who hang around the Pleasance offering him horrendous jokes about sex and crack.

Four radio commercials for the *Independent* – recorded down the line from Scot-FM, a newish station located down at Leith in an old warehouse (I would guess) called Shed One. A very bright engineer called Angus chaperoned me. We did three between nine and ten o'clock and then I had to return at three to do another which was being written during the morning. It was to draw readers' attention to a competition. The first prize was a week in the wine cellars of Burgundy and a year's supply of Crémant de Bourgogne. Ten runners-up will get a case each.

Saturday 19ᵗʰ August

Loose Ends from the Pleasance. Début of a new producer, Jon Rowlands – bright, energetic, full of ideas. He introduced a running gag – Annabel Giles (on tape) taxi-ing around Edinburgh trying to round up *Loose Enders: The Men Who Know* at breakfast; Graham Norton getting up in sordid digs. (The original plan was to discover him in bed with Sandy Toksvig – ruining two reputations – but it didn't make it past the drawing board.)

A nice battle has ensued over who sold out the hall quickest, *Loose Ends* or *The News Quiz*. Apparently we won on speed; but honours were even in that there were punch-ups between disappointed *News Quiz* fans.

I've always enjoyed reading Garrison Keillor but found him difficult to interview. I hope I have now found the answer. He does not like to talk about whatever he's peddling. He prefers to *converse*. So we talked about his recent Scottish holiday. He co-operated entertainingly – as did Liz Lochhead, the Scots poet and playwright who fashions her plays out of monologues she has performed herself. I had not met Boothby Graffoe before. He is a tall London comic. A hot tip for the Perrier – though hot tips rarely seem to win. I hope he does. He is good-looking and easy. The act is partly musical but the chat is unforced and looks effortless – wild flights of fancy about tossing his year-old child up to a ceiling festooned with Velcro so it can stick there. Nick Romero and Dan Freedman had a savage piece about which Edinburgh Fringe comedians to avoid. It was fortunate none of the American comics they were sending up were on the show.

Scot-FM provided Scotty McClue – their fictional late-night shock-jock whom half the listeners apparently think is a real person. His costume makes him look like the late Chic Murray – Scots comic (someone told me that when he died his partner Maidie provided 382 authentic 'Chic Murray caps' for charity auctions). Scotty McClue's real name is Colin Lamont, an ex-director of Scottish Opera's education programme. He was quite untroubled by being unmasked on air.

At five I did the Book Festival in the Post Office Theatre in the big complex in Charlotte Square. Last time I was there, three years ago, about fifteen people turned up. This time it was packed – about 400, I should think. Chaired by a nice plump woman called Lorraine. I did about 30 minutes of *Humorous Quotations* and *Anecdotes*. At first questions didn't come, but after Lorraine had taken me through 'Sherrin – the early years' they were less shy. Mainly 'whither satire?' and favourite interviewee questions. I signed twenty or thirty books.

A radio interview for Scot-FM at the Roxburgh afterwards set some sort of new standard. The interviewer said, 'I don't really know how to do this; would you more-or-less do it by yourself?' Happy to oblige, I did.

Then a TV interview for Janet Street-Porter's ubiquitous 'Live TV' which will be seen by no one.

Sunday 20*th* August

Princes Street packed with pipe bands and tourists all morning. I retreated into the hotel. I decided on a roast beef and Yorkshire traditional Sunday lunch to find that the 'rare' roast beef had been cooked to a cinder and smothered with gravy. The Yorkshire was more like a rock cake. As I was almost first into the dining room there was no excuse. The maitresse d' and the chef offered to take the price off. I accepted.

NYMT charity gala at the George Square Theatre. Rich Hall again – very funny and attacking. Scott Capurro, a gay American with an easy laid-back manner, very successful once the audience's initial shock wore off. It was touch and go for a couple of minutes but he scored with 'gays in the military' jokes. The excerpts from the NYMT production were loyally applauded. Bob Downe and Paul Morocco tore up the second act, as did the extraordinary Margarita Pracatan – the woman who finishes Clive James's TV shows. Somewhere between Carmen Miranda and Zsa Zsa Gabor. She sang two songs. One sounded like 'I will surbibe – I am a surbiber'. She's on the lunchtime show tomorrow.

I've been missing a new TV foodie series, *A Look On the Wild Side*, an eccentric back-to-rural-basics approach to culinary TV. According to one review, the explorer/cook summed up his eccentric programme by saying, 'I'm going back to my roots and if I find them I'll probably eat them.'

Monday 21ˢᵗ August

Jack Sheppard, who is up here with his jazz play *Chasing the Moment* at the Pleasance, talked about that – he might have been a jazz pianist instead of an actor had he been that much better – and about *Wycliffe*, his TV series. He feels it's getting better and he's grateful that it subsidises the play. And we were nostalgic about *The Virgin Soldiers* and our six weeks in Singapore in 1967.

Three smart young Americans from Chicago, calling themselves 'Modern Problems in Science' were funny. They invite an impossible proposition and suggestions of the academic disciplines in which each should consider it and then contrive to improvise their way towards proving it. They reckon establishing that 'Keanu Reeves is responsible for all the world's ills' is the best one they have brought off so far.

Margarita Pracatan came back. She was much more effective in conversation (though incomprehensible) than in her singing and made it very hard for Mark Steele – one of my favourite young comics – to follow her. Her chatter was about 'pardies'; Cuba and Castro (she got out); her celibacy: 'I don't touch dat down dere, not now. I don't need it;' 'I like men to invite me to dinner but then I tell them I don't have sex. I am celery.' 'Celery?' 'Yes. Celery.' Interpreting this as celibate, I suggested that a match with Stephen Fry might be made in heaven. The concept of Stephen Fry proved alien to her.

Dinner. 'The James' (nickname for James Cairncross) and his sister Dorothy. James is an actor just coming up to 80. He is wonderfully alert and witty. Dress dapper – straw hat, white coat and bright stock. Ramrod-straight, he now sports a cane, having cracked an Achilles tendon last year. He was a great friend of Caryl Brahms and a member of the original London company of *Salad Days*. After Bristol, Eric Porter, Basil Henson and Alan Dobie had other engagements and James, Michael Aldridge and Newton Blick, who had all been recent members of the company, replaced them. James is a mine of information on the early history of *Salad Days*. I took him and Dorothy to the Vintner's Rooms in Leith, my favourite Edinburgh restaurant. We were all impressed. I had a beautiful lobster ravioli in a seafood bisque, melting Aberdeen Angus beef in a tarragon sauce to make up for Sunday's disaster, and three sorbets. The beef was so beautiful I took half of it home in a doggy bag and propose to order up white bread and mustard and make myself a couple of really distinguished sandwiches tomorrow.

Friday 25ᵗʰ August

A much better week in George Square. Ros Wolfe has persuaded a wonderful collection of people to come and perform or be grilled – Arthur Smith, Fascinating Aida, Nick Revell, Hank Wangford, Parsons and Naylor, Graham Norton, Simon Fanshaw, Acoustic Mania (Antonio Forcione and Neil Stacey), The Men Who Know, Ben Keaton and Roger McGough, Tom Robinson and Angela Pleasence. The houses have built encouragingly during the week: a good four-star review in the *Scotsman* and another in the *Evening News* – 'The best value at the Festival' – certainly helped. By Friday we had a full house and it was a bit like doing *Loose Ends* with an audience. We had a good bill too. Greg Proops, whom I have not met before, is a San Franciscan who has settled here and scored on *Whose Line is it Anyway?* and live improvisation shows.

He was followed by Richard Eyre, director of the Royal National Theatre, who was up to promote his book *Utopia and Other Places*, a beautifully written memoir. My favourite story in it is his account of his professional debut as Mountjoy, the French herald in *Henry V* at Hornchurch. On his entrance on the cue 'You know him by his habit', he was faced with an English army all standing downstage and miming 'his habit' as violent self-abuse. He started nervous and hesitant about being on a chat show and not coming up to the standard of the comics but he went on to be sage and interesting about the National and Mary Soames's chairmanship. They thought she'd been sent in to sort out 'the lefties' – in fact she 'went native', with tears all round when she left. I asked him about the different approach he adopted after Peter Hall. He said simply that he considered crying wolf too often was counter-productive. He thought a Scottish National Theatre was a good idea as long as it did not become 'tartanised'; and he was wry over Steven Berkoff's 'rubbishing' of him at the Book Fair the previous day. When I asked him about his successor he wouldn't be drawn. I suggested that the 'hot money' was on Jonathan Kent of the Almeida. 'Oh,' said Richard, 'I thought it was Steven Berkoff!'

The show really took off with the arrival of Scott Capurro, whom I had enjoyed so much on Sunday. He is very attractive and quick on the draw and delights in baiting the audience. He has a great rapport with Greg Proops with whom he often works. After flirting outrageously with a blushing Richard, much to the amusement of Richard's wife Sue Birtwhistle, who was sitting in the front row of the audience, he launched into his routine about 80 per cent of British men being uncircumcised and unwashed. He sort of surfs on the great waves of protest and is immediately disarming. 'You asked for it. You know you wanted it!' he is inclined to scream, loving the fuss he is causing. He swears he was interviewed on *Pebble Mill* by Alan Titchmarsh, who asked him how he went down in America. He insists he showed him.

The big hit of the Festival has been the six-man Australian Tap Dogs, whom I saw on Wednesday night at the Palladium. They perform on a versatile, portable set of scaffolding, ladders and girders, all dressed as construction workers. Jeans, cut-off jeans, T-shirts, bare tops, shirts slung around their waists and heavy boots. For all this they are highly disciplined and bristling with talent. They do a non-stop 75-minute show, ripping the set apart and reconstructing it as they go. Every notice sings of the 'testosterone' they generate or cites 'primeval beat, sweat-soaked bodies'. They manage to be every gay man's dream of construction worker camp and every NYMT girl's idea of real men. The city has been divided by arguments about how many of them are gay. I sat on an aisle in the circle. Standing open-mouthed beside me in the aisle was a plump, tiny boy – maybe seven or eight. 'Are you going to be a tap dancer?' I asked him at the end. 'I'm one a'ready,' he said firmly.

Dein Perry, the choreographer and leading performer, came to

George Square with Ben Read, the youngest member and the big pin-up of the NYMT girls. Scott Capurro, of course, had a ball. They were sitting in the front row and he mercilessly directed all his 'Australians are stupid' jokes at them, ridiculing the idea that tap dancers could possibly be straight. When they came on stage he stared fascinated by Dein's boots and made sheep's eyes at Ben. They were bashful and charming and ripped off a few routines, to the delight of the fans. I have no doubt that the full house was largely due to their presence. It was a model show – happy and frivolous with a little weight in Richard's interview and a wonderful rapport with the packed house. Richard and Sue made the point afterwards that taping it (audio or radio) would have ruined it.

It was great to finish on the best show and head for the airport.

Saturday 26th August

Loose Ends back in the basement studio B13. Considering it's still the silly season there was quite a lot of material for Neil Shand for the monologue. Windows '95, and especially the free *Times*, has upset everyone. Embarrassed people were buying the *Sun*: 'We had to have something to hide *The Times* in.' I am computerphobic. To me 'e mail' is something they say on *Coronation Street* when the post is delivered, and Bill Gates is still the host of *Worker's Playtime*. There was also the continuing heatwave, though on Wednesday for the first time in 27 days, the sun didn't come out. To make up for it Michael Barrymore did. I think it was Lynda Lee Potter who suggested in the *Mail* that counselling by Ian McKellen had made Barrymore 'too gay'. Then there was a nine o'clock service New Age church scandal in Sheffield – 80 members of the Rev. Brain's congregation sought counselling for alleged sexual improprieties. Other parsons didn't know you could have so many people in a congregation.

Most of our regulars being in Edinburgh or on holiday, we had no less than three new presenters. They were a bright crowd. Jon Ronson, a *Guardian* columnist and BBC2 presenter, is perky, with a ghastly flat voice, highly quirky. David Quantick is a more sage comedy writer, broadcaster and music journalist, who cobbled together imaginary Beatles interviews inspired by the discovery of Elvis's missing tape.

Vince Rogers I didn't get to know. He was notionally on the roof of Broadcasting House, with an Indian inspiring a rain dance.

Jimmy Mulville came to talk about the new football play he has produced, written by Andy Hamilton. I thought it was going to be a series and had to stay up until 1.30 last night to see it through. It is a very funny, harsh satire on football sleaze – much in the manner of *Drop the Dead Donkey* – terrific performances by Timothy West, James Bolam and most surprisingly Anastasia Hille – she was brilliant in Declan Donnellan's *Measure* and in *Three Tall Women*, but her sharp comedy timing here was a revelation. Jimmy teased me briefly about the success of his (i.e. Hattrick's) *Have I Got News for You*. For the record I tried to establish just when little Yentob jettisoned the revival of my *Quiz of the Week* in favour of *HIGNFY* but got nowhere.

I found Stewart Copeland, late founder and drummer of The Police, interesting. His background is a CIA father and Millfield during R.J.O. Meyer's period. His manner very casual polo-playing rich. He confessed to an inferiority complex when he was just a drummer but has pushed confidently into opera and ballet. He was in to promote an orchestral piece *Genepool*, inspired by *Prey*, a ballet he composed for San Francisco Ballet.

To Guildford to find the *Salad Days* company in very good spirits and garlanded with good notices. The houses are full and a touching number of foyer loiterers wanted to say thank you. Poor Barry James has ricked his back and was being manipulated in order to go on. It meant cutting his involvement in some dance numbers. They survived.

Two wonderful letters. One, at the BBC, from an actress who took issue with my unwise, frivolous, ad-lib suggestion on *Loose Ends* last week that Schiller's *Maria Stuart* was boring. 'It was never boring when I saw it in great productions – among others by Max Reinhardt. According to the critics it was not boring when I played Mary . . . Admittedly, that was a long time ago,' she added sadly. I replied eating humble pie.

The other was waiting for me at Guildford:

Dear Sir,

Having read a report on your forthcoming production of Slade and Reynolds's *Salad Days* in the *Farnham Herald*, I thought that you might be interested to hear of another, and, as far as I am aware, the most recent, production of the musical. I am 17 years old and attend the sixth form. In July I directed, choreographed, designed and took some parts (Classic Don, Mr Dawes, Bishop, Police Inspector, Manager, Asphynxia (a drag role), a pressman, Ambrose and Zed) in three performances of *Salad Days* which was a great success. I intend to watch the production at the Yvonne Arnaud Theatre, and am intrigued to see how certain characters and songs are presented. For example, I cast Mr Dawes as Noël Coward-esque, Mrs Dawes as a be-jhodphured [*sic*] Jilly Cooper type, the Inspector as a senile fool, complete with ear trumpet, the Manager as a leather-clad, brassy American and Ambrose Gusset as a Jean-Paul Gaultier clone, in beret and lacy bodice.

I am also very interested in the dance staging, as I revamped several of them. For instance 'Bishop's Dance', in which I introduced a chorus line of four high-kicking choirboys with *Saturday Night Fever*-style disco dancing from Jane and the Bishop. I cast four waitresses to dance with the Manager in 'Kleopatra' into which I incorporated the whole gamut of Ancient Egyptian sand dance moves coupled with the Manager's lewd and suggestive pelvis wriggling, kicking and cartwheeling. I also streamlined the musical track opening 'Out of Breath' by converting it into a ballet between P.C. Boot and the Inspector followed by a Fred Astaire-esque dance routine from the Inspector, complete with walking stick and police helmet instead of cane and bowler. For 'Sand In My Eyes', Asphynxia was also transformed into a drag queen in black and gold, with an Egyptian gold death-mask, who sung [*sic*] in a husky drawl, à la Marlene Dietrich.

I remained fairly traditional with settings, having a conventional park backdrop with wrought-iron table and chairs and large artificial park trees. To this I added classical columns which served as the entrance to the beauty parlour, dress shop, etc. and various classical statuary. We also constructed a full-scale black, red and yellow patterned 'Minnie', purple and blue glittery saucer and backdrop for the

Nite-Klub, depicting crooks, flails and Tutankhamun in red, blue and yellow paper, to simulate mosaic.

I am also interested in your use of the bandstand motif. I have seen it used in the Yorkshire TV production (1983), where it was largely wasted, along with many of the songs. I enclose a programme from our production, and wish you and your cast much luck in your production. I and many of my cast intend to come and watch it and I know that I myself am looking forward to it with anticipation.

Yours sincerely,

I read it to Julian Slade who thought it must be a leg-pull – as did Kit Hesketh-Harvey. But no. A full programme was enclosed. I love his choice of parts for himself – at least ten – and the almost threatening 'I and my cast intend to come and watch it'!

I wrote to congratulate him on all his invention and pleaded that we were going for the sense of period, the love story and the innocence.

Innocence is not a concept that will find favour with him, I fear. But I daresay we will hear a lot more of the young man.

Later note: Sadly I never heard if he enjoyed it.

Monday 28th August

Bank holiday. A good start – a generous notice for *Salad Days* in *The Times* by Ben Nightingale who was plainly taken over by nostalgia but seemed genuinely to have enjoyed Kit, Richard, and the young people. He was a boy when he saw it in 1954 and the headline 'As Light as Sherbet' won't hurt. Julian phoned to say his brother who has seen it tons of times told him it was the best production ever. I demurred, handing the palm to the original. Kate Bassett wielded an unforgiving pickaxe on poor Stephen Schwartz's *Pippin*, revived by the NYT, in her column underneath.

On to the Benson wedding. Ann and Neil's daughter Harriet married Lawrence Bradley at the North Western Reform Synagogue. The children had planned the service themselves and, according to those who know, had gone for a fuller, religious service than usual. I was reminded of Caryl Brahms's funeral, where the Jewish form of service and particularly the readings from the scriptures were so much fresher than ours. This could, of course, be because I am so much more familiar with the C of E form.

The wedding was a glorious mixture of joy and fun in the religious service and religion encroaching happily into the celebration at the breakfast at the Savoy. Harriet and Lawrence produced a booklet entitled *Welcome to our Wedding*, which explained the stages of the ceremony simply and helpfully. 'I am my beloved's and my beloved is mine,' they quoted. They quoted from *The Song of Songs* at the beginning. As I entered the synagogue (rather proudly rejecting a proffered skull cap, as I had saved one from the last barmitzvah I attended), joyous music was being played by a band. Later there were to be responses and hymns beautifully sung by a choir of soloists. The chupa, a canopy decorated with flowers and supported by four poles, representing Abraham's hospitality – four open sides to his tent – dominated the room. Harriet joined Lawrence beneath it circling him three times to symbolise the creation of a new family circle. They exchanged rings, blessed over wine. Long passages of Hebrew signified the signing of the contract and the Rabbi, who had known Harriet since childhood, made a good joke about their being able to understand a contract – both being lawyers.

The ceremony ended with Lawrence breaking a glass by stamping on it. 'In the midst of happiness this is a reminder of the fragility of life.'

Bride and groom were radiant. Parents likewise. Back at the Savoy, neither Nijinska's choreography for Stravinsky's *Les Noces* nor Jerome Robbins's staging of the wedding in *Fiddler on the Roof* had prepared me for the committed rush of young people to dance and circle on the parquet floor to a pumping Jewish band. It was immensely moving and exhilarating as men circled women and all circled the pair or lifted and carried them on two chairs held high above the floor.

It was fascinating, strange and very special. Impossible to doubt that this lovely and committed pair will make a good marriage. A small prayer to back up the prophecy.

September

Friday 1st September

PACKING PRESENTS FOR the first night of *A Passionate Woman* in Derby. My last day in this oddly impersonal flat in Birchover House. I found two attractive Victorian prints, ballooning scenes, in the King's Road for Gwen Taylor and for David Pugh and Billy Russo, producer partners; mail order ties with a hot air balloon motif for the men. (Gary Webster already has one so he'll have to make do with a bottle of Lanson Black Label.)

Faxed the lines for *Loose Ends* and went into Radio Derby to record three more radio commercials for the *Independent*. One was tricky – it started with an emotional account of Alison Hargreaves's last interview before she died on K2, which the paper has acquired, and finished by saying 'Buy the *Independent* on Saturday and you get the Sunday edition for 10p.' Not an easy gear change but I think we got it as right as possible in the end.

We ran the play on Thursday night after two days of technical rehearsal and it was sketchy so we had a long notes session before the final dress run this afternoon. It was all very low key and the cast were quiet and attentive. As the dress unfolded I was amazed to see how meticulously Gwen had assimilated her notes. She didn't miss a trick and the whole performance came into focus but for a slight hesitancy over the quickfire, almost farcical dénouement on the roof.

I went 'home' to 4 Birchover House to clear the fridge, zip up the case, make a couple of vodka martinis, and finish up the packet of vichyssoise and the Norwich Tesco's Cheddar with an overripe pear.

Derby Playhouse first-night audiences assemble early with a great sense of occasion which they carry noisily into the auditorium. The reaction was as buoyant as the first performance in Bath. Gwen was superb. The cast were all surprised at the warmth of the reception and Derby laid on a party in the restaurant. I had a few sausage rolls, said my thank-yous and farewells, and settled into Paul, the driver's, car at just after eleven. We arrived in London soon after one. Gave myself some hot milk and read Neil Shand's very funny monologue for tomorrow. I was happy to be asleep around two, ready for the six o'clock call for *Loose Ends*.

I awoke during the night and in that moment of half-sleep had, after all the bucketing around the country in different beds, to think for a moment about where the bathroom was!

Saturday 2nd September

An attractive line-up for *Loose Ends*. Craig Charles back for the first time since his stay in jail and his not guilty verdict. He was quieter and grateful for various messages from *Loose Enders*. Apparently he caught me filmed outside Broadcasting House commenting favourably on his release. I think Victoria Mather had wanted to 'spring' him, but we managed to dissuade her.

I had not met Adrian Edmondson before. More low key now than his early knock-about image, he has written a novel *The Gobbler* which his publishers describe, without much justification, as a comedy. I don't like to knock guests' work so I limited myself to suggesting that his publishers had short-changed him by labelling it as comic. In fact it is a depressing read about a failing 'flailing' comedian who is ruining career and marriage and indeed his whole life. It ends in a horribly bloody climax with a mad fan cutting another actor's cock off, and I couldn't warm to it. I asked Adrian about his interview with Kathy Lette, a self-conscious Australian writer. I wondered if she had added her 'jokes' since the interview. He thought not: 'She seemed to have come with them written down on her pad.'

Michael Feinstein came in to play and sing. His one-man show is opening at the Comedy. Jon Rowlands, the new *Loose Ends* producer, conned him into performing a doo-wop version of a Harry Warren ballad without warning me. The result was horrendous and could have done his bookings a lot of damage. I think I restored the situation by getting him to do the male version of the Gershwins' 'The Man I Love' – 'The Girl I Love'. It has been generally believed that Ira G.

never wrote such a lyric and that the brothers regretted the extra royalties they might have collected if he had. No male singer could get away with 'Some day she'll come along. And she'll be big and strong/ The girl I love' or 'Some day she'll build a home/ from which I'll never roam'. However, when Michael worked as IG's musical secretary and archivist he discovered an original lyric buried among his papers. He sang it beautifully and must have reassured his public.

Gurinder Chada, the director of *Bhaji on the Beach*, a controversial film about an Asian women's outing to Blackpool, talked eloquently about *Rich Deceiver*, her new two-part movie for BBC1 – a study of the effect of a pools win on the winner – and confessed charmingly to a teenage crush on Suggs, the ex-lead singer of Madness, who was also on the show. He is now going solo with an old Beatles number, 'I'm Only Sleeping'. Suggs is very engaging and revealed a new facet of Camden Town – apparently the pop world currently considers Camden to be 'where it's at'. 'I was sitting outside a pub a few weeks ago and I saw Blur going up one side of the street, Oasis coming down the other, Morrissey coming out of a drainpipe, all within ten minutes.'

Recently he took his daughters to a Blur concert. They expected to be taken backstage afterwards, as they did at their father's gigs. Sadly he was unrecognised and turned away by unimpressed minders. He reflected ruefully on the transitory nature of celebrity and wondered whether his top ten hit might not make him persona grata again.

My mini-cab driver from the George (where we had our usual drink afterwards) to Chelsea turned out to be an ex-Hammicks's executive, let go by the book store during a recent change of management. The last time we met he was helping to host a literary lunch at Tunbridge Wells. It can't be much fun to have to fill in by cabbing at 50.

The *Telegraph* published an obit of their late literary editor, David Holloway. The last sentence referred to Caryl Brahms's review of one of his later books, *Playing the Empire*, implying that she gave him a bad notice, not having bothered to read it. I faxed off a reply. It will be interesting to see if they print it.

Sir,

In your obituary of David Holloway (Sept 2) you short-change the late Caryl Brahms who wrote the review of Holloway's

Playing the Empire mentioned in the last sentence. (' . . . universal plaudits (except in the *Telegraph* where the reviewer admitted she had read little of it))'.

David Holloway sent the book to Miss Brahms not long before her death when she was very frail. Finding, after reading at least half of the book, that she had written the full number of words required for the review, she closed with a characteristic wit, and indeed an honesty, rare among reviewers, using words to the effect that 'I enjoyed the first half of this book so much that I could not bear to read any more lest I be disappointed'.

To Mosimann's Club, The Gucci Room, where Herbert and Sybil Kretzmer were hosting a small dinner for the second man on the moon, the astronaut Buzz Aldrin, whom the BBC had flown over to appear on Frank Skinner's new show on Saturday night. He is an AA graduate, a rather simple man still obsessed with space travel, according to his effusive air-head wife who insists that his ideas are too unconventional to find favour at NASA. Next to me was the wife of the Egyptian ambassador, an attractive woman who had taught English literature before her husband got his post, but who did not seem to have much knowledge of the modern English novel. Opposite was dear old Robin Day – in a subdued mood. I got him to tell his story about the taxi driver who said to him 'That *Question Time* . . . hasn't been the same since Peter Sissons left.' The Aldrins presented us all with ties patterned on moon rock formations. Pocketing mine I hastened off to the Pizza on the Park to catch the second set by Lilliane Montevecchi and David Staller (a big boring baritone). A mess; naive and ill-conceived. The high point was two songs sung straight and powerfully by the accompanist, Joel Silberman.

Driven home by a taxi-driver who has – fatal words – 'written a play'. I fear it may drop through the letter box at any moment. The only hope is that 'an authoress who lives next door' has promised to read it first.

Disconcerting dream that Edward Snape and David Pugh were withdrawing *Salad Days* and *A Passionate Woman* from their respective tours! What did Anton M. put in his risotto? Or was it the huge chunk of salmon? It can't have been the lovely Mosimannised bread and butter pudding.

Tuesday 5ᵗʰ September

To New Street Square, the Merchant Centre, (conference rooms) for a meeting with Colonel Beatty Royal Signals. I am to give the 75th anniversary address to a Royal Signals audience on the strength of my having been a signaller during my National Service. I was greeted by two elderly gentlemen who turned out to have been cadet officers five or six years after me, which must make them five or six years younger. We reminisced, ate a crab mousse and salmon rolled around with a white fish. (Salmon again!)

To the Barbican for Iain Glen's *Henry V* – directed by the wunderkind Matthew Warchus. A clear, stately production, much better than his *Much Ado*. Glen, who looks magnificent, speaks it intelligently and is much more striking in the less famous passages than in the chestnuts. For example, the chilling ultimatum to the citizens of Harfleur is more thrilling than the 'Once more unto the breach'. Tony Britton's chorus was backed with a wonderful effect on 'Now thrive the armourers . . .' as glittering swords descended from the flies on shiny chains. The proposal scene was beautifully played, something of Glen's innate Scottish reserve pointing up the naive gaucherie. Clive Wood, so sexy as Orsino a few months ago, was a splendidly ragged Pistol – bullied beautifully by the extrovert Fluellen, Linal Haft. By an odd quirk the French ambassador ('Tennis balls, my liege') was played by a woman – short of roles for girls? If so, why give Joanna McCallum two? (Mistress Quickly and Alice.)

I bumped into Jeremy Kingston and recommended that he see Peter Greenwell's show after he has reviewed Michael Feinstein tomorrow.

I couldn't find my letter about Caryl in the *Telegraph*. Though there was one from Charles Osborne complaining that the Headmaster of Charterhouse deserved to resign if he did in fact use the word 'Gobsmacked' when confronted by accusations of entertaining escort girls! Allegations against the Head have been a seven-day scandal in the tabloids and the broadsheets.

Wednesday 6th September

I went to R.E.S. Wyatt's memorial service in St John's Wood Church, a slip catch away from Lord's. 'What are you doing here, if I might so enquire?' asked J.J. Warr politely as we walked away. JJ was going on to the Tavern Banqueting Suite for a drink with a lot of other famous cricket initials. If you can't supply the surname you wouldn't be interested: it's a measure of cricket enthusiasm. There were DCS, MJK, FG, DRW, GHG, Sir MC, EW, DL, TG, Mrs PBH and ACD (Ingle-Mackenzie, the last, was the nearest thing to a boy cricketer in the church).

The setting was perfect. No stain embroiders the glassed windows and a deep cherry-red Madonna and two huge vases of bright summer flowers were the only focus of colour against the unrelieved cricket cream of the walls.

Well, I was there because, unlike Tim Rice, I saw Wyatt play and because I did (for Radio 4) the last interview with him for the series *Ninety Not Out*, when he and Mollie, now his widow, entertained me in Cornwall. His nut-brown pate and twinkling eyes remained a vivid memory as memorialists filleted a past of courageous hundreds, broken limbs, smashed jaws, inspiring leadership, egalitarian example and gentlemanly forgiveness.

'The truth is,' wrote R.C. Robertson-Glasgow of Wyatt (he was so glad that, on second thoughts, Warwickshire named his stand the 'RES' not the 'Bob'), 'He is part artist, part workman . . . I don't know if he is a great batsman: but he is a great cricketer: a great cricketer of yesterday and today in performance and of many tomorrows in the chronicles of fame.'

It fell to his young cousin, Woodrow, who idolised him as a child, and to Tim Rice, his Cornish neighbour, to chronicle a life which stretched from Grace to Gough. They did it with warmth. His son Jonathan, whose scalp will brown up as nicely as his father's given another good summer, read Thomas Moult's 'Close of Play': 'How shall we live, now that the summer's ended/And bat and ball (too soon!) are put aside . . .'

The choir sang Mozart, 'Laudate Dominum,' and Brahms, 'How lovely are thy dwellings'. The hymn tunes were good roast-beef stuff which suited the man – Old Hundredth, Crimond, St Clement. Lord Runcie said the prayers.

I wonder if Mr Major performed the same service for DCS that he discharged after Brian Johnston's send-off? 'Can I get you a drink, Denis?' Compton was famously asked at the reception, and famously replied, 'No thanks, the Prime Minister's getting me one.'

I couldn't go on to Lord's as I had to hurry to Bibendum to see what my new editors at Sinclair-Stevenson have to say about 'the novel'!

Quite a lot, actually.

Two woman arrived armed with the manuscript and ten pages of notes. Helen Fraser, the younger of the two, had arranged the lunch. The older, Penny or Pippa (Penelope Hoare) – I didn't catch which – plump, fiftyish, obviously on a senior level, handed me the notes (by Christine Hickman, 'wonderful cornucopia of characters and incident with a terrific setting . . .' before getting down to the nit-picking). I had ordered refreshing marinated mackerel with red onion rings and sour cream, delicious and excellent veal.

I feel ambivalent about the notes. They are what I expected when I delivered in February and just got a blanket acceptance from Christopher. They asked for a list of characters which I did ages ago and, I thought, submitted; and a division into chapters which I had also accepted and expected months ago. Maybe being away from it for a bit will give me a better perspective – but I had been lulled into not expecting this to be part of my work plan. I suppose it means another week in Devon before Christmas and one afterwards to sort out this.

I suppose what I think is 'Thank God someone has done some editing at last but why the fuck not do it before?' One good thing, they may concede *Scratch an Actor* as a title. Neither knew the source (Dorothy Parker), or the other half of the quote (' . . . and you'll find an actress')!

I went on to Michael Feinstein's first night at the Comedy with Ronnie Shedloe, an old American friend who is having a success with *Carrington*, the Bloomsbury movie he has produced.

Barry Humphries was in the same row. He said how much he had enjoyed the letter about Caryl in the *Telegraph* – so it *has* been published! At home I retrieved the paper and found it staring me in the face right above Charles Osborne's blast!

Barry was back in a gossip column story this week. Dining in a Japanese restaurant during the VJ Day celebrations a waiter asked what he wanted. 'An apology,' he said.

Thursday 7th September

I awoke fuming about the novel. Why could they not have told me in March when I was geared to re-write? I suppose it was easier for Christopher – on his way out – to give it a nod as he went. I went off to record the weekly *Independent* radio commercial with a twinkly new engineer, Fergus.

I decided to bury my annoyance that evening by 'feasting with panthers' (Oscar Wilde's evocative phrase for entertaining prostitutes), which I did – in the singular. It was expensive but highly pleasurable and exorcised the irritation comprehensively.

Friday 8th September

I did a broadcast to Canada for CBC from their studios in Great Titchfield Street to promote *Humorous Quotations*. A pleasant woman, Vicki Gabareau ('a Canadian institution'), who had certainly dipped into the book, asked the questions and had that easy trans-atlantic chattering flow.

The week has been full of coverage and comment on Prince William's arrival at Eton. I hope his induction is a far cry (literally) from that of Lord Holland, the nineteenth-century statesman, who was forced as a fag to toast bread holding it in his fingers. His mother sent him a toasting fork which his fag master immediately broke over his head. Lord Holland's fingers remained withered for the rest of his life.

Disconcerting news from Brussels. According to these metrical moron bureaucrats the 22-yard pitch is to be 20.121 metres; but 22 yards is precisely 20.1168 metres. That extra 32mm could make all the difference to an accurately launched Yorker!

Biked a review of R.E.S. Wyatt's memorial service to *The Oldie*.

Saturday 9th September

Loose Ends produced an enjoyable mixed bag. Bryan Gould has written an autobiography, *Goodbye to All That* (the title shamelessly stolen from Robert Graves's much greater book). It charts his emergence from obscurity in New Zealand, Rhodes Scholar, Law don, Diplomat, MP, Shadow Cabinet – resignation and return to New Zealand as Vice-Chancellor of Waikato University. It presents a very unattractive picture of Labour internal strife, Mandelson plotting, John Smith slagging off Kinnock, Robin Cook, 'shifty in a pub'. In a review Gerald Kaufman called it Pooterish – 'Diary of an almost somebody' – and I did find one line had that authentic ring: 'Our social life extended to the upper reaches of Belgian society'. The book is relentlessly self-justifying, 'my standing with my colleagues rose considerably since there was no one else in the Labour Party capable of understanding the issues'. I quoted Roy Hattersley's judgement in that morning's *Independent*, 'Why would a man who really was so sure that he was usually right go to such trouble to prove that he was rarely wrong'; but Gould is an ex-academic, politician, lawyer *and* TV presenter and there was little chance that he would rise to the bait.

Peter Snow was a perfect reproduction of his television persona – bounding enthusiasm, waving arms and all. He sold, with enormous vigour, his new Radio 4 series *Random Edition*, a lacklustre trek into the past, alighting at random on one day in history – the edition I heard covered a day in 1957. There was much surprise that back in those days TV listings took second place to radio programmes. They wheeled on dear old Bill Ward to talk about life as a sound engineer in television. The last time I heard that voice was in 1958 when he was Controller of Programmes at ATV, and I asked if I could be posted back from Birmingham to London. 'No, Ned,' he said, 'we see you as a Birmingham person!'

Jonathan Pryce was plugging *Carrington*, in which he plays Lytton Strachey. The pre-publicity says that he based the role on a mixture of Muggeridge and me. We played a bit of him: voice much too deep, I thought – and I see that Frances Partridge agrees. She says that when she saw the film and glimpsed him she could hardly believe that it was not Strachey – then he spoke and the illusion was instantly shattered. I look forward to the film. (I wonder if they included my favourite bit of Bloomsbury nonsense, showing the unworldliness of Duncan Grant. Grant thought that the 'L' plates on cars indicated support for the Liberal Party.) Jonathan was very excited – he announced he is playing Peron (opposite Madonna as Evita and Antonio Banderas as Che) in Alan Parker's film. A *Loose Ends* scoop! In the pub he professed to be relieved to be out of *Oliver!* – 'four directors!' I suppose he means Sam Mendes (director); Lionel Bart (creator); Cameron Mackintosh (producer); and Matthew Bourne (the choreographer). He got into a taxi the other day and the driver asked 'Are you still in *Fiddler on the Roof*?' Ah, fame!

Ian Gardhouse – who invented *Loose Ends* and to whom I owe any sort of revival of fortunes in the eighties – we started in 1985 – gave a 'Twenty-five Years in the BBC' party at his home in Kew. A packed garden with a little marquee and God knows how many people. The mini-cab made a farcical job of finding it and I wasn't feeling well so I did a round of the garden, downed one glass of champagne and got back into the cab inside half an hour. I was sorry not to linger. All Ian's BBC radio past was there: but a scrambled egg on toast steadied the stomach for an early night.

Monday 11th September

Lunch with Belinda Harley and Neil Shand at Harry's Bar. Exquisite warm, uncooked, clear tomato soup with basil and very good veal off the trolley. The free lunch had been a mystery – soon explained. Belinda, ex-high-powered PR, then aide to Prince Charles, now high-powered PR and publisher, has a deal for the Albert Hall, a Sunday in November, to put on a concert in memory of Peter Cook to raise money for the Cambridge Arts Theatre. She wants a massive bill of ex-Cambridge entertainers. Neil and I agreed to go into her office for a brainstorming session. With the new work on the novel I'm not sure how much time I can give.

Tuesday 12th September

Paid to talk to clients of IBS, a computer firm, at the House of Commons – in the Churchill Room booked by David Rendel, Lib. Dem. MP for Newbury. I think they would have preferred my usual knock-about but I had been steered towards Parliamentary stories and did rather more work than usual to accommodate them. Rendel was supposed to do five minutes but expanded to fifteen so I had to do fifteen to twenty as they all had to go on a tour of the House at three. For this relief much thanks.

Bonused with a box of House of Commons Victorian Mints, an H of C money clip and an IBS brandy flask!

To the Sloane Club in the evening to talk for Joyce Hytner at a fund raiser for the Royal Court. *Theatrical Anecdotes* for an hour. They seemed to enjoy it. Too shy to ask questions. Went on to the Caprice with Henny Gestetner and Neil Benson's sister, Clare, and brother-in-law. A packed restaurant with Hugh Laurie and the returned Stephen Fry who, thank God, seems to be letting his dyed blond hair grow out.

Henny is remarkable. She must be approaching 90. Her devotion to theatrical good causes is legendary. She lives in Bosham, but also in Arlington House above the Caprice, which she treats as a canteen, amiably bossing about the staff who plainly adore her. We left around eleven as hordes of after-theatre-goers were still arriving.

Wonderful thick bortsch, cold with a biting horseradish cream infusion which set it up marvellously, and a starter portion of Eggs Benedict. Nursery food.

Wednesday 13th September

A euphoric lunch with Victoria Mather, Carol Thatcher and Jon Rowlands (*Loose Ends* producer), who didn't know the two girls. They came to the flat and we went up the road to Lou Pescadou. The girls were very impressed by Jon. I have still to find out what he thought of them. I am writing this several days later and he has retired to his bed. I hope this is not a reaction to my lunch. I wondered about the oysters but mine were so wonderful and Carol had six – no ill-effects – and even Victoria, who had a bad experience at Quag's a year ago, braved one and has shown no signs of decay. It was only spoilt by the absence of my favourite maître d'hotel in the whole of London, but everyone must have a day off. They gorged on mussels. I pressed the best apple tart on Jon and the girls, who had poo-pooed it, had a taste and looked envious. Daniel, the owner, treated us to liqueurs – not a bad idea as I had clocked up £166.

To the National Film Theatre in the evening to see Ronnie Shedloe, today known for *Carrington*, but at the age of fifteen Errol Flynn's last secretary, who, with Patrice Wymore (Flynn's widow) and Jack Cardiff was to answer questions after a screening of Flynn clips. A unique collection of anoraks – especially a man who went on endlessly about some ghastly footage of Flynn as William Tell, an aborted TV series. Apparently there are miles of film – no sound – sitting in a vault in Boston. We saw bits of the best and it should be burnt instantly. It is using up valuable space. Cockroaches would occupy the shelves to more advantage. I slipped away before the 'party', fortunately meeting Ronnie on the way out so I could tell him that he was good and avoid telling everyone else that the evening had no purpose.

Thursday 14th September

My film for Mark Greenstreet has long fallen through. They took my advice, dropped me and booked Leslie Phillips. But I have been summoned to play a judge in John Thaw's *Kavanagh QC* TV series.

Measured for suit to be worn under robes for this. Some five days' filming at the end of the month for a few odd lines scattered through and a brief summing-up. As I remember it from *Orlando*, the filming process is infinitely boring but it might make a couple of diary entries and I can do my reading for *Loose Ends*. Sue Yelland, the big jolly wardrobe mistress, proved that my waist is undeniably 42 and my neck 18.

To lunch with Neil Benson at Green's with King Constantine. He was interesting on his relations with Nelson Mandela, Botha and Chief Buthelezi, and unaccountably fascinated by the mental state of Stephen Fry. I told him Stephen's dyed blond rent-boy look was in retreat.

I took a train to Derby to see *A Passionate Woman* and do a talk-in. *Backchat* they call it, with the theatre-goers. They haven't had an empty seat and the show was in fine shape.

A lively question and answer session and none of those 'How do you learn your lines?' enquiries. Morale is so good, I hope it holds up under the vicissitudes of touring.

To bed at the Midland Hotel by the station. Soup and sandwiches in my room. Lots of noisy young men in the public rooms.

Friday 15th September

Straight off the train to Saunders and Gordon – fry up breakfast – for a single *Independent* radio commercial. Just 20 secs – took two hours to record, with constant re-writes and re-thinks.

A drink at the Groucho. I bumped into Brian Izzard, the noisy TV director. He specialises in Armistice Day sentimental South Bank shows. Having done Vera Lynn and Thora Hird, it is Barbara Cartland this year. The mind boggles.

Lunch at L'Epicure with Keith Waterhouse. He wants to pin down Duncan Weldon to definite dates for rehearsals of *Bing Bong*. So do I. The spring looks busy with re-vamps of *A Passionate Woman* and *Salad Days*, and possibly Michael Linnett's farce. Keith maintains his habit of always ordering the same food in his favourite restaurants. At L'Epicure it is their home-potted shrimps in a sharp sauce on toast. And he has them without the sliced mushrooms. Then he has deep-fried goujons of sole – with a green salad on the side, which he simply looks at and feels healthy. I had a delightful partridge off the bone and a bottle of Fleurie. Keith had his usual bottle of white.

I arrived nicely oiled for a medical for *Kavanagh QC* in Harley Street. A form to fill, a couple of taps and a bit of listening and I was pronounced fit for filming.

I see the row about gays in the navy continues. It reminds me of the remark of a rent boy during the trial of Oscar Wilde, who said he was going to mend his ways and join the navy. This caused considerable laughter in court.

Saturday 16th September

Our dynamic young producer was laid low by some mysterious bug, so the onlie begetter of the programme, Ian Gardhouse, came in to chaperone the show and, reviving an old custom, to pick me up at home instead of sending the now habitual taxi.

Debbie Barham the very bright 23-year-old, is succeeding Neil Shand as writer of the monologue, a hard act to follow.

We led off with dear old Patrick Moore who, when I got down to the anteroom area of the studio, was hunched in a chair, fast asleep like an elephantine dormouse. We were on strict orders not to break the news that his house in Selsey had been broken into. His agent did not want him worried until he had done the last two interviews on his book tour. His *Guinness Book of Astronomy* – the fifth edition – is crammed with facts. He dealt effortlessly with all my questions about the intriguing minutiae – names like 'The Sombrero Hat Galaxy', 'The Coat Hanger', 'Bode's Nebula' – they are obviously all old friends. It might have sounded as if I was trying to catch him out. I wasn't, and questions like, 'What was the Dirty Ice Ball Theory proposed by F.L. Whipple in 1950?' and 'What does "star with the greatest known proper motion mean"?' triggered off beautifully clear and simple answers. He is obviously a born teacher and an unstoppable enthusiast. I did try to surprise him by asking him ('on information received') if it was true that he possessed a bootleg copy of the notorious pirate recording of Ann Driver's music and movement keep-fit class, 'Now, children, toss your balls in the air . . .!', etc. He owned up with glee and proudly announced that he had another, even more suggestive record.

Meanwhile Tony Benn ('The incredible shrinking name') joined in and claimed that he had acquired the Driver classic while he was a BBC producer. Politically at opposite poles they plainly relished each other's enthusiasms and expertise in a warm exchange.

Benn was at his popular, humorous best. He would have been easy to converse with for the full hour but also took a lively interest in all the other items. Frances Barber did a spirited plug for a new Channel 4 series *Blow Your Mind – See a Show* and I'm afraid I left Tim Pigott-Smith with only just enough time to promote his play – Maugham's *The Letter*, with Joanna Lumley in Gladys Cooper's old role at Hammersmith. I squeezed in the exchange between Maugham and old Ernest Thesiger who asked him, 'Why do you not write parts for me?' Maugham replied, 'I do but Gladys Cooper always plays them.'

Kevin came in to clean and left a note saying 'There's something rotten in the living room fridge.' It was the grouse I bought early last week. I had it for lunch – beautifully high and tender. I boiled up the carcass and legs for a delicious clear consommé.

Magdalena Buznea came by with her lovely Romanian bread and

some exquisite lilies. She has been to see Joyce Nettles about a film role to be shot in Russia. Much hangs on it. She thinks she did badly. 'They did not ask me to read . . . I do not think she liked me . . . She did not greet me like she did a fat Hungarian actor . . .' I do hope she gets it – she deserves a break. Her acting is wonderful. Her audition/interview manner is plainly nervous.

I see the Princess of Wales is to visit a Cézanne exhibition in Paris. She should say nothing. Opening the Tate extension in the 1930s George V stopped in front of a Cézanne and said to his wife, 'Come over here, May, this will make you laugh.'

Sunday 17th September

To lunch with Gaye Brown. A large piece of pork with brilliant crackling. Her son Charlie, and Eric, a Chinese school friend, were there on a long weekend, also two young Brazilian lodgers and two old friends. Gaye wants to revive the Dorothy Fields/Dorothy Parker programme she did for D. Kernan at the Donmar. I recommended Joe Harmston to direct as I shall be overrun in the early spring when they want to do it.

Stephen Sondheim rang. He's here for *A Little Night Music*. We met for dinner at Orso's. I got there first and was surprised to see Derek, who used to be a waiter there, in shiny black leather pants, heavy black boots and spikey, black 'golliwog' dressed locks. He was very excited (high?) and insisted on kissing on the lips twice before going. Stephen came with PJ, his companion, a quiet, serious man who, brave soul, is writing a 'serious' musical (i.e. not a camp romp) based on *Peyton Place*. Stephen's thriller has just opened in San Diego. He's very pleased with it. His musical, based on the Mizner brothers – Hollywood wit and Florida entrepreneur – is becalmed but John Weidman is getting on with the book. I suspect that the fire which destroyed so much of his home in Turtle Bay has caused a block. At least all his manuscripts, sketches, etc. are intact. He is camping out in a luxurious apartment at the bottom Corner of Central Park West, high up with wonderful views every which way you look. He was very calm about the show at the National, although it is overrunning its technical rehearsal time and they will have to have dress and first preview tomorrow (Monday), all in rather a hurry.

Monday 18th September

Met with Neil Shand at Belinda Harley's new offices to discuss the Peter Cook concert. It's put off to the spring which *may* help and it may now be at the Festival Hall. Lin Cook (widow) arrived and looked very frail and sad.

On to the Theatre Museum for a Development Committee meeting. All seems to depend on the National Lottery for which we have an impressive entry. We also discussed other rich chaps and trusts who might be squeezed. Lady Hollick seems to know *everybody*.

A drink at the Groucho with Leo Rost, an old friend of my late friend Burt Shevelove. He lives in Florida and is here to see Victor Spinetti in *The Relapse* at Stratford. He looks like Ernest Hemingway and many years ago won an Ernest Hemingway look-alike contest in Key West. Now he goes along to judge. Leo is rich. Leo is 75. He wheezes. He is a cousin of the Bronfmans of Seagrams, the liquor people. He is scholarly about the history of gin and particularly about bootleggin. He is something of a satyr. He has published novels which he is enthusiastically promoting and is trying to interest his MGM cousin in his movie script of the latest one. He once financed Tony Shaffer in his first venture and says he did a lot to promote *Sleuth*. His cherished project is a Gilbert and Sullivan compilation – a riot in Cleveland. He financed it there in a town where he is unknown, and lurked in the loo during the interval, lapping up the comments of the punters which were all of the order of 'Fuck! Shit! What a show!' Leo is a character and he was very entertaining for an hour. Then he left. I think I bored him.

On to Elena's L'Etoile in Charlotte Street for dinner with Stephanie Cole – back from her Scottish and Tuscan holiday. Energy and humour renewed. In great form. David Pugh has approached her to do a second tour of *Passionate Woman* after Christmas. (Gwen has a TV series.) She is dickering with other TV projects but *just* might do it.

Tuesday 19th September

Alicia Markova's *This Is Your Life* recorded at Teddington. I was doubtful about doing it – not for any lack of admiration for Alicia, but I could not feel myself appropriate or authoritative except as an appendage of Caryl Brahms, who loved and valued her both as friend and dancer. I fear I stumbled over my inadequacies. Thames did it very well. They had corralled Jimmy Tarbuck (dance isn't rarefied). Milorad Miscovitch, whom I remember as a Festival *danseur noble* and is now richly wed in France, told a long story about dancing with Alicia in the open air in Italy and not knowing what the music was doing because of the noise from a passing train. Alicia then repeated it. It will be interesting to see which version survives in the final cut. The family of sisters and nephews, etc. came on and Alicia looked faintly unhappy about her sister Doris's story of how she had stolen her sweets when she was a baby and still had a sweet tooth. Dame Ninette de Valois (filmed at 97) paid generous tribute after remembering resenting the job Diaghilev gave her as chaperone when the fourteen-year-old Alicia joined the company. Make-up might have tidied her hair. Perhaps Madame said 'no'. Danilova (filmed in New York in 1993) paid ambiguous tribute: 'You dance little flower-cactus.' Dame Beryl Grey and Wendy Toye were good, particularly Wendy who has fallen again, and has a sore left cheek and a damaged arm. Freddy Franklyn was flown in from Tulsa. He is 81 – four years younger than Alicia – bright and snappy. He looks like a 50-year-old Vincent Price. He danced on tour with Markova in America in the forties on one-night stands when she used to hire a hotel room, order extra towels and have the whole corps up for a bath. The great last entrance was the incredibly stately and emaciated Ram Gopal. When someone asked him backstage where he had come from, he said, 'From God.'

At the post-show party I sat with Wendy, Freddy, Wayne Sleep and his companion José ('I am Basque'); and the two young, pretty Estonian stars of Festival Ballet – sorry, English National – Thomas Edur and Agnes Oakes, who were enchanting.

Wednesday 20th September

I interviewed the American film star Billy Crystal on tape for *Loose Ends*. His new film *Forget Paris* is about a baseball referee who falls in love on a quick jaunt to Paris. I wasn't brave enough to mention one review of his last movie, *City Slicker*: 'If you like male bonding, arrested developments and poignant moments (big smile, please, Billy, and cue the music), you'll like the movie' – which applies equally to

Forget Paris. However, I did risk another judgement which suggests that he increasingly represented 'Mr Menopausal Manhattan' which threw him for a rare wordless loop – but he was interesting and literate about his grandfather, a touring Yiddish Hamlet; and his father, a concert promoter who got him into Louis Armstrong's box to watch his first baseball game and into Billie Holloway's lap to watch his first movie – *Shane*. He wanted to be Brandon de Wilde.

There's a lot of 'control freak' there – but he has a valuable career to control.

In the evening, to the Carrington exhibition at the Barbican and then to the screening of *Carrington* the movie. Frances Partridge has been complaining that they didn't use Ham Spray, 'which was offered', as a location, but another house. I talked to Christopher Hampton about it. 'Too far from London,' he said, very reasonably. 'We'd have had to pay for everybody's overnight accommodation!' An impressive film. Jonathan Pryce excellent as Strachey. A performance full of witty detail. Of course one missed the fluting voice – would it have made the movie or would it have driven audiences mad? Certainly it held the attention when Dan Massey did it in Peter Luke's play *Bloomsbury*, at, I think, the Phoenix. Emma Thompson was excellent, but defeated, as Carrington. A line-up of young men starting with Rufus Sewell pretended to be obsessed with her but the script gave no hint as to why. Maybe if Christopher had given her all Lytton's lines it might have been credible.

Thursday 21ˢᵗ September

Indie radio commercial nine to eleven, much to-ing and fro-ing about what the Broadcasting Standards, or whoever decides these things, would admit. They were uncooperative and unhelpful. I went home to be summoned back straight away when a decision had tardily been made.

Friday 22ⁿᵈ September

A delightful day. The happiest of lunches at Lou Pescadou with Sondheim, and Peter, his very bright, inclined to silence, travelling companion. Peter wouldn't have the oysters. Stephen and I had nine each and they were wonderful. A bowl of thick fish soup was more than enough to finish. I had the apple *tarte* and gave them each a slice to prove that they were wrong not to have ordered it. Stephen and I once had a little froideur over an arbitration after the New York run of *Side By Side By Sondheim*. We have edged it back gradually and he has been the main motor for the now easy relationship.

It might have foundered at the National in the evening. I took Lindsay Dolan to see *A Little Night Music*. We both love the show and the score. The book comes up bright and burnished, especially when Judi (Dench) is rejecting anything but an instinctive desire to zing her lines out to the house. But the Olivier is the wrong auditorium for a chamber musical, and Stephen Brinson Lewis, who has served us – and the director, Sean Mathias – well in the past, has not provided a single moment of relevant beauty. However, the score is so enchanting, romantic, questioning, disturbed, it could not fail to make its magic. Judi was definitive, Pat Hodge lovely, and Lambert Wilson is a revelation as the Hussar.

The weak point is the American import to play Lawyer Eggerman – the male lead. God knows why Mathias imported Laurence Guittard – the dullest dragoon in the original production and now the dullest lawyer. Why not David Firth, elegant, lively, handsome, and a beautiful native English singer? Oh well, young men must do it, if they come to it – and that includes miscasting.

This led to my disagreement with Steve. We bumped into one another at the stage door and I foolishly let my view slip. He pursued us to Joe Allen to argue the case. We had a very jolly fight about it and neither convinced the other. Later he said, 'Where are the stagers of musical numbers these days? Jerry [Robbins] was the best. Michael [Bennett] next . . . and I suppose Gower [Champion] . . .' It is the important difference between choreography and staging a number. In *Night Music* he is lumbered with a choreographer who hasn't a clue about staging; a clever director, not much more. The irony is that he was talking to Lindsay, the best stager (if not the best choreographer) in Britain.

Saturday 23rd September

Very irritated by a fax from someone at Carlton in the in-tray at the *Loose Ends* office. It was unsigned but seems to have come from one Peter Rushton. I had berated them on *Loose Ends* last week for not continuing their funding for the Donmar beyond a writers' scholarship. He cited their mediocre 'hits' and their continuing mini-support. I fired off a card saying that Carlton's record was 'shameful and shameless . . .' The funding might 'not change my opinion of your programmes; but it might change my opinion of your good intentions, sabotaged, plainly, by the craven incompetence of your shows.' Sadly, of course, letting off steam will do no good.

That done, *Loose Ends*. An edition I particularly enjoyed. It almost got out of hand, so relaxed were the contributors – Scott Capurro, Jenny Eclair, Stephen Duffy, Maureen Lipman and Alan Coren. Scott was in great form. He's still on his Love & Affection Tour. He listed the various synonyms for 'gay' he's come across in England. In America hecklers usually simply call out 'Faggot!' The English phrases are more varied and the one he was most fascinated by was 'Turd burglar'. He joshed very nicely with Jenny Eclair who beat him in the Perrier finals in Edinburgh. I was anxious to see her close up as Keith Waterhouse wants her for the secretary-cum-standup in *Bing Bong*. I have revised my reservations. I think she'd be great – and in the pub afterwards it transpired that she's dying to act, having auditioned unsuccessfully for Childie in the revival of *Sister George*. She describes her typical audience as usually consisting of 'Christians who try to talk me out of it afterwards, transsexuals, teenage runaway slags and debauched grandmothers with fag-ash down their cleavage and breathing gin fumes. I bring out,' she added, 'the old slapper in everyone.'

Maureen Lipman was also pleasantly relaxed. After the first two items, Scott (gay) and a Phil Cornwell jokey report on drug references in pop-songs, she wondered aloud if she should have told her mother Zelma to switch on in Hull. Her autumn offering is *You Can Read Me Like a Book*, another of her collections of essays. We played a trick on her – running a track from the album of *Tyger* in which she played 'Second Randy Woman'. Alan Coren, the other Robson Books author, was almost squeezed out. I had let everything overrun, but Alan managed to squeeze back in some neatly funny pieces about the video of his wedding, his scheme to make Jeffrey Archer King of Estonia and his wild plan for making education more interesting; *Hamlet, Prince of Nintendo* as a teaching aid was the burden of it.

We all retired to the George for a particularly happy drink. Maureen reports that Codron is bringing in the *Shakespeare Revue* from the Barbican – which should mean royalties of two pence a week from our 'Ladies of London' song.

Sunday 24*th* September

I finished reading and thinking about Philip Hoare's biography of Noël Coward. There have surely been enough already. Morley's covers most of the ground – life and plays. Cole Lesley wrote an affectionate insider's *Life* having worked first as factotum and later friend. Graham Payn's *My Life with Noël Coward* gave yet another perspective; and there was an eccentric memoir, heavily anecdotal, by William Marchant.

Hoare's main new research is in two fields – he has discovered a much grander family tree, with admirals involved, in the early part of the nineteenth century – and he has been at pains to list all the sexual involvements from the clergyman who gave Coward sixpence and patted him on the knee in a railway carriage ('of the two I preferred the latter'). Hoare lists early meetings with Robbie Ross, Siegfried Sassoon, Scott Moncrieff and Edmund Gosse and imagines that there was a liaison with Prince George, Duke of Kent. (After the Duke's death his cousin, the Marques of Carisbrooke, told Coward cattily, 'You know, of course, Noël, that you can never be Dowager Duke of Kent.') He pooh-poohs the notion of a fling with Laurence Olivier during *Private Lives*, and details the despair provoked by an affair with a handsome, straight young actor during Coward's last Broadway appearance in a lacklustre *Nude With Violin*. (The boy took an overdose, but survived.)

Philip Hoare sets out the limits of Coward's sexual requirements early on. 'A revulsion against penetrative sex remained with Coward all his life.' This has the ring of truth. I once entertained a guardsman in the early sixties: 'Have you heard of a bloke called Noël Coward?' he asked. I had. The guardsman had visited him the week before. 'Nice old boy,' was his verdict. 'Only likes the schoolboy stuff.'

Hoare quotes the American composer, Ned Rorem, on whom Coward in his sixties once pounced in the early hours in Paris. 'He likes to be held . . . he likes to be childlike and pushed around a little bit.' Rorem reluctantly acquiesced but commented wisely, 'There is no such thing as a sophisticated sexual person . . . no matter who they think they are – when it comes to sex, especially when a person is as old as he was, they know they can have everything they want, except someone who will lust for them.' When I told Soudheim, he said Rorem had made much the same advances to him – but had to face rejection.

The book makes one acutely conscious of the sadness of Coward's last twenty years. There is a sad vignette of Coward sitting in the William IV, a gay pub in Hampstead, wearing a little Tyrolean hat. Spotting a nineteen-year-old youth, he said 'Of course you know who I am?' 'I hadn't the foggiest,' the boy confessed.' He said, 'I'm the man who wrote *Bitter-Sweet*', which didn't mean anything to him either.

I've done a notice for the *Literary Review* and shall bike it off on Monday.

Magdalena, recovering from heavy flu, brought bread and heart-rending accounts of interpreting for Romanian gypsies in police custody for immigration offences.

I listened (on Radio 5) to the Ryder Cup golf. A game I barely understand, and certainly couldn't see, became almost unbearably exciting before we won by a squeak.

A spirited – almost too spirited – start to the TV *Pride and Prejudice*. Alison Steadman pushing Mrs Bennet to the limits, Jennifer Ehle lovely and thoughtful as Elizabeth, and Colin Firth brooding as Darcy.

Monday 25th September

A young designer, Craig Hewitt, came to show me his portfolio. He is a product of Central School of Art and the splendid Pamela Howard. Very nicely mounted designs and very imaginative sets for Oldham, Bolton, Manchester, Perth and Edinburgh. There's nothing at the moment but he is well worth keeping in mind.

To High Wycombe to see *Salad Days* and talk to a tiny group of theatre Friends in the Dress Circle bar – twenty at most but very sweet and appreciative. The company are in fine spirits. A couple of spats endemic to touring seem to have burnt themselves out. They took a terrible pasting at the enormous Sunderland Empire – 1,900 seats and some nights fewer than 200 occupied. The new Wycombe Swan is a better size and was about two-thirds full. The advance for Richmond – a month away – is already £45,000. Edward (producer) is mystified as to why booking has not even opened for Chichester the next week. I set Deke on to Duncan Weldon who books Chichester but he is elusive and Deke is complaining about how hard it is to get hold of anyone in the business around Jewish New Year.

Tuesday 26th September

A very convivial Saints and Sinners lunch (proceedings are confidential), followed by a somnolent train journey to Brighton to see *A Passionate Woman* on its first touring date. Apparently things went well on Monday – David Pugh has had a white ribboned Rolls driving around Brighton to whip up trade. It certainly seems to have paid off. There was a packed and expectant house. I met the Person from Plumpton and we went to English's for oysters (me) and smoked salmon (him). Pugh threw a very pleasant party for cast and crew at 1 Paston Place – which used to be Langan's. I talked to Kay Mellor's agent – just back from seeing the play in Germany – very impressed by an apparently rather expressionist production and seven curtain calls. P from P dropped me off at the Old Ship.

Wednesday 27th September

Some reading for *Loose Ends*.

I took the Bunns, Douglas and Tracy Brook, to the play. Another full house. Tracy had been at the first night in London, Douglas, not. I *think* he enjoyed it, but he wasn't as immediately enthusiastic as he usually is. However, he kept returning to it over supper – again at 1 Paston Place – so I think it must have had a good delayed-action effect. Paston Place was a great success. Douglas knew it twenty years ago as Le Français but they both treated it as a great local discovery. It certainly is a find in Brighton and indeed in East Sussex.

A deep sleep in the Blue Room at Hickstead.

Thursday 28th September

Up in time to see godson, Charlie Bunn, off to school. He has shot up again, hair slicked down.

Paul, Douglas's batman (I think the right word), drove me to Gatwick. Lunch with Michael Linnett and Neil Morrissey at the Ivy to talk about Robert Hawdon's farce *Quiet Wedding*. Linnett would like the entire cast of *Men Behaving Badly* to play it. We fenced enjoyably through the meal while it became clear that Neil thought there was no chance of persuading his co-star Martin Clunes, whose current ambition is directing. They are doing a new series in the spring and a cinema movie. Michael moved brilliantly at the end to suggest two weeks at Guildford followed by a v. short, limited West End run. After that, he reckons, he might be able to re-cast. It's an interesting gamble. Neil agreed to talk to Martin that night before he flies off to Spain for a week's filming on some promotional jaunt. I suspect we may have to think of alternative casting.

Friday 29th September

Indie radio commercial at 9 a.m. – less than the usual fuss to get it OK'd. Back to lunch with Alistair Beaton. Tomato, basil and mozzarella and then *osso buco* and fruit. Alistair very impressed and well oiled by a bottle of Perrier Jouet and the second of Douglas's Christmas fine wines, a 1982 Château Latour. We discussed the Clark *Diaries* and agreed that the central tension, the drama, is his ambivalence. There is huge political ambition fighting fits of disgust with Westminster, mediocrities, civil servants, etc. Last time I hadn't been able to convince him about my theatrical bookends. The idea is that we should start with an imagined Foyle's lunch – top table across the stage. Perhaps some six guests and a toast master. As Alan makes his speech the table dissolves and the others fall into whatever characters we must have. The Alan actor continues to talk and we need never see him sitting and writing a diary as he walks in and out of scenes. We reckon we need two pages of text to bring the Birmingham offer to a head.

I read that Chancellor Kohl (all of 18 stone) is a cook and writing his own cookery book. He recently ate a second dinner after a Guildhall Banquet. Rather like our first PM Walpole, equally heavy, who relied on only one cookery book, *Lamb's Cookery* and managed to spend £1,000 (some £200,000 today) on food annually as well as £1,200 on wine.

Saturday 30ᵗʰ September

Another packed *Loose Ends*. The day started badly. The driver hadn't turned up by 8.10 and when I went down I found a rather elegant woman in black shawl parked well down the road and still searching. After some gesticulating she found me. She didn't look like one of nature's chauffeurs and I wondered what rebuff/tragedy had brought her to it; but didn't like to ask.

Mike Harding opened brilliantly. He has a collection of newspaper articles out, and retails amusing vignettes with great good humour as soon as you turn on his tap. He is perhaps the easiest person in the world to interview to good effect. Buy the book.

Sara Paretsky, author of the V.I. Warshawski crime novels, is a poised and amused Chicagoan. Politely she tried to bolster her good behaviour in Britain by praising Dorothy L. Sayers.

Kenneth Baker was effortlessly smooth – and interesting – about his anthology of political cartoons. The two or three young 'alternatives' around the table made the usual confession afterwards that they had found the 'monster' extremely pleasant and 'interesting' in the flesh; 'I used to watch him on the telly and want to throw things at him!'

Mark Rylance came in on the backwash of his *Macbeth* at Greenwich which has been savagely slaughtered by the critics. He has linked his production with some sort of modern cult – shades of Guyana or Koresh's Waco, Texas. Once he got going he made a very quiet and lucid case for it, but not, perhaps, one which will draw me to Greenwich. Sadly, I did not have time to ask him whether the board of the Globe – which he takes over as Artistic Director in January – had seen it or commented!

A bizarre letter from 'a fan'. He is about 24 now and has been writing for a couple of years. At the beginning it was an open plea for sex – 'I like older men. My current partner is nearly 60.' I did decline straight away but we have continued to correspond.

I realised ages ago that we would never be having sex together, but there's always been a few things that I've wanted to ask you, some sexy questions! I just wondered what you thought of the idea if I was to type out some questions . . . and left room for you to answer them and sent them to you if you would answer them. It's just an idea, but as we'll never be together in bed, we could have told each other some of the things we would like to have done! . . . Phew! I'm not shy am I!!?

It wasn't hard to reply, 'No, I don't think a questionnaire is a good idea. Dream on! It'll be much more exciting than the real thing.'

October

Sunday 1st October

KIT CHAPMAN'S LAUNCH party for his book *Great British Chefs II* at the Garrick, with canapés by a selection of the chefs featured – Rick Stein, Phil Vickery, Simon Hopkinson, etc. I wasn't feeling 100 per cent so I took a turn of the room with one glass of champagne and talked briefly to Isla Blair and Julian Glover – who, like the Timothy Wests, have done Kit's after-dinner entertainment at the Castle, Taunton – and headed for home.

Monday 2nd October

Met David Pugh at his office. He confirms that Stephanie has said 'yes' to the spring tour of *A Passionate Woman*. Gwen's due to be recording a TV series.

Sonia and Andrew Sinclair's party in the evening. The L-shaped room packed as always with the usual suspects.

Tuesday 3rd October

First day of filming *Kavanagh QC*, the John Thaw series in which I am a judge. I have been carrying around my longest speech – six sentences – for days, trying to learn the legal jargon. I'm here for six days so I ought to get it by the time I have to deliver it – it is the final judgement.

Here it is:

I have therefore made two crucial findings of fact. First, the plaintiff was ordered out on to the barge by Mr Dale. Second, the machinery was switched back on without any check being made as to the whereabouts of the plaintiff. These amount to a gross breach of the duty of care owed by the defendant to Mr Lomax and the defendant is therefore solely liable for the accident. As a result of the findings I have made with regard to Quantum, I propose to award the plaintiff the full amount of the damages claimed. Further I propose to refer the question of the material on board the barge to the proper authorities.

Well, I just wrote that out without reference to the script so maybe I'll be able to remember it on the day. My inability to learn lines is ridiculous. Mercifully, as a judge, I can have my other interjections written out on slips of paper before me. God knows how John Thaw manages one cross-examination after another with the same sort of technical, banal non-sequiturs.

We were filming at the Chiswick Town Hall. They had a few shots to do elsewhere so I wasn't picked up until 8.45 a.m. It'll be seven for the other days. The driver had got it into his head that he was taking us to Heathrow – in fact it was Heathcliffe Terrace, Chiswick, and we had some difficulty in disabusing him. The other passenger was the principal protagonist in the plot, a boy disabled by an accident at work. He is very young, virtually straight out of drama school in Edinburgh. He's called Kevin McKidd, very open and unassuming, and troubled about moving down from Glasgow which his agents would like. His 'relationship' doesn't want to leave her cat which she feels could never settle in London.

I had remembered from *Orlando* how boring filming can be and came well provided with books: but it's always fun to turn up on a set and see who else is in the piece. Caravans and honey-wagons and caterers' vans were piled up on the green opposite the town hall and I spotted the names on the tiny dressing-room doors. Alfie Lynch, who was in *A Passionate Woman*, is here. T.P. McKenna is the rival barrister; Frances Tomelty is the victim's mother. David Schneider, who is part of the Armando Iannucci team, is a solicitor, so is Tim Bentinck (who is also David Archer in the radio soap).

Nothing much happened – except reunions – until early afternoon. I put on my rather splendid costume. Pinstripes, white shirt and wing collar, black robe edged with rabbit-ermine, red sash and a wig which looks like a badger perched on my pate. The director, Andrew Grieve, came to call and reminded me that about thirty years ago John Gorrie brought him to see me to find out if I had a job for him in movies. I had forgotten the incident but he has changed so little in that time that it gradually came back.

The atmosphere on the set is very efficient and low key. The producer is Chris Kelly who seems to have a finger in so many pies. He has a restaurant in Cambridge, compères a food show on BBC2, was fronting a radio spoof comedy series the last time I saw him and then spent a year on business in Hong Kong. *And* he's got a novel coming out in the spring!

John Thaw is immensely affable. His white hair is so brightly, whitely, lustrous that TP (who also has an impressive mane) asked him what he put on it.

Location catering yielded cottage pie. When we did start at about three I had quite an impressive entrance, clomping into court looking sour on 'The Court will rise'; I was shot from below, looking like a real legal ogre. There are quite enough folders, etc., to hide my script – a great relief. They are a little bit behind on the first day's shoot but should pick up the time easily now that they've sussed out the location.

We added David Schneider to the car load on the way back. He said, 'Armando sends his love.' I took good-(I hope) humoured exception to this as I have never met Mr Iannucci and he misses no opportunity to slag off *TW3* when interviewed. David thinks it's because he would like his show to be as successful. I explained that it was very hard to be first a second time!

Wednesday 4th October

More filming. The car was prompt at 7 a.m. The routine of filming continues. My reading redoubles. There's Michael Parkinson's *Sporting Profiles* – I have to talk to him on *Loose Ends* on Saturday – and a lengthy tome by one Lyle Leverich – *Tom: The Unknown Tennessee Williams*. Like Philip Hoare's new Noël Coward biography it's fuller but not much more revealing than the other books and never catches Tennessee in the way that Maria St Just did in her book of his letters to her. Leverich has been complaining that she blocked publication until her death. I think he's been lucky. Her fierce and loyal steward-ship of Williams's estate has placed his reputation now on a plateau where less careful control might not have taken it. Now Mr Leverich's book will gain wider currency because Williams's reputation as Ameri-ca's leading poetic dramatist is unassailable.

We finish filming at seven but the traffic between Chiswick and Chelsea is so thick that I never seem to get back before eight. Before I left we got the O.J. Simpson verdict at six o'clock – I 'announced' it in 'Court'. It's a bit like when Kennedy died. I'll always know where I was when the OJ verdict was broadcast.

I thought I'd taped the Alicia Markova *This is Your Life* but found that I had taped half an hour of *Das Boot* on BBC2 instead! I just wanted to see what they cut and what they left in. Now, no chance! In a way it's a relief. I'm sure I stumbled embarrassingly.

I took the Arlons to Lou Pescadou. A great success. It is exactly their sort of real French fish bistro and they quickly made friends with Daniel, the owner, who has shed the prickly skin he used to present to customers. Deke has a new battle on his hands. He now represents Michael Flatley of *River Dance* and has pulled him out of the Hammersmith season after a row about who controls the show he devised. 'You don't tell Judi Dench how to act. You don't tell Michael Flatley how to dance!'

Thursday 5ᵗʰ October

Lunch at Alastair Little's restaurant with Frank and Jo Coachworth who look after my accounts. It has been a good year so I must look after next year's tax. Lovely food but I must have my stomach looked at. The appetite is not there. I had a splendid rough bortsch and a really delightful wild mushroom open lasagne with the most delicate, gossamer pasta. Alastair's Italian influence I suppose. I was furious that I could not eat it all.

Two of the OJ jury have now declared that they thought he did it. It's a new sort of justice when the jury make up their minds after the verdict is announced.

Friday 6th October

No *Indie* radio voice this week. Have they decided on a new approach? We shall see. I did a bit of *Loose Ends* work and lunched very happily with Edward Snape and Charles Stephens at Chez Gerard to talk to Julian Slade about next year's tour of *Salad Days*. Most of the company are staying. Critically the two young leads are with us. I'm sad that Gary Fairhall, who has been wonderful as the common policeman – looking like a young Tommy Trinder – wants to go. I hope it is for another job.

It must be hard being a young manager. Theatres keep you at arm's length. Agents ignore your calls. But Edward – with Charles – battles on and the New Year tour looks much more southern – where *Salad Days* is doing especially well. I had a very odd call yesterday from a man who thinks he is buying the Ambassadors Theatre and wants to revive revue. He lacked gravitas (always important in mounting a frivolous exercise). Julian said the man had called him yesterday twice. Once daytime; once very late at night, sounding vague and merry. He kept telling *me*, 'Only us oldies can do it. The young people don't understand it. We'll have to teach them.' I doubt it. I doubt also if it's possible to revive an out-of-date genre. It *might* be possible to make the Ambassadors a venue for alternative comedians, their sort of revues, etc. However, I don't think pumping life into a dead art form is going to work and I doubt if our impresario can get it together.

I was trapped earlier last week into going to the Café Royal after the Soho Jazz Festival ball. I would *love* to have stayed at home – especially when I found that dinner started at nine and there's *Loose Ends* in the morning. Oh well, it was good to sit next to Tim Spall who is as nice as he is clever and wants to do his Falstaff. I've no doubt he will. I followed a big band, did ten minutes of old jokes and gave a bravura introduction to Alan Price. As I regained my seat it was announced that Alan hadn't finished his set in the Green Room. I had already been announced before the Big Band had time to clear and so had to chatter on as they removed their instruments. Fran Landesman was dealt in and filled the gap with a couple of poems. I fled as soon as Alan started, having an early call.

John Prescott managed quite a good joke at the Labour love-in at

Brighton; 'Michael Heseltine is the Kama Sutra of the Tory Party; he's been in every position except No. 10.'

Saturday 7ᵗʰ October

A rather hairy *Loose Ends*. Normally the problem is squeezing every-thing in: but this time we had two reluctant double acts. Interviewing them was blood-out-of-stone time. Fortunately Michael Parkinson was on hand to plug his book of *Sporting Profiles* and when we got to the last ten minutes there was nothing to do but turn back to Parky and Victoria Mather and Carol Thatcher, who had been to Brighton to report on trying to get the Labour Party to return to Socialism. The original idea had been to thread their report with the Cagney and Lacey theme tune. This was dropped but it still worked well. They had some trouble trying to get Carol accredited at Walworth Road (Labour Party HQ)!

Only a short time to drink at the George as I was off to Kavanagh QC for some more filming in leafy Chiswick. They'd been shooting reverse angles all morning with a 'body double' topped off with my wig if they needed the judge in the corner of a shot. Again I only had one line to deliver so I got on with revising my six-line verdict which refuses to stay in my mind. I'm due to deliver it on my last day, Tuesday, but I hope to be ready the day before just in case. We finished at seven. I was taping *Blind Date*, and Magdalena came with more of her beautifully aromatic Romanian bread at eight. Over a drink she told me her son Andrei is having a difficult time rustling up the money for his barrister's wig. The irony of my earning silly money for a few lines as a bewigged judge on *Kavanagh QC* was not lost on me. Perhaps I can help.

Sunday 8ᵗʰ October

As there is no traffic on Sundays the studio car was ten minutes later – 7.10 a.m. Hardly a lie-in but welcome. I enjoy the chatty atmosphere of the make-up trailer. My *Mail on Sunday* reveals that Tim Bentinck is not only David Archer of *The Archers* but also Lord Woodstock, heir to the Earls of Portland. Teased about it, he explains that his branch of the family are poor relations of the Dukes of Portland –

another title he rather fancies which has now fallen into disuse is Baron Bolsover. Portland heirs, on the Duke's side, are called Viscount Euston. I suppose they owned the land on which the station stands. There was a wonderful misunderstanding today. As Frances Tomelty left the trailer, one of the make-up girls appeared to say, 'I can't stand Frances.' There was general astonishment and disbelief – Frances is *so* nice – it turned out that what she was saying was that she had 'a touch of arthritis'. General relief. It's a good thing make-up artists don't depend on their diction!

Alec Douglas-Home has died. Speaking as a Scotsman he once asked Robert Menzies, the Australian Prime Minister, 'Why don't you pronounce your name properly, Mr Mingiez?' 'I'll look into it,' said Menzies, 'when I get Hume!' An obit programme repeated Home's comment that *TW3*'s attacks were the only criticisms that got to him as PM. I once commissioned a very hard piece with Frost as Disraeli attacking Home's ascent to office rather than Butler. He was a genuinely pleasant and honourable man; but I would have much preferred to see what sort of fist Butler made of it.

Monday 9th October

I've discovered a handsome pub across the green in Chiswick, to which I go for a single half-lager before the location lunch. This comes in huge portions but is edible.

As feared, the judgement was brought forward to this afternoon. The joy of being, as a judge, able to refer to notes took away any nerves and I was able to deliver it to empty seats which was much more relaxing than keeping a court full of actors while I fluffed away. I managed a satisfactory third take. Andrew Grieve was very patient. He has shown great restraint and enthusiasm all through, trying very correctly to get me to mug less and less.

We broke early. Back in time to hear *The Archers*. Usha's assailants go to jail. As a judge I found it a highly satisfactory verdict.

Tuesday 10th October

Last day of shooting. I had a couple of lines to do before my departure at four. We had agreed this in the contract. I had the Cheltenham

Book Festival and John, the OUP driver, arrived to pick me up. Said an affectionate farewell to my 'fellow actors'. It has been an enjoyable digression. We got to Cheltenham ridiculously early. I found I wasn't due to go on until 8.45 so I went to the Queen's Hotel and gave myself dinner – delicious teal, after bacon and lentil soup. It's a handsome hotel and I had forgotten what stately streets Cheltenham possesses. We had had some small trouble finding the theatre. It is quite recently restored. The auditorium is warm and enchanting and backstage is spacious. Plenty of room for the set of *A Passionate Woman* which tours there week of 23 October while *Salad Days* is in Richmond.

Humphrey Carpenter introduced me. The programme was titled *Theatrical Anecdotes*, but as OUP had arranged it I thought I ought to do something about *Humorous Quotations*. A good thing, as a director of OUP turned up in the audience. A good crowd. Nearly 500 in a 600-seater. There's a great impression of something literary going on all over Cheltenham at all hours. When I arrived the Archers (literary?) were in full flow. Rabbi Julia Neuberger (literary?) was about to give an address just before me; Oleg Gordievsky (literary?) was at the Town Hall, etc. It seemed to go very well. I did about an hour and then ten minutes of questions with Humphrey. I don't think I got past 'E' on the alphabet of anecdotes so I could always go back. I signed about 30 books and was home soon after midnight. It was an exhilarating drive – both ways. A wonderful blue sky trip through the dark green autumn Cotswolds on the way out, and great scudding, herring-bone, Payne's grey night skies on the way back.

The Tory Party Conference listed a motion submitted by the Sheffield Attercliffe Tories ... 'capital punishment for the murder of children, castration for repeat offenders ...'

Wednesday 11th October

A ten-second *Indie* flash in the morning. An infuriating tooth cap came off when I sucked a jelly baby on the set of *Kavanagh* yesterday. No pain but my inquisitive tongue kept seeking out the jagged bits underneath. Apparently it's the last tooth which was to be root-canaled before I go on to my implants – ouch!

To *The Rat in the Skull*, the first Royal Court classic to open this season at the Duke of York's. I missed it the first time. It is a debate between an IRA man and a Protestant policeman from Northern Ireland who has been sent to turn him. At first I thought that with the peace process it had missed its moment: but it considers the generations of antipathy and misunderstanding between the two sides in emotional, and often witty prose – well acted by Rufus Sewell and Tony Doyle.

The set (Bill Dudley) is the big shock. The stalls are covered over to provide a huge metal floor onto which guards can run and tramp. In the centre is an earth patch which represents the prisoner's cell in Paddington Green police station. The stage space is similarly occupied with more audiences in temporary boxes and circle seats making it a complete 'in the round' experience.

I took Rick Kerwin. We went on to see Richard Rodney Bennett's first set at the Pizza on the Park. He was at his most winning. He talked charmingly, producing a lot of under-exploited or unknown songs – some his own. The programme included his very funny 'Paris *again*' song (by Dave Fishburg), 'I'm Ending Up with Me Again', 'End of a Love Affair' and 'I'm Talking to my Pal', dropped from *Pal Joey*. In the Paris song there was a cute rhyme – 'hunchback' with 'Get your lunch back'.

Thursday 12ᵗʰ October

To Swansea to do a *Desert Island Books* programme at the Arts Centre – hosted very efficiently by Professor Tony Curtis. I shared the reading of extracts with Joe James, the son of the late Emrys – who read lightly and highly intelligently. The extracts I chose were 'Mr Vuffin on Giants' from *The Old Curiosity Shop*, and 'Hunting the Thatcher' from Walter Raymond's *Book of Simple Delights*. Raymond was a Somerset author and I love reading the piece and slipping in and out of dialect. Then there were two bits of criticism. Shaw on Augustin Daly's ghastly *A Midsummer Night's Dream*, after which we had an interval and started again with Tynan's paean of praise for Edith Evans – which gave me a chance to air my Dame Edith anecdotes. I then read the 'Consumer Guide to Religion' from *TW3* by Charles Lewsen and Robert Gillespie which still stands up surprisingly well; but I must put in a few cuts the next time I use it. We finished with the scene from Brahms and Simon's *No Bed for Bacon* where Bacon comes to Shakespeare to commission *Twelfth Night* for a command performance before Gloriana. The audience was very warm: but I was reminded of what Nellie Wallace once told Wynford Vaughan-Thomas: 'If you don't go in Swansea, you'd better give up because you won't go anywhere.'

A nice nervous man, David Lambert, organised it and put me in a pleasant private hotel where we dined afterwards. As I was on expenses (train fare and bed), I thought I'd better pay for the wine at dinner. Five of us (the Prof's wife driving and not drinking) got through three bottles of Fleurie and one of Chardonnay so I don't recall much of the spirited conversation.

It is the anniversary of the birth of Lillie Langtry. In his magazine *Truth* the Liberal MP Henry Labouchere one week printed a harmless item of gossip that there was nothing between the Prince of Wales (later Edward VII) and Mrs Langtry. The next week, in the same place in the same column he printed the simple sentence, 'Not even a sheet.'

Friday 13ᵗʰ October

We arrived at Paddington fifteen minutes early so I had time to buy my tickets for Saturday's journey to Somerset for a wedding.

Finished my reading for *Loose Ends*. Harry Thompson on *Richard Ingrams* and Ingrams on *Muggeridge*. Ingrams quotes Mugg's interview with Salvador Dali. He opened with: 'I know we're supposed to discuss modern art, but first of all might I ask what happens to your moustaches at night?' 'They droop,' replied Dali.

A wonderful rumour from the city. Ever since a newspaper described Sir Iain Vallance, the highly paid, high-profile chairman of BT as 'having occasional flashes of personal warmth', his amused children are said to be making his life hell by taunting him with cries of, 'Go on, give us an occasional flash then.'

Saturday 14ᵗʰ October

I think Jon Rowlands must have been compensating for last week's uphill work on *Loose Ends*. He booked Eddie Izzard, Ingrams, Thompson, The Men Who Know, a report by Emma Freud on political defectors, a very funny surreal musical comic, Bill Bailey, Richard Rodney Bennett and David Soul of *Starsky and Hutch* who only got five minutes at the end. Eddie has now got the measure of interviews. When he first came on to the show he hardly dared to be funny. I think he saw the light after I interviewed him in front of an audience in Edinburgh. When we talked afterwards he asked if it might not be better if he got a few laughs. I reassured him that it would be *much* better. Now he rattles on engagingly – without exposing any of his material. He was funny about his first night. A button popped off his Gaultier jacket and when a woman threw needle and thread on to the stage he sewed it back on, carrying on with the act at the same time. Richard Rodney B. had a success with 'Paris *Again*'.

I had to forgo the George in order to get to Paddington in time to catch the 11.25 for the wedding. Alfred (my brother) met me at Castle Cary station. The train was about ten minutes late. We had stopped outside Bruton. The guard announced, 'Some children have been putting large objects on the line. We have to go slowly because we're not allowed to run over them – unfortunately!'

Alfred is three years older than me. We could hardly be more different, or get on better. He never considered doing anything but take over the farm from our father. I never thought of staying in the country. Alfred retired a few years ago. He was beginning to tire of second-guessing the various Common Market ploys and regulations; and he was increasingly bothered by arthritis. He has slipped happily into retirement and divides his time between cursory glances at the garden, gently exercising his replaced hip and studying the racing colours of point-to-point owners. His big hobby is doing on-course commentaries to point-to-point all over the south-west of England. I've only heard him once, and he was splendidly fluent and efficient. Obviously the thorough homework pays off.

We lunched (soup and a sandwich) at a pub nearby. Alfred, just like our father, on tenterhooks about being late. We were joined by Alfred's younger son David, who has a business in Castle Cary.

The marriage was that of my second cousin Frances Drewett to her long-time fiancé Harry, a barrister and ex-soldier. They had taken enormous care over the highly individual and personal service. Frances belongs to a London choir and 30-odd of them had come down to support and sing. None of that 'Here Comes the Bride' stuff. She entered to Parry's 'I was glad'. Before that we had fanfares from three trumpeters outside the church from the band of the Royal Gloucestershire Hussars, the Royal Wessex Yeomanry. Another was waiting to blow inside.

The Cary vicar, Patrick Revell, was in wonderful absentminded form. To Harry he said, 'Do you take this man ...' before realising his mistake. I wasn't sure about the charismatic sermon by the Rev. Rico Tice, who went to school with Frances. He started with a rugby football which he lobbed around the church to various members of the congregation and then preached on the theme that God is as important to a marriage as a ball is to a game. He described himself as 'a non-combatant in the business of marriage'. Oh well. During the signing of the register the choir gave us the anthem 'Like as the Hare' from Psalm 42, and the couple left to a Trumpet Tune (Stanley) and the Lefébure-Wély Sortie in E flat. The reception was in a marquee in the grounds of that lovely, mellow, butterscotch-yellow Castle Cary stone, great house, Brympton D'Evercy. A couple of hundred dined and then danced, but we had left by then. The bride's father, my cousin John, a solicitor, gave an immaculate toast, measured, grave – his wife Rosemary died recently – and often very funny and affectionate. The groom did what grooms do and perhaps thanked too many people. The best man, introduced by the nervous MC (an hotelier from Cambridge) as the funniest man imaginable, was a sad disappointment and went on far too long. John confirmed my suspicions about Markova's *This is Your Life*: 'Your brother and I thought you were less fluent than usual,' he said!

Sunday 15*th* October

Back to London, after breakfast cooked by my brother. Nancy, his housekeeper, has dislocated a shoulder and he is discovering domesticity and rather enjoying it. He gave me some beautiful fresh beans and leeks from his garden. I had them for lunch with some partridge, delicious. In the evening I succumbed to an escort ad. for 'American hunk – porn star quality' and phoned. Stallone-ish, Brooklynish, and highly satisfactory, Sicilian, late twenties, swaggering in, in black boots, jeans and a chunky leather jacket, with a provocative line in chat in a gravelly Brooklyn accent, and a great sense of humour. We'll meet again.

Monday 16ᵗʰ October

Saints and Sinners annual whitebait supper at the Trafalgar Tavern, Greenwich. A trip down the Thames in the *Mayflower Rose*. Club rules decree no reporting these private occasions but since *The Times* will list the guests tomorrow I can say that they included Lord Callaghan, General Sir Michael Rose, Francis Edmonds, Rabbi Julia Neuburger, Peter Snow, Sir John Mills, the Recorder of London, James Molyneaux and Rev. Roger Royle.

I got back to watch the tape of Gore Vidal's second instalment of memoirs. Some time was spent on his cameo film appearances. In the light of my *Kavanagh QC* appearance I liked his summing up of the lure of the occasional acting engagement for a non-actor. Gore likes to emerge from a period of solitary writing into a movie role where 'you get to know people quite intensely: but for not too long. That suits me.'

Anniversary of the death of S.J. Perelman in 1979. At 75 Perelman was dropped off at his home in New York by a taxi-driver who said, 'Have a nice day.' Perelman barked, 'I'll have any sort of goddam day I want.' He died later that evening.

Wednesday 18ᵗʰ October

I finally returned to The Novel. I am not sure why. I was quite keen to potter into the study and attack it. I find it easier to have a different table for a different project. The Novel is in the study, the floor is covered with reference books – Australia, Hollywood, the theatre – and I can pick my way past the piles. Our block of flats is being painted and the windows repaired. I think the study window may have to come out altogether. I do not look forward to sorting out and tidying up the books. Letters get done in the kitchen and this diary lives on the hall table.

I am finding the reader/editor Christine's notes sensible and constructive and often stimulating. Would I had had them before. Maybe not, perhaps the distance helps. I am not as embarrassed by the book this time around.

Darren Ramirez – my old house guest in Chelsea in the early seventies when he was Rachel Roberts's boyfriend – came by to be taken to the Barbican to see John Osborne's *Patriot for Me*. We just made the seven o'clock curtain to find that it was going to run four hours with two intervals. Well, it is one of my favourite Osborne plays: but I did not remember it running that long. The reason was soon apparent. Peter Gill's stately, detailed production was in no hurry. A sock once taken off in a bedroom had meticulously to be put back on. Likewise shirts. Likewise trousers. It is an impressive performance, no nuance goes unexplored, but I often wanted to reach for the fast-forward.

One of the fascinations of the play is trying to work out Osborne's attitude to homosexuals, and to homosexuals in the army. Sometimes he puts a passionate plea in an actor's mouth, at others he points up the threat to security and discipline. In the light of his later shafts it's difficult to work out his underlying point. The play is, of course, the story of an officer in the Imperial Army of the rotting Hapsburg dynasty. Alfred Redl has been played by Maximilian Schell who was not fluent, or at least easy, in the English and by Alan Bates who was. I had not realised until I saw James Wilby tonight how important the man's youth was. He goes from cadet to senior colonel with great leaps between many scenes. With the two older actors (as cadets) their obvious maturity warred with their gropings towards understanding their sexuality. Surely they ought to know by *now*! (It's a bit like the *mariage blanc* in *Salad Days* when the lovers are being played by 30-somethings). James Wilby – of whom Hugh Grant famously said after sharing a love-scene with him in *Maurice*: 'Nobody kisses like James Wilby' – starts *looking* the right age (even though *he* must be 30-something); vulnerable, puzzled and desperate. His vocal range is limited, light and, in emotion, rasping, but he ages easily and in his ability to chart the progress of Redl's homosexuality he is very moving. Denis Quilley dominated, as he must, the drag-ball scene as George Devine did. The difference is that Devine made no concessions to campery and it worked – Denis does play it camp but it still works. He provided a wonderful ad-lib when one of the young drag queens, overcome by meeting Redl, accidentally dropped a clattering earring.

Confusion and uneasy laughter. Denis covered it simply with 'You see, you're so excited, you've lost an earring' – and got a round. Will they keep it in?

We left at 11.10! We went to Orso's for a quick course. Helen Osborne arrived just before we left on Tony Palmer's arm with John's agent Kenneth Ewing and his assistant. We had no time for more than the pleasantries on the way out. Palmer has directed John's posthumous *Purcell* for TV (in the person of Michael Ball).

Red Rum died today. I recall that when he won his third Grand National such was the outburst of emotion that Ron Pollard, a director of Ladbrokes, burst into the Press Room shouting, 'We've lost a quarter of a million and I simply don't care!'

Thursday 19ᵗʰ October

A 'show case' of Ivor Novello's *Glamorous Night* in the Dress Circle Bar at Drury Lane – 60 years after the first production opened there. 'Revised book and new material by Daniel Christie'. I couldn't work out what was revised as there was only a very skeletal book linking the four or five great swooping tunes. Apparently they hope to revive it in the West End. I don't fancy its chances. There was a chorus of keen young babes all got up in Ruritanian uniforms and long dresses, and four principals – two plainly had operatic pretensions and attacked the big songs with a flourish – acting about up (or down) to D'Oyly Carte standard. I took Alistair Beaton because someone (the D'Oyly Carte, I suspect) has asked him to consider a new book for one of Novello's shows. This may have convinced him that it can't be done. Duncan Weldon was in the audience. He has no intention of being involved. He confirmed that we are moving ahead with Keith's play *Bing Bong* and said, 'You know that show you're doing at Guildford for free? D'you want to do it in Chichester for money?' It's the Minerva studio threatre, not the main house, but it might be a good way to find out if *Theatrical Anecdotes* stands up to a paid audience. I keep doing it for nothing!

Sandy Wilson (also at the *Glamorous Night* show) announced that he's coming to Richmond to see *Salad Days*. He was taken to see the original *Glamorous Night* 60 years ago. He shares the general feeling that the books will be impossible to reconcile with modern tastes.

Saturday 21st October

A highly entertaining *Loose Ends*. Lily Savage dropped out. Officially injured during rehearsals for the musical *Prisoner Cell Block H* – due to open on Monday. I suspect general despair about the state of the show, overworked and overtired and quite sensibly not wanting to get up early and come out and plug. We substituted a wicked tape of Arthur Smith interviewing Paula Yates about her new opportunist autobiography – making a big point that she was 'flashing her knickers at him'.

The rest of the programme was three interviews – John Mortimer, Keith Waterhouse and Nick Revell. Waterhouse told a wonderful Xmas tale. In the first flush of success he was drinking one evening at the Salisbury pub when he remembered he'd forgotten to buy a tree. So he bought the big one in the pub. He and Willis Hall were reluctant to go home at closing time so they took the tree to a night-club. The doorman objected that it had no tie so they bought the taxi-driver's tie, took the tree in, introduced it to a hostess and sent a bottle of champagne across to it. When Keith eventually got it home the kids voted it the best tree ever!

Nick Revell, a clever, personable writer-comic, was eloquent about his new show at Hampstead, *Liberal Psychotics*, and vivid about a punch-up in the bar at the Assembly Rooms during the Edinburgh Festival. Lee Evans lost his temper when a punter moved on from insulting him to being rude about his wife. The punter was unaware that Lee had been a boxer before becoming a comic and found himself on the floor. Nick intervened, saying, 'Come on, Lee, you're too *good* for this!' Now the story has snowballed and whenever it is told back to him involves a riot, squads of police and even platoons of soldiers drafted in to restore order.

My bill for the first round at the George has escalated. It came to well over £40 this week – helped on by three bottles of Australian chardonnay.

The *Spectator* has a letter about child abuse amongst the Christian brothers and the joke about clerical child molestation in Ireland is going the rounds again: 'What do Catholic priests hand round after dinner?' 'The under-eights.'

Sunday 22nd October

I phoned Keith to arrange a rendezvous on Monday. He's coming to see *Salad Days*. He told me that Kingsley Amis has died. I was surprised not to have heard the news on breakfast or lunch news bulletins. Keith was on every evening news bulletin, glass in hand, extolling Kingsley's reputation and saluting his memory – standing outside his door, slightly flushed and possibly swaying. It seemed very appropriate.

Monday 23rd October

I think one project has bitten the dust. I phoned Peters Fraser & Dunlop to ask Charles Walker, Alan Clark's agent, if the synopsis we submitted for the *Diaries* had moved things on at all. 'As I told your agent,' a cold voice said, 'I think he's lost interest.' I'll get Alistair to ask Mark Berlin (*his* agent), who has been handling it, to find out what, if anything, has happened. Do I regret its passing? I'm not sure I do. So much seems to be piling up for next year. I must also let Birmingham know.

To Richmond to see *Salad Days* and do some sort of bookshop 'do' – the opening of the Richmond Books Now Literary Festival. Apparently it's good PR for the theatre to provide free speakers for the Lib Dem council's events. They aren't getting much financial support from them.

Keith W. came down to see the play and so did the Redingtons (Michael, producer of *Jeffrey Bernard* etc.). The cast were in top form to a full house – we are sold out throughout the week. The juveniles – Simon and Nicola – will stay on for the post-Christmas tour and Kit and the Widow are firming up. Julian Slade was introduced from the stage and bowed and waved 'graciously'. He is *so* happy about the way it is playing. One more week to go – at Chichester. I'm not sure if I can get down but I shall try. Julian is throwing a cast party at his house on Thursday night.

Train back from Richmond with Keith and a melancholy drunk who had walked to Richmond from Hammersmith, stopping for pints at two pubs on the way, and then imbibed a good deal more around the town. We lost him at Hammersmith.

Tuesday 24ᵗʰ October

A wasted morning at a BBC seminar at White City. A staggeringly useless public relations exercise. John Birt waffle was followed by Liz Forgan (Managing Director, Radio) on digital development, exploding competition and the global market place. Will Wyatt (MD, TV) followed, repeating Birt's plea for more licence money – costs going up, income pegged. He also listed BBC awards worldwide proudly. A man from Scotland blew the regional trumpet.

All this under the vague brief 'How can the Corporation help the creative community?' We were variously flattered as creative, artistic and the Great and the Good.

Questions had nothing to do with the creative links. The first question was why were no Afro-Asians present? Then Andrew Davis asked a typically pugnacious question about the line-up of the Director-General's apparatchiks and the self-congratulatory speeches which had preceded him. Most writers and producers – Carla Lane, Peter Flannery (whose 1982 project *Our Friends in the North*, is just being filmed), Edward Woodward, etc., concentrated on their own projects which had foundered or been dropped when executives moved on. Ben Elton was the only satisfied customer, loyal to Alan Yentob to the point of brown-nosing – a strange development from his earlier persona.

There were two good moments. Jimmy Nail, who is filming *Evita* with Madonna – he plays Magaldi – told me at lunch that they have been pre-recording the score. On Friday they had a row which ended with Madonna saying, 'Go fuck your mother!' James said, 'I take particular exception to that as my mother is currently staying with me. Go fuck yourself!' He is looking forward to resuming hostilities tomorrow.

And I *was* interested in a brief demonstration of Digital Broadcasting and Post Production. Digital editing is a million miles more advanced than the last time I was in a TV studio. I think I now know what e-mail is and I sort-of understand CD-ROM – hitherto one of life's great mysteries.

A ghastly mixture of the BBC pleading for support and patting itself on the back to an audience conned there on the suggestion of some providing support for the arts.

Roger Royle – the Rev. – came for a cup of tea to ask about broadening his broadcasting career. He is a natural, charming, funny talker with more than enough gravitas under a candyfloss manner. I gave him a couple of names and promised to write to back him up.

To *Volpone* at the National. Terrific performances by Michael Gambon and Simon Russell Beale and an ingenious, inventive break-neck-pace staging by the wunderkind Matthew Warchus. The magnificent opening 'Good morning to the sun but first my gold!' ruined by a wild and incomprehensible flurry of movement all over the whirling set which left Volpone half-hanging from his bed post. Very odd and an unnecessary way of bringing attention to the director and taking it away from the actor. Wolfit would not have let him get away with it. Gambon is the finest Volpone I've seen since Sir Donald.

Cheryl Campbell as Lady Politic wildly over the top and unfunny until her superb exit line: 'Lend me your dwarf!'

Wednesday 25th October

Well, well, well! Today a postcard from Alan Clark from Saltwood, saying, 'Dear Ned, sorry not to have acknowledge your card and treatment. As far as I'm concerned that's on [odd writing, could be OK]. But "terms" have to be negotiated with PDF [*sic*]. It seems there is still quite a lot to do. Are you really . . . [content? corpulent? comment? – can't read the last word]? Alan.'

Charles Walker at Peter Fraser & Dunlop didn't return my call all morning so I faxed him the text and set Mark Berlin and John Stalker of Birmingham Rep, who initiated the whole thing, on him.

There was something called 'Books for Giving' – a 'celebrity' reception at the RAC Club. John McCarthy and Sandi Toksvig the 'star celebs'. Sandi blotted her copybook by asking me if *Loose Ends* was back on the air. Roy Hattersley said he was grateful for my help in getting him to Stephen Sondheim. He interviewed Stephen at the Savoy and asked him why he was often so critical of Lorenz Hart as a lyric writer. Apparently Stephen then made him sing 'Take Him' ('I won't put a price on him/Take him, he's yours/Take him, pyjamas look nice on him/But how he snores'), and then speak it – highlighting how unhappily some words sit on the music. Steve comes back in September (for *Company* at the Donmar, I imagine). He's never 'done' the House of Commons, so we're both to be invited to lunch there. Hattersley was full of admiration for Stephen's canny reply when he asked him if 'Anyone Can Whistle' was a gay anthem. Stephen said, 'It's a song for minorities. Gays are a minority so it's all right by me.' Tony Benn came over later saying, 'I saw you across here talking to Hattersley . . .', implying that he'd waited until the Rt. Hon. Roy had gone away. There being no tea he drank Coke.

Benn couldn't make up his mind about his book of the year. Usually when asked for his favourite books he says the Bible and *Das Kapital* with a bookmark permanently placed at page 11. I asked him the other stock question: 'What would you like your epitaph to be?' He said he'd got that off pat: 'He tried to help.' I told him my lucky find in Kenneth Williams's *Diaries*. I'd gone to be civil to his mother whom he'd left at a table in Joe Allen. Kenneth's entry read, 'What a kind and considerate person he is!' An enviable epitaph which would come as a surprise to quite a few people. Ken Follett called me a 'champagne Tory' and proudly announced that he'd sold many – I can't remember how many – millions of his new book in Italy. 'Bigger than the Pope?' I suggested. He smiled almost modestly. We had to nominate a favourite book of the year for Sky TV. I chose Keith W's *Street Ahead*. 'Why did you choose that?' 'Because I'm mentioned in it so many times.' Saw dear old Spike Milligan looking very frail on the way out – 'Not *the* Ned Sherrin?' he managed in his Goonish voice.

Thursday 26ᵗʰ October

Recorded quite a funny *Independent* radio commercial. They replayed in reverse the first paragraph so that it sounded like some Slav language. It was on the lines of 'Ringo's gone dry, George needs the money, Paul's wife makes vegetarian pancakes. John's dead.' Then in clear the copy went on, 'There's a coded message in there which will tell you what's happened to the Beatles – 22 pages in Saturday's *Independent*.' Then they reversed *Independent* to read 'tnednepedni'. It actually sounded quite funny.

Brian Conley's *Jolson* in the evening. A big glitzy four-square production with all the usual faults of a biographical musical; but with the great virtue of Conley's performance in the title role. The book faced many of the problems we had in *Ziegfeld*. (I took Alistair Beaton, with whom I wrote *Z*.) Both Ziegfeld and Jolson were eminently dislikeable. The advantage of this show over ours was a terrific display by Conley, who was able to make the selfish character sympathetic and charismatic while still playing the text faithfully. At the end he did a virtuoso 20 minutes with the band on stage – totally barnstorming any of the audience still unpersuaded. We left as the curtain calls were developing into a party with usherettes and waiters materialising from all over the theatre bearing trays of champagne and canapés.

We went on to Bar Central in the King's Road. After dinner I looked in at Julian Slade's cast party for *Salad Days*. Everyone turned up except Rosie Ash and Barry James, who are already rehearsing for takeovers in *Oliver!* The company have stayed in remarkably good spirits. No empty seats at Richmond and advance bookings of £75,000 already at Chichester does wonders for morale.

I was saddened to see that Peter Casson, the great hypnotist, died this week, aged 73. In 1947 a friend of mine, Michael Hill (then editor of the *Isis*), took him for morning coffee at the Kemp Café in Oxford. Those were the days of rationing: one cake per person. Casson unintentionally hypnotised the waitress, causing her to serve them happily with a vast plate of eclairs to the dismay of the managers and the delight of Hill, who would live on eclairs if he could.

Saturday 28*th* October

A busy morning. *Loose Ends* – good guests. I had not met Tully Sahib (Mark Tully, ex-BBC India correspondent) before. Eloquent, of course, but also modest and funny about his book *Heart of India*. He uses it to retell a lot of news items (unbroadcastable as fact) in the guise of short stories of village life. They are riveting and read like an Indian Chekhov.

Rich Little, the American comedian I talked to a couple of times in Edinburgh, spoke about his funny little paperback *Self Help for the Bleak*, a highly effective antidote to all those American self-help books.

Matthew Kelly I haven't seen in years – except as being a personality on the screen. He made a brilliant comic debut back in the seventies in a play called *Funny Peculiar* and I used him in a TV sketch in *The Rather Reassuring Programme* in 1976; now at last he's back in theatre and doing *The Cabinet of Dr Caligari* at the Lyric Hammersmith. There's never been a stage version of the old movie. Now suddenly there are two! This one comes from Nottingham. The *Stage* reports the Liverpool *Dr C* has 'a very swishy cloak for furling at his exits'. Matthew sounded envious when I quoted that to him. The final interview was a pleasant bumptious Radio 1 type called Danny Kelly. He used to edit the *NME*, then *Q*, a pop monthly and now he's starting a very glossy total *Sport* monthly.

After the usual wind-down at the George I got the 12.25 to Taunton. After-dinner for Kit Chapman who was throwing one of his 'gourmet' dinners – his young chef, Phil Vickery, is a wiz. I did *Theatrical Anecdotes*, having done the usual topical one not too long ago. We started drinks at 7.30 and I did not get on my feet until 11. I stopped bang on 11.30 reckoning that that was enough!

I enjoyed sitting next to Fay Maschler and opposite her new*ish* husband, Reg Gadney, a writer. Gadney has a TV series about to hit the small screen after years of hanging about.

Sunday 29*th* October

To Guildford to close their Book Festival at the Yvonne Arnaud. Again I did *Theatrical Anecdotes*. They wanted 75 minutes. I just managed to string out the stories, having hurried rather quickly over the early letters of the alphabet. I signed about 50 copies of *Humorous Quotations* and *Anecdotes*. It was a very warm house. Downstairs Duncan Weldon was throwing an eighteenth birthday party for his daughter. James Barber, who runs the theatre, elbowed me in for a chat as Duncan appears to be dragging his feet over *Bing Bong*, pleading that the combination of Dennis Waterman and Robert Powell may not be strong enough. We need to be moving if we are to start rehearsals in good order in February. I must speak to Deke.

Monday 30*th* October

Cell Block H – the Musical – a disgrace at the Queen's theatre. I took Rick Kerwin. We both hated every minute except the occasional bit of stand-up by Lily Savage who was playing herself incarcerated on a murder charge. Lily (Paul O'Grady) *is* funny but this show did as much as it could to conceal the fact. We left for the Groucho slipping out at half-time for a quick snack. It was a huge relief to get away. How can such an abortion, badly written, acted, designed, directed, sung and choreographed, land up on a West End stage? The mind *boggles*.

I see Alan Clark has been rejected as a short-list candidate for selection by the Chelsea Conservative Association. One member asked if he had any skeletons in his cupboard? He replied, 'A whole grave-yard full.' I wonder if it will affect our dramatisation of the *Diaries* if he gets a constituency?

Tuesday 31st October

Gerard Kenny at the Green Room, Café Royal. I took Gaye Brown. Gerard in fine ebullient form. Porter, Gershwin, Elton John's 'Honky Cat'. Slowing tempos effectively on standards like 'From This Moment On', 'Johnny B. Goode', 'Every Time You Go Away', 'I Made It Through the Rain', 'I Could Be So Good for You' (which he wrote with Dennis Waterman), 'New York, New York' – 'so good they named it twice', and 'Nickels and Dimes' (lyrics Drey Sheppard) and 'I'm Dancing My Blues Away' – a number he wrote for an uncompleted score with Alan Jay Lerner. There was also one he wrote with Lynsey de Paul. I was a little dimmed that he didn't do the one we wrote for *Small Expectations* – 'Not Funny'. Heigh-ho!

It's the 20,000th *Times* crossword. A little research revealed that the first – on 1 February 1930 – was compiled by a farmer called Adrian Bell. He said it was 'the ideal job for a chap with a vacant mind sitting on a trailer harrowing clods'.

November

Wednesday 1st November

STILL WORKING ON revisions for *Scratch an Actor* and enjoying it.
I have to invent some more early background for Zelda Fame, my
Hollywood movie singing star. As she's a dyke I suppose I'd better
give her an affair with Garbo or Dietrich or perhaps both.

Lunch was at Bibendum with the Tabasco Club. President Paul
McIlhenny flew in with his wife Judy whose voice – Louisiana –
sounds as if it's been marinated in some fierce pepper sauce. Simon
Hopkinson and Matthew Hall (now head chef) provided lovely Colchester oysters, generously tabascoed, and soft goujons of sole while we
drank tabascoed Bloody Marys. Then we had a delicious thin tart
with onions. It was like eating onion soup on Melba toast. Then
home-potted shrimps. Roast beef with the best Yorkshire pudding I've
ever tasted, roast potatoes magically boiled fluffy before roasting,
asparagus and finally a luxurious treacle pudding. The wines were
Spanish from Frexinet.

Sadly I lost my menu, and also my intention to work, and succumbed to at least an hour and a half of heavy sleep.

In the evening I went with Joe Harmston to see Alan Bates in *The
Master Builder* at the Haymarket. I had not seen it since Redgrave
(uncertain) and Maggie Smith at the National. I retain nothing else of
that production. I've missed John Wood and Brian Cox recently. It's
one of Peter Hall's stately productions with a barnstorming performance by Alan. It is hard to recall the Bates of *Look Back in Anger* –
virtually 40 years ago. There is an agonising exchange about the death
of the twins which must be so painful for him to deliver. Gemma
Jones impeccable as Mrs Solness. The new girl, Victoria Hamilton,
took all the notices playing Hilda Wangel as a back-packer, but she

was none of Maggie Smith's scorching attack in the role. She's straight out of LAMDA and should do well. I'm not sure it'll be *that* well; but she is impressive in this. The theatre was half empty but the audience was bolstered down in the front of the stalls by a large party of extrovert young Americans on some sort of concession deal. At the second interval one girl was terribly impressed by Ms Hamilton's appearance, 'I just love her. She makes me miss my hair!' Another could only talk football. 'Arsenal are playing Manchester United on Saturday. That'll be awesome!' Another wanted to know if it was at 'Wem b-u-ly'?

Saturday 4*th* November

An odd *Loose Ends*. The funny Irish Australian comic, Jimoen, fell out at about 8.30 this morning – sick. First of all we thought we would just spread the others – Warren Mitchell, Eric Sykes, John Shuttleworth – a fictional, musical, comic, the creation of Graham Fellowes – and Jerry Herman (*Mack and Mabel*). Then we decided to do a quick edit on a Billy Crystal interview I did some weeks ago. On the air Warren was so lucid about his new Lear, Eric so anarchic and John Shuttleworth so musically expansive that we had to junk Mr Crystal after all and still only had eight minutes for J. Herman of which three minutes were taken up by a song.

Warren apparently plays the storm scene naked and says his daughter has labelled it The Wind in the Willies – Edgar is naked too and Warren says this distracts most of the attention from him. He spoke the reunion with Cordelia: 'We two alone will sing like birds i' the cage . . .' very tenderly. He is about to film *Death of a Salesman* and said that playing Lear is much less exhausting once the storm scene is over.

I have never been able to laugh at the John Shuttleworth character on television though I am told his live performances are very funny. This was borne out in the studio. He plays a ridiculously incompetent musician who shouldn't be allowed to perform outside his garden shed. He has a fictional wife and agent and in the flesh one could see the charm.

Eric Sykes, who has long been going deaf, now says he's going blind as well – no great help to lip reading. His fourth novel is a piece

about UFOs landing (*UFOs Are Coming Wednesday*). I quite enjoyed
the book until a criminal hoax was revealed. I then lost interest. He
has an amusing, rather old-fashioned attitude to chat shows – trying
to throw the interviewer, shooting off at a tangent, etc., which led to
a good deal of happy giggling. I hope it wasn't too impenetrable for
the listener.

Jerry Herman played and croaked 'I Won't Bring Roses' from *Mack
and Mabel* and submitted to interview as readily as always but there
wasn't really time to ask him anything at all off-beat.

A small group at the George. Apart from Graham all the guests
were hurrying off to other plug programmes. First round still came to
£35.

Sunday 5ᵗʰ November

An afternoon and evening at the Prince Edward Theatre. *A Handful
of Keys* was the name of the late Martin Smith's one-man-at-the-piano
show. He died of AIDS last year. He was a composer, actor, singer,
orchestrator, arranger, conductor – and often a leading man in flop
musicals – though he did play Che in *Evita*, and both Marius and Jean
Valjean in *Les Miserables* – a unique achievement. He was volatile,
promiscuous, loyal, very talented and extremely attractive, which
ensured a high turnout of West End names. One friend used to recall
one of those blazing rows with Martin – the sort which is so violent
that it ends with a more potent making-up – the climax had Martin
shouting at him, 'You're a nasty, evil, deceitful person – and don't you
ever forget, I made you what you are today!'

Julia McKenzie had put together an enormously ambitious production – big, staged dance numbers and song scenes. She was looking
distraught by the end of the afternoon. However, as always, everything
slotted in neatly. I was in the corner in case of a hitch but only needed
to emerge for planned appearances.

I had a drink with Sheridan Morley and Jack Tinker in a Soho pub
before the show. Morley is having trouble with his late-night TV
theatre show – every time he criticises a play or an actor in the
Spectator they withdraw from their spot on the show! He's in
the middle of his Gielgud 'official' biography and Sir John keeps
ringing up to ask how it's going. Sheridan is avoiding this and

keeps saying he's just got as far as age 21 or something absurdly young. Sir John is now becoming suspicious. 'Not surprising,' I said bitchily. 'Everybody knows how long it usually takes you to turn out a book!' Personally, I think he's finished it.

'Back in the knife box, Miss Sharp,' said Jack. Sheridan wrote his father's life in six months of conscientious research and writing. He wanted to do Robert justice and felt when he had finished that he had. The next day his publisher asked him to do a rush job on a book about Audrey Hepburn. He ripped off some 20,000 words to go with a lot of pictures which the publisher already possessed. The Hepburn scissors-and-paste job did infinitely better than the conscientiously crafted proper biography.

Reunions are half the fun – no, *more* than half the fun – of these occasions. Our dressing room had Millie Martin, Siân Phillips, Dale Winton, Lily Savage, Clarke Peters, Angela Richards, Pet Clarke. There was a beautiful *a capella* version of 'Bring Him Home' from *Les Mis*, a very funny *Phantom* extract with Michael Ball vamped by four identically costumed heroines and a simple staging of songs from Martin's best piece of writing, *King*. His version of the Martin Luther King story was sabotaged by a rival version which failed horribly at the Piccadilly Theatre but put the knockers on Martin's infinitely superior show.

They prised dear Lis Welch out of her hermit-like retreat in her flat to present the cheque to Crusaid. She is very frail and hugely forgetful but she appeared to enjoy the outing until the heat at the post-party got to her.

Monday 6th November

In the late afternoon to Broadcasting House for the first of a new series of *Counterpoint*. A new producer, Steve Doherty, recently established as a Light Entertainment trainee. Very sweet, very nervous at his first-ever recording, amiably cocking up his warm-up and introductions but doing it with such charming diffidence that he 'won all hearts'. Quite a high standard of contestants; as usual they were beautifully behaved and sportsmanlike.

Tuesday 7ᵗʰ November

First night of *Mack and Mabel*. Jerry Herman's musical has taken 21 years to get here. I doubt if it will last. It got a rapturous reception and the score is beguiling but the book is still soft and silly and fails to justify the chauvinistic bully, Mack Sennet, in the way that they bring off the trick with Brian Conley as Jolson at the Victoria Palace. Howard McGillen as Sennet is tall and elegant. He looks so haunted and sensitive that he should be playing one of the writers whom his character terrorises. He has a ravishing voice but is totally unconvincing in the role. Great hollow, sallow cheeks will make him perfect casting when they produce *Michael Ignatieff – the Musical!* Caroline O'Connor, an Australian who has been struggling to make it here for years, is also clever but not nearly clever or winning or funny enough. I fear they are all in for a horrible disappointment tomorrow morning. Dear little Marie, the octogenarian, regular first-nighter, clutched me on the way out and asked, 'Have we seen the birth of two stars tonight?' and I had to whisper sadly, 'No.' She was unconvinced.

I saw Darren Day, who sang 'Love for Sale' on Sunday, during the interval. I had wanted to tell him and the audience that Lis Welch was the first person to sing it solo 70 years ago but did not have the chance. So I took the opportunity to tell him today. He had no idea and was amazed and delighted to hear it.

Rick Kerwin and I walked across Piccadilly Circus to Marco Pierre White's Criterion. A lovely room now seen in its full splendour. Wonderful service. A chatty waiter explained the provenance of his colleagues: 'He's from the Manoir, I'm from the Canteen, there's another from The Restaurant, etc. . . .' Marco Pierre at his most genial and relaxed came across. He was dining with a pretty *Standard* journalist. We had one course each. Mine was langoustine and spaghetti, Rick had haddock on a potato base – both excellent.

Wednesday 8ᵗʰ November

Jack Tinker's notice in *The Mail* confirms my fears for the morale of the *Mack and Mabel* company. Very dismissive of the book, unimpressed by the girl and highlighting the miscasting of poor McGillen.

Soon after I read Jack's notice a messenger arrived from Michael

Owen at the *Evening Standard* with the judge's comments on the *Standard* Drama Awards. Best musical *Mack and Mabel* – but I note from the comments that it wins almost by default and Nicholas de Jongh the *Standard*'s critic abstained. That'll make his notice interesting when I go out to get it at lunch time.

LATER
De Jongh trod a neat tightrope, reporting the enthusiastic reception and keeping his reservations, modestly expressed, till towards the end.

At Jonathan Harvey's new play *Rupert Street Lonely Hearts Club* at the Donmar, he told me that his award would have gone to *A Little Night Music* but as it wasn't eligible, he abstained. Harvey's play is marvellous, constantly funny and moving. I'm not sure if its violent climax is justified or, perhaps, if it is adequately prepared; but it *is* a wonderful evening; a fine play, beautifully acted and directed.

Thursday 9th November

Did some early reading for some of the re-writes to *Scratch an Actor*. I am enjoying filling in the past of the American film star Zelda Fame.

I did a 20-second radio commercial for the *Independent* and got to Paddington early for the 12.35 to Newton Abbot (an after-dinner for the Booksellers' Association, West of England at Torquay). There was a scare – lorry hits bridge at Slough – and we thought we might be delayed for up to three hours while insurers assessed the damage. I was prepared to hole up in the new first-class 'transit lounge' only to be called on to the train bang on time. Asparagus soup and oxtail for lunch. Rather good oxtail, something I've never seen on a railway menu before.

I had rung to warn them in Newton Abbot that I'd be late and when I wasn't I had to wait five minutes to be picked up. Torquay is looking rather run down. The Grand commands a splendid view of the bay and my windows overlooked it. I signed 100 copies of *Humorous Quotations* before dinner. Much concern about the Net Book agreement and the BA honcho was flown in from Glasgow to rally the troops. Speech went well, early to bed, having to be up at six to catch the 7.36.

Friday 10th November

A great bonus on the return journey. Stella Watson, the bookshop owner who arranged the dinner and drove me in from Newton Abbot last evening, gave me a magical book. *Through the Window* – a facsimile version of a book describing the views on the line from Paddington to Penzance – first published in 1924. I can't wait to read it coming down from London. Going back you have to start at the bottom of each page and work your way back up which is fairly irritating. All sorts of familiar landmarks from my childhood are listed. High and Low Ham, near Langport, between which I was born. Kingweston, to which we moved when I was three. You can see the church from the line and the fields near Charlton Mackerell where, during harvesting, I used to watch the Torbay Express and the Cornish Riviera. In the evening as it got darker I used to be horribly envious of the pink lights in the restaurant cars where people seemed to a child to be dining in circumstances of incredible sophistication. From Charlton Mackerell I would train to Taunton to watch Somerset play cricket. Just before Castle Cary we pass the house to which my parents retired. After Cary the train speeds through Bruton. Above it are the buildings of Sexey's where I went to school. I always look out for a clump of trees on the left where the head of school seduced me pleasantly one summer's evening as the trains thundered by. The spot is not marked on *Through the Window*. Even so there is an immense amount of interesting material to absorb. Every line should have one.

Saturday 11th November

Our first 'theme' *Loose Ends* – the starting point is Philip Hoare's biography of Noël Coward. I still relish the exchange in which Lytton Strachey got the better of the very young Coward. Coward said, 'I met you a few years ago.' He received the cool reply, 'Rather a nice interval, don't you think?' David Quantock and his writing partner Jane Bussman did a quite funny extrapolation of Coward's cinema career as it might have extended into the eighties. Judy Campbell was funny about wartime touring with him. On one occasion in the frozen north she found his hands under her top holding her breasts. As the curtain fell on her tremulous excitement he said, 'First time my hands have been warm all night.' Peter Greenwell sang 'The Bar on the Piccola Marina', 'Alice Is At It Again' and 'The Party's Over' as a play out. We hadn't timed it and I thought they would fade it gently; in fact he finished bang on time to the very second. We were all so amazed by this that we totally forgot to honour two minutes' silence called for at 11 on the 11th day of the eleventh month.

À propos the Enoch Powell TV profile tonight, I once read that Harold Macmillan always had Enoch sitting on his side of the Cabinet table because he said he couldn't stand Enoch's staring eyes.

Sunday 12th November

To Denville Hall in Norwood to talk to the old actors. Arranged by Joan White, who is in her eighties. Doris Hare (90) was there looking twinkly and Peter Brough (of Brough and Archie Andrews) very frail but delighted that we had talked with Eric Sykes about him on last week's *Loose Ends*. I did *Theatrical Anecdotes*. Many seemed surprisingly new to them and nobody came up with any fresh revelations. There was one serene, pale, wraith-like woman well in her nineties, Aimée Delamain, and also Cecil Trouncer's widow, pleased that I knew about her daughter, Ruth.

A very sweet, gentle evening. Miss Delamain was touching. 'Thank you so much,' she said. 'An hour of lovely stories and not a single mean-spirited one.'

Monday 13th November

Robert Styles came by for a drink. He and Tim Higgs, who was one of the pianists on *Side By Side By Sondheim*, have written a splendid adaptation of Waugh's *The Loved One* which they workshopped some time ago – now it seems becalmed. I couldn't offer much advice beyond trying Chichester. Robert's adaptation and lyrics are impeccable. He's very attractive and displays most of himself in the drag ball scene in *A Patriot for Me*.

To the RSC's *Shakespeare Revue* which Michael Codron is presenting at the Vaudeville. 'Ladies of London', the song Caryl and I wrote for Doll Tearsheet, Doll Common and the Mistresses Overdone and Quickly, is still in. They are coming from Falstaff's funeral. It was beautifully sung and heard by a hushed house – the atmosphere heightened I think by the sad coincidence of the death of a recent Falstaff – Robert Stephens – the day before.

I don't know if the show will survive the current climate; but an old-fashioned first-night house gave an old-fashioned welcome.

Tuesday 14th November

There was a reception at the Theatre Museum to launch Philip Hoare's *Coward*. A big crowd of hardened Cowardites turned out. Judy Campbell and Neil Tennant, Graham Payn and Sheridan Morley, of course. I talked most to Elspeth March, who was in a wheelchair. We wondered what was happening to Robin Phillips. His parents were Elspeth and Stewart Granger's gardener and housekeeper when Robin was small. He's just been over to direct Britten's opera *Owen Wingrave* at Glyndebourne and got very good notices. He has not contacted either of us. Black mark! Joan Hirst who does a lot of the administering of Coward's estate was there and her brave nephew – early 20s – gamely sang Coward songs, accompanied by Stephen Bednarcyck while everybody talked their heads off and drowned him. I moved in to hear his 'Wild Wild Weather', from *Waiting in the Wings*, which he sang very charmingly.

Wednesday 15th November

I had lunch in the King David Suite under the Synagogue in Great Cumberland Place with 400 members of the Jewish League of Women. Very moist salmon, pickled cucumber and salad. They all profess to be dedicated Radio 4 listeners and addicts of *Loose Ends* – though some demanded a repeat because, of course, it clashes with synagogue. The Chief Rabbi's wife and I compared notes about Rabbi Julia Neuberger whom I had heard saying that, although she didn't approve of a lot of things that Dr Sachs says and does, she thought he had been splendid about the death of PM Rabin. Apparently her friends had all rung Mrs Sachs to say 'Switch on "4" – she's saying nice things about your husband!' One of my hostesses – they were all past presidents – said she always switched off Julia and Lionel Blue! It was their annual literary lunch so I did *Humorous Quotations* and *Theatrical Anecdotes* for 30 minutes and then signed 50-odd books, maybe more.

Straight to Euston for Coventry and a taxi to Stratford-on-Avon. I have to host a sort-of *Loose Ends* at the Swan theatre with RSC actor guests tomorrow. The treat is to see Victor Spinetti's Foppington in *The Relapse* tonight. They are putting me up in a sweet little hotel-cum-guest-house run by a Frenchman and his wife. A charming actor, Peter Holdway, who is on the committee for the RSC fringe programme, was waiting to greet me. The object of the lunchtime chat is to raise money for the fringe season in January. They need £5,000.

I have a delightful room. A big double bed, Laura Ashley-type blinds, dried flowers in the fireplace and a sitting room effect at the bottom of the bed. The shower is a bore (I like a bath) but the only room with bath had been booked by 'someone who has been here before'.

The Relapse was a joy. Victor, who had some good and some divided reviews, has plainly explored his way into his part with all his customary extravagance and with more vulnerability than usual. There is a brilliant cameo by Christopher Godwin as Coupler, the matchmaker, who is played as a treacherous, disreputable, old queen who grabs at the crutch of any passing youth, especially young Fashion, the hero, and is constantly massaging his own. It gives the audience a clear signal that though Foppington is effete, selfish, vain and obsessed by fashion, he isn't gay. By now Victor has found a very real character under all the campery. Susan Tracy beautifully incisive as the predatory widow Berinthia; Hugh Quarshie, flashing enormous teeth and charm as her victim, Loveless, and Jennifer Ehle delightful as his faithful wife, Amanda.

It lasts three hours – is any play at the RSC allowed to run for less? – but the full house was enchanted.

'The Committee' gave me dinner at the Dirty Duck with some of tomorrow's cast – Diana Coupland, Jennifer, Victor and Don Gallagher who is going to sing 'Take Me to the World' – an obscure Sondheim number from *Evening Primrose*, Stephen's early television musical.

Peter Holdway walked me home for a reasonably early night – 12.30.

Thursday 16th November

Declan Donnellan appeared at breakfast as I was leaving. He's starting a tour of *The Duchess of Malfi* at Warwick. Must see it when it comes to Wyndham's.

We had a full stalls and quite a lot in the circle. They took something over £2,100 so that starts the fund raising quite well. It was a very responsive audience. Victor gave us a wonderful kick off, doing fifteen minutes, largely from his one-man show. However, he sneaked in quite a lot of stuff which he'd left out for time in his full evening. The first time he was kissed on the lips by a man was in a rugby scrum when he was playing for the Royal Welsh Fusiliers. Don Gallagher sang 'Take Me to the World' splendidly and was followed by the ebullient John Nettles. This year's Romeo, a marvellously cheeky Indian – Zubin Varla – sang 'Leave You', the song from *Follies*. It is delivered in the show by a bored wife who is threatening to leave her rich husband. David Kernan changed the sex of the song for his climactic solo in *Side By Side By Sondheim* and it was good to hear it sung by a man again. Zubin made it very funny – and cocky and dismissive, hitting the notes perfectly. Definitely to be watched. I forgot that I'd seen him earlier this year in Jonathan Harvey's *Beautiful Thing* at the Duke of York's.

Diana Coupland and Jennifer Ehle were more hesitant in interview but Diana sang 'My Man' – 'Mon homme' – with great passion and pathos, and Spinetti and Nettles had stayed on hand and chimed in amusingly when things looked liked sagging. When I plugged the Fringe season Victor recalled his early London Fringe experience at the Drill Hall in a play called *Vagina Rex*! His mother said, 'What's it about?' Victor explained that it all took place in a woman's vagina, prompting her to say, 'Ooh! Your father'd like that!'

Everybody seemed delighted and packed me off in a taxi to Coventry.

Friday 17th November

When I got home last night I switched on the radio and heard that a newspaper had folded. Could it be the *Independent*? I waited fully five infuriating minutes before the departed sheet was declared to be *Today*. Today is its last.

Another alarm about *Bing Bong*. Weldon is going cold. James Barber wants to make a meeting with him and Keith on Tuesday. It sounds like nerves about the casting.

I was interested to read in the *Spectator* that the failure of Malcolm Muggeridge to commit suicide by drowning himself in the bay at Lourenço Marques in 1943 was actually not due, as he claimed, to lack of resolve – but to lack of water. The bay is much too shallow.

Saturday 18ᵗʰ November

A fairly chaotic but enjoyable *Loose Ends*. I had to talk to Leonard Nimoy – Mr Spock in *Star Trek* – never having seen the series; and to Tony Warren who created *Coronation Street*; I've never seen an entire episode of that either. Fortunately they have both written books. Nimoy's *I am Spock* – a mixture of autobiography and the story of *Star Trek* – and Warren's *Behind Closed Doors*, another of his thick, unpretentious chronicles of Northern life. Most interesting was David McAlmont, a young black singer with a beautiful, high soul-flecked voice who sang 'I Only Have Eyes for You' and then talked wryly about growing up gay in Guyana where he 'stood out like a peacock amongst crows'. When he confided his feelings to a woman in the choir to which he belonged they sent for a faith healer 'to cast the demon of homosexuality out'!

A panther evening, featuring the return of the American hunk who has the most attractive low, gurgling, giggle which is very sexy. Not really feasting – he is very abstemious – but definitely a panther. I miscounted the fee and he checked. Ended happily.

Sunday 19ᵗʰ November

Cold. I did not stir out.

The letters – too many. Two were hard to write. Two distinguished actor/writers, both somewhat older, perhaps a decade, had sent scripts. Both had merit. Neither did I want to do. How does one make genuine appreciation of bits not seem like faint praise and the damning which goes with it?

I must swot up for my Royal Signals 75th Anniversary address on Thursday. The audience sound like a lot of generals, mainly younger than me. Next day it's going to be the *Evening Standard* Drama Awards. Thank God we have a theme show on stand-up comedy on *Loose Ends* and I have no novels, biogs, etc. to read. I might take a holiday, reading a book with no other purpose than enjoyment tonight!

Monday 20*th* November

Lunch at the Halcyon in Holland Park Avenue to go through the procedure for Friday's *Evening Standard* awards. Simon Cherry and Dan Niles from LWT, and Michael Owen and Caroline Mulcahy from the *Standard*. Sadly, no real gossip except that last year Maggie Smith, proudly presented by the editor Stewart Stephen to some young aspiring actors, looked unimpressed and said simply, 'Family, I suppose.' It was dead-on and not expected. Lunch far too rich (foie gras and confit of duck) but afterwards we only had to look at the clips – excerpts from the winning shows. It's a different format this year: 90 minutes and they will be editing in a judge's discussion around each award.

I came back via Harrods – three pairs of black socks: $3 \times £8.95 = £26.85$. A pound of tripe more reasonable, just over £1. Then I explored the leather case department. I want to replace my much-treasured, much-travelled Gladstone bag. I inherited my grandfather's which pre-dated the century but lost it when I moved house in 1965. You always find something and lose something when you move. My then movie partner, Terry Glinwood, bought me the replacement at Asprey. It's been round the world a few times since then – 30 years ago – and is now held together by string. I took it to Asprey who quoted £3,250 to repair it. They no longer sell them. A very helpful man at Harrods pointed out two but they didn't look quite large enough. I said I'd get the old one back from Asprey and the Harrods man said he'd see if they could find a new one or even repair the old one for a reasonable price. He was shocked to hear the quote. I must retrieve it from Asprey and make the new or reconditioned one my Xmas present to me.

I watched the Princess of Wales *Panorama* interview with a sense of shock, mesmerised by those huge revolving eyes and the sense of revelation – I wished neither she nor the Prince of Wales had embarked on their two broadcasts. Certainly Nicholas Soames would have been wiser not to come on *Newsnight* immediately after and confirm by example all the things which she said about her husband's friends. We shall hear nothing else on the airwaves for days.

One rumour is that Camilla has told a friend that in no circumstances will she take on the job of Queen. Charles is determined to marry her, and apparently wants to be King. Something of an impasse. Will he do an Edward VIII? This may be what Diana was hinting at. The rumours grow wilder.

I don't suppose it is significant that Diana is broadcasting on the anniversary of the death of Queen Alexandra (1925). As a new Princess of Wales in 1863 she wrote amusingly to Princess Victoria of Russia: 'You may think I like marrying Bertie for his position but if he were a cowboy I would love him just the same.' King Edward did indeed become something of an amorous range rider.

Tuesday 21st November

We might have heard of nothing else but for the Rosemary West verdict – so the headlines were shared. Nicholas Soames got his comeuppance and the judge said of Mrs West, 'Take her down.'

Dinner at the Royal Lancaster. Duke of Edinburgh's Award arranged by Deke Arlon. Maria Friedman sang – a rather oddly arranged programme. I had seen Duncan Weldon with Keith Waterhouse earlier at Duncan's offices in the old Ivor Novello flat above the Strand Theatre. He still says he wants to do Keith's *Bing Bong* but not with our cast. There was little we could do other than agree that he would speed a script to Robert Lindsay – his suggestion, his move.

In the week of the premiere of the Bond *Goldeneye* I recall that when Ian Fleming used 'Goldfinger' as the name of the villain in *Moonraker*, the celebrated Hungarian architect Erno Goldfinger threatened legal action. Fleming replied by offering to change the name to 'Goldprick' and insert erratum slips in each copy. No legal action.

Wednesday 22nd November

Saw Mark Bailey and his portfolio – he's a talented, established designer with a very clear, simple line – especially in his costumes. He has just done the successful *Importance of Being Earnest* at the Old Vic (via Birmingham). Then, after lunch to Lionel Bart's *Quasimodo* at the Soho Laundry. The impresarios turned out in force, Cameron Mackintosh, Duncan Weldon, and Bill Kenwright. I think Lionel started on this musical of *The Hunchback of Notre Dame* in 1961 – maybe completed it then. Hal Prince once told me he thought it was Lionel's best score. Somehow he could never move it. I have always cherished the tale of Lionel's last throw with a Hollywood movie producer. They were closeted in a cabana at the Beverly Hills Hotel, surrounded by secretaries and assistants, 'Tell me, Li,' said the Hollywood producer, 'how do you see this show – visually?'

'Oh,' said Lionel, 'somewhere between Gustave Doré and the elder Breughel.'

The producer turned to his team, 'See if those guys are available,' he told them.

The Soho Laundry is a plain white box – a platform in the ceiling girders represented the Hunchback's belfry. Lionel had played it to me some years ago. The story is well-known and (as in *Oliver!*) he tells it simply and sparely with easily communicating songs. The three leading roles were beautifully done. Ray Shell, warm and heart-breaking as Quasimodo; Frances Ruffelle, a clear, surprisingly witty, cockney Esmerelda; and Peter Straker, terrific in repose as Frollo. Its opening is strikingly like *Oliver!* – a baby abandoned at the Cathedral doors. We had entered to the smell of incense and most of the cast standing like statues around the room behind the single rows of seats. Tim Hopkins, a young opera director, staged it simply and swiftly in an hour and fifteen minutes. There were some witty narrative plot jumps and a very warm reception.

Its future? It needs a huge production. It would have worked well in the sixties with a Sean Kenny set. It'll need a lot of commitment from a very rich impresario. Several of the songs could slot into the repertoire – like the score of *Oliver!*. Will someone take the chance? I'm not sure. Cameron sounded equivocal as we walked towards the brief party. Robert Lindsay was among the throng. 'Has Duncan sent the script?' I asked. 'What script?' I told him; and told Duncan I had told him. We will see if he gets it by the weekend.

On to Channel One, the Associated Newspapers cable station, to do a pointless interview to promote the *Evening Standard* Drama Awards.

The news that Lord Rothschild has now completed the restoration of Spencer House in St James's at a cost of £13.5 million recalls the great days at his family home, Waddesdon Manor, when a footman would greet each waking guest:

'Tea, coffee, chocolate or cocoa, sir?'

'Tea, please.'

'Yes, sir. Assam, Souchong or Ceylon?'

'Souchong, please.'

'Yes, sir. Milk, cream or lemon?'

'Milk, please.'

'Yes, sir. Jersey, Hereford or Shorthorn?'

Thursday 23rd November

I spent most of the day fretting about my 75th Anniversary speech for the Royal Corps of Signals at the curiously characterless International Press Centre in Shoe Lane. I need not have worried – a very welcoming selection of generals and their ladies and lesser ranks. I did 45 minutes on the general theme of communicating and not communicating – largely autobiographical – an undistinguished career in the Signals and a varied one trying to communicate more successfully in radio, television, the theatre and books.

We ate afterwards with my host-general, his very beautiful wife and two extremely attractive young daughters.

Friday 24th November

Evening Standard Awards. This is, I suppose, my favourite gig of the year. So many old friends and colleagues in front of whom to show off. Neil Shand had given me some good jokes – mainly Princess Diana's broadcast.

London Weekend TV, having taken over the event from Thames/ Carlton, were determined to make it an event. Ninety minutes instead of sixty. The panel of judges explaining their choices. A crane camera panning down from clever shots through chandeliers. There was a running theme of filth in the speeches which was filtered out in the edited version. Steve Coogan and Eddie Izzard were New Wave presenters and very funny, but Eddie was quite censorable. Steve presented his friend and colleague Patrick Marber with the gong for *Dealer's Choice* (Best Comedy). Felicity Kendal gave the Best Director award to young Matthew Warchus for *Volpone* (R.Nat) and *Henry V* (RSC). No rudery there. Eddie gave Most Promising Playwright to Jez Butterworth for *Mojo*. LWT had cleared the excerpt which was a virtuoso piece of filth and very witty with it. Butterworth's speech was in the same vein, but quite endearing. Not, I thought for the home viewer. *Mack and Mabel,* twenty years after its Broadway opening, won Best Musical – almost by default. *Jolson* couldn't grab it in spite of Brian Conley's towering performance. A hundred pounds on it running longer. Poor Jerry Herman was not well enough to fly to collect, so the leading players did. Placido Domingo, presenting, said that the best tunes these days were in musicals. Best play – David Edgar's *Pentecost*. Best Actress, Geraldine McEwan for her (from the clip) very funny and credible Lady Wishfort. Maggie Smith presented Best Actor to Michael Gambon (*Volpone*), opening with a beautifully judged, spare, dignified and moving mention of Robert Stephens, the father of her children. Pat Quinn – Lady Stephens – his widow, was there with her son Quinn by my old friend and Virgin Soldier, Don Hawkins. Quinn Hawkins is reading law to be a barrister. The resemblance is extraordinary and takes me back 30 years. I find I did my first *Evening Standard* in 1983 so, with one year out, that must be eleven. I took Jon Rowlands (*Loose Ends*) to give him a crash course in West End Theatre.

On to Guildford with Edward Snape to see Peter Greenwell in *A Talent to Amuse*. He had a full house and Michael Codron wants Edward to bring him in. Edward confirms that the spring tour of *Salad Days* will now probably end up in the West End. Oh well, as long as he doesn't lose money. The out-of-town reaction has been *so* enthusiastic. I know it would thrill Julian.

I got back to fast-forward through the Awards. The 'F' word had been largely excised except in the *Mojo* excerpt and a couple of times in Eddie's and Gambon's speeches. I recalled teasing Melvyn Bragg that the IBA could fine LWT £1,000 per 'F', 'but they can afford it.'

'They can't,' Melvyn twinkled, 'but I can!'

Saturday 25th November

Loose Ends. An edition with an audience in the new BBC theatre in Broadcasting House. A jolly show, with two eccentric bands, Beer Gut 100 and L. Kipper. I must ask Jon to be careful about booking more than one band in future. The first-round bill at the George came to a record £61.

A Spanish panther evening. Very disappointing. I paid the fee agreed over the phone, made my excuses and he left.

Magdalena Buznea had come to tea and brought me a loaf of her Romanian home-baked bread. I told her that the Romanian government had forbidden parents giving children 'ridiculous' names such as those of TV characters. Apparently some Romanian kids were being christened 'J.R. Ewing'!

Monday 27th November

Worked on the novel. I did a plug on GLR for *A Passionate Woman* which is at Woking (I shall see it tomorrow). Pleasant lad – Jeremy Nicholas, not the grizzled regular Radio 4 man. We had a little fun with today's *Independent* feature on Britain's 40 most influential gays and why I was not on the list. I said I didn't know the two authors but assumed that they had slept with the 40 and not with me.

Recorded two *Counterpoints*. As always, the contestants were sweet and civilised and competitive only with the questions – though one lady did say too many times of another contestant: 'Oh, if only I'd had his questions, I could have answered all of them.'

Tuesday 28th November

More novel; and starting to work on an introduction to a CRUISE charity book about Memorial Services, *Remembrance*. As 'Memorial Services Critic' of the *Oldie*, I have to turn my various reviews of these services into an introductory essay. They bring back a wave of memories of the people and the occasions – Sybil Thorndike, Mervyn Stockwood, Kenneth MacMillan, Brian Johnston, Caryl, Ken Williams, Geraint Evans, Harold Hobson, Gwen Ffrangcon-Davies, Sidney Nolan, Sam Wanamaker . . .

Off by train to Woking for a performance of *A Passionate Woman*. No sign of the famous graffito on the Waterloo–Portsmouth line under the notice in the lavatory which asks passengers not to use it when the train is standing in a station. Under it somebody with a grudge once wrote, 'Except at Woking'! In what a ghastly *Clockwork Orange* shopping centre the theatre is confined! The auditorium is large and impersonal. To get to it you go first to a box office ('How's it going?' 'Well, we've had some big shows here lately' – rubbish as far as I could see). From the box office you walk miles to another bar-cum-foyer and finally into the hall. Actually it wasn't a bad house. For the first time ever the revolve stuttered and stopped in Act Two; but after a brief halt the curtains rose again and all was well. It seemed much enjoyed by the house, many of whom said 'thanks'. I had a return ticket but Stanley Lebor very kindly offered me a lift. We got lost five times getting out of Woking!

The anniversary of the birth of Nancy Mitford in 1904. Nancy only just made it to adulthood. At the age of two a doctor chloroformed her to treat an infected foot. Her father, Lord Redesdale, suddenly noticed she seemed to have stopped breathing. 'What did you do then?' asked Jessica Mitford later. 'I seized the doctor by the neck and shook him like a rat.' Nancy survived but no one knows if the doctor did.

Wednesday 29th November

Grey Gowrie lunch for Arts Council. Diana Rigg, Brian Glover, David Bintley, Sue McGregor (hot from a tea morning with Hillary Clinton), Julia Neuberger and Colin Tweedy ('one of the country's 40 most influential gays'), the Business Sponsorship in the Arts man, and some others. It's all a 'private and privileged conversation' so I can't report it other than to say that everyone was pissed off about the Budget – £5 million off the Arts Council money. I arrived amidst wonderful confusion. Greg and Mary Allen (secretary) were scurrying around comforting their staff. Mary Allen, who is impressive, turns out to have started life in Cameron Mackintosh's third tour of *Godspell*! Excellent canapés and very good cold buffet.

On to Belinda Harley's office in Bruton Street to discuss the Peter Cook concert at the Festival Hall in April. A very boring nuts-and-bolts meeting enlivened at the end when she spotted my raddled old Gladstone bag which I had just picked up from Asprey's. Belinda was shocked by their repair estimate and says she has a man in Hungerford who specialises in restoration. I have given her *carte blanche*.

A funny letter from James Cairncross prompted by our Noël Coward *Loose Ends*. Two stories about Clemence Dane, painter and playwright, friend of Coward's and famous for her gaffes – the result of her monumental naivety.

Dear Ned,

A couple of Clemence Dane stories you may not have heard. The first was told to me by darling Joyce Cary:

At a dinner party the conversation had turned to small London gardens, and in particular to the rockeries and statuary that various people had placed there. The usual providential silence having fallen, Miss Dane's voice was heard to ring out with, 'Mine's an enormous erection, covered in everlasting pea!'

And this one came from the late Lionel Harris:

Toward the end of all their careers, Miss Dane wrote a play for Sybil Thorndike and Lewis Casson. The beginning of the Third Act proving recalcitrant, she invited Lionel to come to her country cottage for the weekend, while she struggled with it.

On the second morning of his stay, he was summoned to her bedroom just after breakfast. She was sitting up in bed, triumphant. 'I've got it!' she cried. 'Just listen to this. *The curtain rises on Martin, alone at his typewriter. He types a few words, then stops, tears out the sheet of paper, crumples it up and throws it into the wastepaper basket. This process is repeated (perhaps twice).* Martin: *Oh dear, oh dear, there was a time when I seemed to be able to toss anything off . . .'*

I'm not entirely sure what I can contribute to the Cook evening as I'm likely to be involved in the theatre during the lead up but I nudged Hugh Wooldridge towards the position of Director of the Day and fortunately the Director of the Cambridge Theatre Company had the same idea, Hugh having been his best man. Hugh organises, lights, and generally 'gauleiters' brilliantly.

Thursday 30ᵗʰ November

I finished the introduction to *Remembrance* and failed to find some-body to take to *Hysteria*, Terry Johnson's 'Royal Court Classic' which is opening at the Duke of York's. Just as I was about to call to turn in one ticket Stephen Sondheim phoned, having arrived for *Company* final rehearsals. He accepted with delight.

I saw Carol Allen (now an independent radio producer) at the Groucho about doing a 'Yip' Harburg programme for Radio 2 – which she has had accepted. Quite keen. Upstairs at the Groucho there was a party for 25 years of *With Great Pleasure*, the Radio 4 show where you pick your favourite literary extracts and share the reading with actors. I did mine in the early seventies at my old school in Somerset with Robin Phillips to read. Mrs Hammond Innes once told me, at a private lunch of Christina Foyle's, that her husband had just recorded his edition. I said what a good programme it was and foolishly added that I had done one. 'You couldn't possibly have,' she snapped. 'They only ask extremely well-known people!'

I had to rush to the Duke of York's so I had barely time to say hello to Roy Strong and Robert Runcie – the room was just filling up as I left.

Hysteria was a bumpy riot. Johnson hasn't quite balanced wild farce with the serious stuff but when it does work the laughter is explosive. Stephen was almost out of control at times. He took me on to Marco Pierre White's Criterion. Again, excellent. We talked mainly about the play – its excellences and its structural faults: but it did make for an exhilarating evening.

December

Friday 1st December

SAINTS AND SINNERS annual lunch. A privileged and so unreportable occasion; but I can say that Alistair Beaton wrote some splendid updated cards – especially the reply half of the second verse of 'Good King Wenceslas': 'Ma'am, his name is Fatty Soames/Though he's not a peasant/Eighteen stone of gastronome's/Not exactly pleasant.'

Saturday 2nd December

A routine *Loose Ends*. Brian Patten whose couple of poems produced an avalanche of telephone requests from listeners, and Cottonmouth, a good breezy Manchester band about to release 'Don't Come Crying to Me', who curiously sang 'Stand by Me' – but theirs, not Tammy Wynette's song. John Sessions defended Ken Branagh – not that I had attacked him. Derek Griffiths did a mime with Sessions doing a cod commentary, Sarah Stockbridge was twice as good as she had been before (disaster).

I finished Robert Stephens's autobiography, *Knight Errant*, as told to Michael Coveney. It's a charming, slim volume, very direct, honest and honestly prejudiced. Much happier reading than the serialised excerpts had suggested.

Panther time after some work on the novel. 'Sly' is going to America and won't return until Easter. Oh well, time for celibacy if not hibernation – he has become a very funny, engaging, and uninhibited companion, very pleased with having appeared as one of several James Bonds behind Mr Motivator on GMTV!

Monday 4th December

I've started to sicken for a heavy cold. I hope it's not flu. Anyway, I used it as an excuse to listen to the most gripping Test match on the radio – all day! Something I have not done for years. It was riveting with Atherton and Russell's incredible stand forcing a draw. Atherton battled for nearly eleven hours for 180 something. It was a wonderful, *Boy's Own* captain's innings.

I pulled myself together in the evening to go to the Royal Academy at Burlington House to auction three Hockney prints of Glyndebourne programme covers and posters and three Hockney exhibition catalogues on which David has done three different drawings of his dog. The Reynolds Room was packed. There were ambitious canapés and delicious cranberry Bellinis. Delia Smith's cranberries are everywhere. The crowd was friendly and generous – all the proper auctioneers were working professionally. We made about £12,000 on the works – helped by Sybil Kretzmer, who frequently forced the bidding up to £3,000 but didn't get anything. There was an odd group of young men whom I christened 'The ring', who seemed to be taking it in turns to bid. I never did work out what they were up to.

The Kretzmers gave me a lift home in their taxi. Herbie has withdrawn from the musical *Martin Guerre*. One of Stephen Sondheim's Oxford lyricist protégés is taking over. Ironically it echoes Cameron's decision to replace James Fenton with Herbie on *Les Misérables*. Herbie, I think, feels a weight has fallen from his shoulders.

Tuesday 5th December

I felt really ropy. *The Times* printed a piece bemoaning modern comedy and extolling 'the Vassall sketch on *That Was The Week That Was* with John Bird and John Fortune'. Neither of them appeared on the show – they were in America with the Establishment Club. I fired off a fax to *The Times* and a jolly woman rang to ask if she could cut one word.

I dragged myself to the Lloyds Private Banking offices in Grosvenor Street for a genial judging session for this year's playwriting award. We produced a long short-list of candidates. It is a rich year and the final decision won't be as easy as last year. Melvyn Bragg told a nice tale of plugging his Richard Burton book on local radio. The neighbouring TV show lost a guest and called him in with no briefing. As he expanded on Burton's drinking with some enthusiasm he was suddenly aware that he was talking to an audience of alcoholics, sponsored by AA!

I junked the BBC Radio Light Entertainment party, the launch of Willie Rushton's book *Humphrey, the Nine Lives of the Number 10 Cat* at Jack Duncan's cartoon gallery and Bron Waugh's *Literary Review* Bad Sex in Fiction Award; came home and curled up in front of the fire with potions, pills and vitamins.

Wednesday 6th December

The Vassall letter is in:

VASSALL SKETCH
From Mr Ned Sherrin

Sir, I am sorry to have, reluctantly, to correct your columnist, Nigella Lawson (article, December 5), about the John Vassall sketch on *That Was The Week That Was*. Both Johns (Bird and Fortune) were in America during the 39 editions of the programme.

The excellent sketch, written by Peter Shaffer, was brilliantly performed by Lance Percival and David Kernan. Ms Lawson will have been too young (if born) to see it; but, of course, her point about comedy nowadays concentrating on showbiz and soundbites, is well made.

One totter out to the fishmongers in the Kings road to get a quarter of smoked salmon, a £5 pot of caviar and a soft roe to go on toast – the only things I fancy. I had two ounces of smoked salmon with scrambled egg for lunch and slept most of the afternoon.

No news of who won the Bad Sex prize in *Mail*, *Times* or *Standard*.

Thursday 7th December

I thought the cold was lifting but no such luck. After going to the dentist David Croser to have a cap (yet another) refitted I cancelled going to *The Glass Menagerie*. Better to stay in. Read a lot of David

Blunkett's autobiography, *On a Clear Day* and P.J. O'Rourke's essays *Age and Guilt* (*beat Youth, Innocence, and a Bad Haircut*). They are both on *Loose Ends* on Saturday. Blunkett's is charming and simple. It sounds as though 'told' to a tape recorder. I find it impossible to imagine a life which starts by being sent away to blind boarding school at four. O'Rourke's book covers 25 years of his journalism – 'underground' press, *National Lampoon*, motor car stuff and now *Rolling Stone*. The essays later in the book – more funny reporting and less funny fantasy fiction – are infinitely more rewarding.

I picked up two *boudins noirs* from the House of Albert Roux on the way back from the dentist but couldn't face them and shall wait until tomorrow.

The bloody phone is on the blink. I can ring out but I cannot hear anyone ringing in. Twice I have conveniently picked up the receiver to find a caller hanging on! At least BT say they will send someone round between eight and ten in the morning.

Friday 8th December

A nice big black man came along and solved the problem – spent batteries in the main phone causing shorting. Luckily I had new batteries.

The cold lifted a little during the night.

My suspense about the Bad Sex Award is over. Won by Philip Kerr for *Gridiron*, a novel for which he has a $1 million movie advance. The hero's tremulous thumbs pluck down the panties of the object of his love revealing the 'twin golden orbs of her behind'.

Saturday 9th December

Better – not that one would know and only for a little! I *felt* splendid but great hacking, wrenching coughs brought up huge dollops of . . . oh, well.

There is a flick-off button in studios: but you never press it in time and anyway I thought I'd got it all up before we went on air with P.J. O'Rourke, Patsy Kensit, Jack Dee, a group, Teenage Fan Club, and David Blunkett. I had not realised until I read the cuttings that O'Rourke's first grandmother-in-law was Lena Horne and he was so admiring, amused and amusing about her and the Lumets (his first wife's parents) afterwards that I wished I'd talked on air to him about her. Next time, perhaps.

Patsy Kensit's agent issued a threat to the office last night – 'This interview is only conceded on the understanding that there is no mention of Ms Kensit's private life.' Nothing was further from my mind so we faxed a reply, 'Mr Sherrin is not and never has been interested in Ms Kensit's private life.' One is, of course, but not to repeat every gangland, louche behaviour story. Her film, *Angels and Insects*, is slow but worthy and she looks lovely.

On my sick bed last night I watched Jack Dee telling Clive Anderson the story of his humiliating time as manager of a restaurant in Fulham, so I couldn't ask that again after half our audience had seen it; but he had a good 'My four hours as a motorcycle messenger' tale I'd gleaned from another rag. And a sob story about being a sous-chef at the Ritz. One of his early-morning jobs was to cook and deliver bacon and eggs to the doorman. The ultimate humiliation was to find a 50p tip on the tray when he collected it. Comics I've talked to more than twice are a problem. Jack is enchanting – but he must be bored with the anecdote-fishing ploy. Maybe I should call next time and say, 'Is there anything new you'd like to be new about?'

David Blunkett's new book threw up lots of stuff – and his new dog and he judged perfectly (being blind, presumably with no eye on the clock) a tale of a policeman who arrived at his door and accused him of driving a Mini Minor around Sheffield with his blind dog in the back seat. Blunkett asked if he knew what day it was? 'No,' said the copper. 'April 1st,' said Blunkett. 'What is the significance of that?' asked Plod! He finished exactly on time for the end of the show.

Sunday 10ᵗʰ December

Kept to my bed more or less: but I indulged myself with a two-pound joint of splendid rare beef and have not yet started making mad cow noises. It was terrific.

Monday 11th December

The cough/cold has not lifted at all. I wanted to stay in but had to go to dentist (cap off); to Sinclair-Stevenson to discuss the cover of the novel – I was surprised they'd taken my advice and called in Antony Pye Geary from Dewynters, the leading West End theatre advertising poster people – he's gone off to think. The title seems to be agreed at last after one last suggestion of *Encore*, which sounds like several theatre magazines; and on to *Counterpoint*. I coughed and spat my way through two episodes. The usual congenial contestants. Raced home to bed.

Tuesday 12th December

A dreadful night of coughing. I limped to the Grosvenor House for a TV and Radio Industries Club Xmas luncheon. I have to be president next year. They are what they say they are – Radio Industrial. I sat pleasantly between Will Wyatt, MD BBC TV, and Esther Rantzen who was collecting charity money for Childline. Felt ghastly and went home to sleep. I was committed to see Sam Mendes's production of *Company* at the Donmar. The show stands up brilliantly. It doesn't seem as harsh as it did in New York 25 years ago. I don't think Sam has softened it, but we take rocky marriages more in our stride these days. The book/sketches lacked a bit of bounce but I think that was the playing. The songs work imperishably. We used six of them all the time in *Side By Side* and three more off and on so I must have heard the six over 500 times. They have inserted 'Marry Me a Little', which I love, to close Act One. It works triumphantly. And the birthday party is played as though it only happens in Bobby's mind – he can't face his own surprise party which is also convincing. Adrian Lister, the first black Robert, is great. His voice much improved since *Sweeney Todd*. Sheila Gish, triumphant in Stritch's old part of Joanne – 'The Ladies who Lunch'. I kept thinking of Larry Kert, almost the original Robert. We shared a dressing-room at the Music Box on Broadway after David Kernan left. He died of AIDS a few years ago.

I took Joe Harmston who (like most younger people, I realised) knew the score but had never seen the show. He was ravished by it and took me to the Ivy. A quick Martini, a starter portion of eggs

Benedict, a glass of wine and home to bed, elated by the play. Will Dr Theatre work his magic?

Wednesday 13th December

No, Dr Theatre didn't. But at least I spent a day wrapped up and plugging myself with hot lemon and honey and my recommended pill. It wasn't entirely an idle day. *The Times* asked me to do an obit for Eric Glass who died on 4 December. He was a Mittel-European agent of the old school – born in Vienna, knew Schnitzler, when he came to London in the thirties he represented him and an incredibly varied list of clients. Richard Tauber, Wolfit, Edmund Purdom, Anna Kashfi (mother of Brando's child), Edward Woodward, William Douglas-Home, Noël Langley, Eric Maschwitz, Oscar Homolka, Rodney Ackland ... He collected an incredible list of French authors when he became the English representative of the *Société des Auteurs et Compositeurs Dramatiques* – Camus, Feydeau, Gide, Guitry, Sartre. Someone once told him he had on his books the best list of dead authors he'd ever seen. *The Mousetrap*, *See How They Run*, and *Seagulls over Sorrento* were three of his long-running hits. His wife, Blanche, died fifteen years ago and he married his very capable assistant, Janet, three years later. I met him first in the late fifties when Caryl Brahms and I made a musical of Schnitzler's *Anatol* dialogues which we called *Parasol*, with Malcolm Arnold. We also had to deal with him over all our Feydeau translations for theatre and television. Caryl could be guaranteed to giggle at Eric and Blanche Glass's way of referring to their prize clients, 'Ah, yes, Donald [Wolfit], he is one of our darlinks!'

I was a little surprised to find Caryl and I were both still on his client list; but since technically he controlled the Feydeau and Schnitzler estates I suppose it figures. I phoned the piece through amid coughs and splutters. I hope it was decipherable.

Decided it wiser to miss the National Youth Music Theatre new office-warming, and BBC Director-General John Birt's Xmas party. Still coughing horrendously.

I see old 'Wrong Way' Consign has died in the States. He became a folk hero in 1938 when he set out to establish a flying record from New York to California – and ended up in Ireland! We all know the feeling.

Thursday 14th December

I was paid (quite generously) to launch a new Disney Channel TV series *Stick With Me Kid* to the press in West Kensington. Very groggy, I waited for the car which, of course, forgot to materialise. I tottered down, well-wrapped, and by a brilliant stroke a cab dropped someone off next door after only a few minutes. Lots of nervous Americans and confident English girls and me with no voice.

I fled to bed, or rather couch, for two hours before going out to chair the judging panel for the Oldie of the Year contest. Fellow panellists were Ingrams (ed. – natch) Rhodes Boyson, Dr Thomas Stuttaford (*Times*) and Clare Short, MP. Stumbled through, well below par, but picked at smoked salmon, blini and cheese. What did we decide? I've lost my notes and must wait for the official letter. I think we said Sean Connery – largely Clare Short's idea – with Frank Bruno (old for a boxer) as runner-up. The Longfords – a sort of Dunmow Flitch award. Mrs Merton – Wannabee Oldie of the Year. There was a lot of support for the old boy who shot a persistent burglar and keeps losing his court cases; but it appears they've tried him before and he never replies. The social question of who might sit next to him also arose. The woman who rode Cossack ponies across Russia is, I believe, Sportsperson of the Year. It's all a bit vague. If I get the official list before the end of the year I'll record it.

To sofa, with honey and lemon, shivering, and did the linking script for *Loose Ends*.

Friday 15th December

An *Independent* voiceover on a day I could have done without it. At least it was postponed from 11.30 to 12.00. Got to Grand Central Recording Studios and kept the cab. A cruel day, not one to go coughing to the corner for a car. A brand new Saatchi team arrived at 12.30 with an undecided script. It was fiddled with and recorded and phoned through and rejected and re-written and fiddled and fuddled and recorded and then it was 1.45 and no chance of a decision. I went on to Broadcasting House to record the trail for *Loose Ends* – leaving the phone number. It rang, so I went back to find – at about 3 p.m. – no decision. There was a bit more to-ing and fro-ing on the phone but neither Amanda Platel (*Mirror* Group) or Charlie Wilson (ed. *Indie*) were back from lunch. We moved to Saunders and Gordon in my cab. I finally left after recording an unauthorised script just before it had to be delivered if it was to get on air. Fell into waiting cab, stopped at supermarket to buy soup. The widow Glass phoned. Apparently she approved the obit. Always a relief. I tucked up on huge sofa sipping soup in front of *Have I Got News for You* and Clive Anderson – also a very funny Steve Coogan half-hour earlier. Coughed the night away.

Saturday 16ᵗʰ December

Dragged myself to *Loose Ends*, David Cassidy, here to play in *Blood Brothers* for four weeks, touchingly grateful that I knew and referred to his father Jack – the elegant Broadway performer whose life ended tragically (and literally) in flames. David withdrew his hand from a shake very quickly when he learnt I had a heavy cold. He's 45 now and like so many American showbiz people can talk endlessly to no purpose – but he was pleasant. A wonderful 29-year-old pianist, Julian Joseph, who has had a prom (this year) at the Albert Hall and a whole weekend at the Barbican the year before, played exquisitely. He talked lightly and well about his luck in being suddenly summoned to play with Branford Marsalis at the Jacksonville Jazz Festival and finding himself surrounded by all the musicians he idolised and unable to speak. He came with his handsome, pleasant younger brother, James, who manages him. Also Gary Rhodes the chef. I'd found two good quotes about him from Kit Chapman for whom he worked at the Castle, Taunton. One was simply complimentary – to soften him up; but I loved the other: 'At moments he appeared to behave like a blind kangaroo.' ''E must have caught me on the hop,' said Rhodes, laughing it off neatly.

I only stayed for one drink at the pub. Kept the car while I did a rapid Waitrose, and put myself on to the couch and slept for a couple of hours before making a bowl of tomato soup. Fortunately I found a few tattered Panadols in my sponge bag.

I wonder how Tom Stoppard's *Rosencrantz and Guildenstern* will stand up in its revival at the National. When he was asked in 1967, 'What's it about?' he said, 'It's about to make me rich.' It has.

Early night.

Monday 18th December

Better.

There was reference to John Barrymore in the evening paper. I'm always telling the Barrymore chestnut – when asked by an earnest girl at a seminar if Hamlet and Ophelia had a physical relationship Barrymore is supposed to have said, 'Well, they certainly did in the Chicago company.' I suspect it's apocryphal – the English version is 'On tour always – in the West End, never!' but my Deal friend, Michael Hill, reminded me of a story – a different story – a shocking story – he'd heard from Anne Fleming.

Barrymore was sitting with Errol Flynn and said, as his daughter Diana passed by, 'Ever fucked her?' Flynn had, but as the girl was sixteen he thought it wise to deny it. 'Don't miss it,' advised Barrymore. 'She's terrific!'

Tuesday 19th December

Certainly well enough to go to Maureen Lipman's Foyle's Lunch. Strangely, she'd never been asked before. She drew a much larger crowd than usual – perhaps aided by Christmas. Terrible traffic in Chelsea. I arrived at about 1.05 and found everyone seated and my empty space conspicuous beside the guest of honour. Ruth Morley-Leon on the other side, then Derek Nimmo and Victoria Wood. Jane Asher and Janet Suzman were even later than me. Maureen was extremely funny and Victoria, who proposed the vote of thanks, did a full five minutes of beautifully judged stand-up which made up for the unripe frozen melon, bland turkey, and rock-hard sprouts. I enjoyed the flamed Xmas pud.

Having had to miss so many parties because of the cold (if I'd been fit I'd probably have missed most by choice), I was furious when the mini-cab didn't arrive to take me to Lady Rothermere's annual bash at Claridge's. It finally got to me half an hour late – so that I would have arrived at turning-out time. I sent it away and sulked. It seemed a good idea to turn in early – so I did and kept on sulking.

And, so doing, missed the *Omnibus* on Peter Cook which I was dying to see – not for my contribution – but because he was so good. I'd simply recorded a piece about being on his disastrous chat show. It was the miscasting of all time. Cook, unique, a really original entertainer, asking three of us questions. It must stand as a classic example of a genius trapped in an art form which demands the presenter's mediocrity. I got a bonus: not only did I get a fee for appearing, but the show was taken off and replaced by repeats of Caryl Brahms and my adaptations of six Feydeau one-acters under the series title *Ooh-la-la*! starring Patrick Cargill. I have to say that, limp as our texts were, they were caviar to the misuse of Cook's genius.

Wednesday 20ᵗʰ December

Dentist 9.30. Cap is back on.

Haircut, 10.30. Jack Lee in ebullient Christmas form. Very proud of his new joke. The last client he told it to nearly fell out of the chair. I laughed but, of course, I can never remember jokes. Stories, yes. He told me about his first job in Charing Cross Road, just after demob. Val Parnell was dropped off by a particularly beautiful woman. A colleague cut his hair. Parnell at the time controlled the Palladium and was Mr Variety. Jack had no idea who he was but, as he was leaving, said, 'Excuse me, sir, but that lady is the most beautiful woman I've ever seen.' 'You've got taste,' said Parnell, 'and it agrees with mine. What's your name?' 'Jack Lee,' said Jack Lee. The next time Parnell phoned to book a haircut he asked for Jack Lee. It was an opening door for Jack who went on to his own business at the Piccadilly Hotel and used to turn up every Sunday at the Palladium to clip the hair of whichever stars or Moss Empire execs needed a trim.

To Dr Billy Bishoff for my flu jab, now I reckon that my cold/ cough is sufficiently in retreat. Also a blood test.

Having forgotten the P. Cook programme I was determined not to miss tonight's on Ray Davies. Fascinating old footage and good quotes from Ray and Dave Davies and a curiously silvered Mick Avory, their old drummer, with the Kinks. Far too much of me, presented as an expert when the most I would ever claim is enthusiasm – I looked like a fat white slug. I watched from bed and kept drowsing off and then awaking to find myself reaching for, and frequently failing to find, the right words. Rock authority is not my most convincing role.

The Blairs are off to Australia for Christmas, I read. I'm still not sure of my prophecy for the next General Election. Last time in the *Loose Ends* lottery I was one guess outstripped by Carol Thatcher in getting the correct Tory majority. Will Blair have the same rapport with the Monarch as early Labour leaders had? When the first Labour Government fell in 1924 Lord Esher, a friend of George V, said shrewdly, 'I am sure the King is sorry to part with MacDonald. Radicals and Socialists are much nicer to Sovereigns than Tories.'

Thursday 21ˢᵗ December

I saw Mr Bashaarat about the hated implants for teeth – with only time to be X-rayed and then rush to Saunders and Gordon for another *Independent* commercial.

I stopped off at Harrods on the way home to get my godson Charlie Bunn's Xmas present and some books for the other children. Charlie wanted a 'Hector' remote-controlled car. They were out so I got the next best thing, which looks very grand – 'by the same makers,' the assistant kept saying.

I couldn't resist tripe and trotters from the Food Hall.

At 5 p.m. I visited Miss Godfrey, my old housekeeper from the late sixties/early seventies. She is well over 90, looks incredibly well and stately with beautifully dressed white hair. However, she thinks she has had a slight stroke and occasionally has blackouts. She is in a residential home in Prince of Wales Drive, Battersea, where she is well looked after. Having always been active and involved, however, she finds the company sad and unrewarding. I can remember her telling me of boat trips in Battersea with a very young Rex Harrison who was romancing a friend of hers. Later she nursed her parents for years, and at various times ran households for Selwyn Lloyd and a judge whose chambers were opposite Lord Goddard's. One can sense the frustration in an enquiring mind, comfortably looked after but dying for stimulation. We reminisced, as always, about some of my more colourful house guests – Paul Jabarra, Hiram Keller, Jonathan Kramer and Darren Ramirez. Hiram, Paul and Jonathan were all original members of the Broadway *Hair* cast. Of these three only Hiram survives – raising horses on a ranch in America; poor vulnerable Jonathan committed suicide and Paul died of AIDS two years ago. Darren, whom I first met as Rachel Roberts's lover, comes through from LA a couple of times a year on fashion business.

Friday 22nd December

Recorded the New Year weekend version of *Loose Ends* with Emma Freud in Broadcasting House. It was fun but I kept remembering the last time I was in that particular studio, a few years ago doing a *Loose Ends* recording with Peter Cook and Dudley Moore when their *Derek & Clive* video tapes were released. Very funny, very filthy.

We had a drink at the top of the St George's Hotel – a very sweet dry vodka Martini in my case (far too sweet); and then I shot home to wrap the Hickstead parcels.

Tomorrow's *Loose Ends* is to be a rather unstructured affair so I decided to write all my questions tonight – breaking the habit of a lifetime (well, at least ten years) – so that I could get straight in my mind what was to happen in the studio tomorrow. We have this fictional society for the Authentication of Tall Tales and I want to check if Ken Russell really did buy his first condom from his local chemist in Southampton, who was Benny Hill's father. Apparently Hill père advised Ken, 'Wash it out with Lifebuoy after each use and it'll last you a lifetime!' Ken has made a highly personal 60-minute movie of *Treasure Island* with his third wife Hettie Baines as Long Joan Silver. Bits of Monroe, Mae West, *Great Expectations* and *Snow White & the Seven Dwarfs* keep breaking in – echoes of Ken's film-struck childhood re-creating his variations on the movies he'd seen as a child. Royce Mills outrageous as Squire Trelawney in pink and Charles Augins as a black, tap-dancing, Blind Pugh. I rather enjoyed it. I suspect the press will not.

Saturday 23rd December

Ken Russell struck down by flu. Will Mrs Russell? Oh, yes, she will! Oh no! she won't! Their tiny son now has the flu too. All this happens between 8.30 and 9.30. Eventually Jon Rowlands (producer) gets Bill Bailey, our inspired musical comic, to stretch from five minutes to nine. Alexei Sayle, whom I have never met before, proves charming, funny and expandable. He says he's always wondered why he's never been on before. Later Rowlands tells me he only got him because he agreed to have another of his agent's clients, who's peddling a duff musical, in the new year. Another case of agent obstruction it sounds like to me.

A couple of good monologue jokes from Andrew Nickolds and Richard Stoneman. Labour won a victory in the Fisheries debate by bringing in their walking wounded – particularly John Fraser, MP who was much photographed with his broken neck in a brace. According to Andrew and Richard, the final vote was 'No's to the right, 297. Ayes to the left 297. The eyes straight ahead 1.' And Pamela Anderson is amongst us – courtesy of the *Sun* – leading to increased sales in the Baywatch Barbie Doll. 'However, purchasers of the doll complained that it was a poor likeness, containing far less plastic and several more movable parts than the real thing!'

Emma interviewed a game Tony Slattery, bearing up under disappointing notices for his performance in *Privates on Parade* at Greenwich. Aled Jones has recorded a duet between his new baritone voice and his old treble. However, it was embargoed until after his Radio 2 show on Christmas Day so we codded up a verse of *Walking on Air*. I did an appalling deep baritone echo which sounded quite funny. Quick drink at the George and off to the King's Road to pick up fifteen live lobsters for Hickstead and the rest of my baggage. I got there in time for a cheese and pickle roll before the cars left for the Theatre Royal, Brighton. Poor David Land who owns it has had a sudden heart attack and is languishing in hospital.

The Brighton *Cinderella* has, as usual, the great virtue of brevity. It starts at 2.30 and comes down at 4.50. No stars this year. Elizabeth Power and Nicola Stapleton from *East Enders*. Miss Power as the Fairy Godmother sang an extraordinary parody of 'Broadway Baby' in the process of getting Cinders to the Ball. Sondheim would have been apoplectic.

Charlie Bunn got his demand to be in the box gratified. When we got back the total household numbered 17 so far and increasing. Lovely tomato and mozzarella salad and casseroled pheasant. We appeared to demolish (the nine grown-ups) an Imperial (nine bottles) of claret. Pinchon Longueville Comtesse de Lalaude, Pauillac '83.

A record for Hickstead in that everyone tottered up the stairs before midnight including, nay, practically led by, Douglas.

Hickstead Christmas

It was pleasantly odd to be down for a whole day before Christmas with this curious, spread-out festival. The household, apart from family, consists of Ross Benson, the *Express* columnist, and his wife Inge who edits *Majesty* and is always called upon to be expert in all media at every royal crisis. They have a daughter, Arabella, a model Belgravia beauty aged about six or seven. Laura and Martin Levy came up from The Prospect on the Isle of Wight with Sonny – Laura's son by her first marriage to David Mallett, the commercials director, and their own two kids Lucci and Louis. The visiting party is completed by Julie Sampson – recently widowed – and her son Jonathan who has been training for hotel management and is now hoping to be a ship-broker.

My lobsters – necessarily augmented with five obtained locally – were wonderfully hot and soft and smothered in hot butter. Tracy (Brook) had cleverly ordered vast bibs from a shop in Walton Street which made eating them much less dangerous. Washed down with lots of a Mersault Charmes '87, they were a big hit. I must order 25 next year. I noted my favourite pretentious remark on the back of my cheque book but foolishly forgot to record who made it. Can it have been Douglas? 'It was considered rather vulgar in Prussia to wrap presents.'

We did church parade at the lovely Twineham church – where Douglas and Lorna's little son Douglas, who died of a cot death, is buried. Hickstead Place has a large 'loose box' pew at the front of the church into which we crammed. Five grown-ups and six children – three of whom are grown-up size. A new young parson, obviously nervous, brought considerable warmth and informality to the service. His very simple, direct sermon was well judged on a theme of Christmas and gifts. The congregation responded happily. After a dodgy first hymn which no one knew we had a selection of favourites – 'Shepherds', 'Royal David's City', 'Hark the Herald Angels', 'Oh Come All Ye Faithful'. Ross and I sang so lustily we were reproved by Tracy who thought we were sending the carols up – we weren't. I do like to sing out in church. There was some very ambitious and not entirely correct descant singing from the little choir. Peter Ryan, Douglas's doctor, had joined the household when we returned and James Villiers and his wife Lucy arrived. 'Jimbo' is a magnificent bonus at a party. I remember one Hickstead Christmas – last year, I think – when I found a lovely poem about West Sussex by Hilaire Belloc in the library. He sight read it beautifully after dinner and the dining room which had been awash with hilarity was suddenly silent and deep in sentiment. This year he was in his clown mood. He is firmly entrenched at the Palladium playing Mr Brownlow beautifully and very acute about the struggles and weaknesses of his fellow players. Jim Dale has taken over as Fagin and although he gets more laughs than Jonathan Pryce, Jimbo's heart sinks every night as he comes forward unable to resist the lure of the curtain speech – Jimbo has a train to catch. I was teasing him about being 35th or 38th, or something like that, in line to the throne – which he is through the Buckingham line. 'I don't want to be King of Hearts,' he said in his immaculate, patrician drawl, 'I want to be King of the Port Manufacturers – pass the '55, luvvy!'

Yet another Imperial had accompanied the feast – a Château Lafleur-Pétrus (Pomerol) '83. There was a good deal of sleeping off lunch and then a festive supper, attacking the enormous Harrods ham which Julie brought (I sneaked a look at the bill which was still inside – £103) and some delicious cheeses which the Bensons brought from Elizabeth Street.

There was another groaning buffet on Boxing Day. Douglas's dining room table can seat 25 but this was a more informal meal. It was good to see Lorna's brother Neil and sister, Nicky, and her husband Christie – I hadn't seen them since Lorna's death in January. The children, Chloë (fifteen), Daisy (twelve) and Charlie (eight) have borne up so bravely. The two girls look like beautifully groomed nineteen-year-olds. Both are academically promising. Chloë is beginning to win at show jumping. Daisy is a star at school. Both are ravishing to look at and remind me irresistibly of their mother. Charlie is still at his Just William stage and will surely shoot up in a year or so. Not over-pleased with the radio remote-controlled car I gave him, preferring another one which fires dummy bullets!

I fell asleep remembering W.C. Fields's topical ad in *Variety*: 'A Happy Xmas to all my friends except two.'

Wednesday 27th December

I sorted out the questions for the National Theatre *v.* RSC annual quiz. Infuriatingly, in the Quotations round I forgot my favourite: Alan Bennett, described by the *Independent* as 'winsome', turned down the paper's request to interview him with the acid riposte 'Win some – lose some!' Curses! I only found it on the back of my cheque book later. John Mortimer captained the RSC team – Desmond Barrit, Caroline Blakiston, and Simon Callow. Nicky Wright was the National's skipper – backed by Issy von Randwyck, Simon Russell Beale and Ben Whitrow. The scorer was Janie Dee who was judged impartial, having been in the National's *Carousel* and now appearing in the RSC's *Shakespeare Revue*. Simon Callow clinched a victory showing off brilliantly on Shakespeare and music – 53 against a score in the low forties.

The prize is Anthony Sher's *Richard III* crutch. The RSC have now won it two years in succession. They get it outright if they win next year. Anthony Sher arrived to present it and gave it to Desmond Barrit saying he'd always wanted to give his crutch to Desmond's Bottom! (Desmond has just been filming the role in Adrian Noble's movie of *The Dream.*)

Tracy brought her two children, young Douglas and Lottie, up from Hickstead with Charlie and Daisy. Chloë was show jumping and Douglas had retired groggily to bed with flu. They enjoyed the quiz in a mystified way and we then held the fort with lemonade until 7.30 when it was time to see O'Keefe's *Wild Oats*. This proved to be a bit uphill for Charlie who departed for the loo half-way through Act One and asked at least ten times in Act Two how much longer it was going to go on! Daisy was very good with him.

The high point was the interval with ice-creams in the Governor's Room. There is a bust of Shaw in the room. None of the children had heard of him. I said, '*My Fair Lady*' – they'd all heard of that. Maybe Daisy had heard of Shaw. Perhaps she wasn't in on the conversation. Would not Shaw be furious?

I'd never seen *Wild Oats* before. I'm not sure it's worth another revival. The RSC exhumed it a couple of decades ago and had a success. It's the story of a roving actor who lands up in a Hampshire village. Anton Lesser was charming and inventive as the actor – a relief after his Hamlet for Jonathan Miller years back, which I thought the dullest I had ever seen. Jimmy Bolam energetic in a Michael Hordern part. None of the kids recognised Manuel under Andrew Sachs's make-up as an eccentric sea dog. Ben Whitrow excellent as a hypocritical Quaker with a splendid vulgar bit of business, hanging his hat over his crutch to make an exit in embarrassment when aroused.

Jeremy Sams directed and although the scenery moved swiftly and ingeniously, somehow I never thought it took off until the dénouement (some three hours in) when everybody turns out conveniently to be related to everybody-long-lost-else. Then that was dissipated by an extended re-creation of a country-house production of *As You Like It* as a finale.

I took them to Joe Allen – a new departure and a definite hit. The children snapped up large steaks in no time and the house non-alcoholic cocktail 'Shirley Temple' was a smash with Charlie and Lottie. Charlie was determined to stay out until midnight and we left *on the stroke*.

I talked briefly to Simon Russell Beale about *Jules et Jim*. I started to think about it in the late seventies – as a musical. Caryl B. and I had a screening of it for Andrew Lloyd Webber who was then committed to Garnett's *Aspects of Love*, a prodigiously inferior account of shifting emotions and relationships. After Caryl died I decided to write through it – *sans* composer – to prove to myself that I could. I finished it some eight years later and ever since I have been trying to pin down the Truffaut estate to some sort of deal. God! The French! Deke and countless reps have failed to flush them out. I want to do it with Glen Roven, who has composed a splendid setting to the opening song. It is a chamber work for three soloists and a back-up group of maybe five singers. Simon, who sang at Cambridge and at Guildhall, would be a perfect Jules. I asked if he was still singing – he said 'no' – then admitted that he'd flirted with *Oliver!* and talked about *Martin Guerre*. He seemed interested. I *must* press for action. I can't let Glen write any more until I've sorted the rights. Oh, at last a worthwhile New Year's resolution! It's heartening that I've shown it to Alistair Beaton and Herbie Kretzmer, both of whom are sceptical of my lyric writing ability, but who were nevertheless most encouraging.

There was a brilliant anti-review in the *Standard* for Ken Russell's Christmas *Treasure Island* – which I rather enjoyed in its homely way.

Referring back to Ken's previous effort, casting himself in the title role of his own film *The Secret Life of Arnold Bax*, Victor Lewis Smith wrote that he 'gave a performance so dire that I suspect he may have had to perform sexual favours for himself on the casting couch in order to get the part'.

Thursday 28ᵗʰ December

I was determined to go to the Comedy Theatre to see Zoë Wanamaker and Clare Higgins in *The Glass Menagerie*; but as the time got nearer I kept feeling guilty about the final draft of the novel, which I've promised to submit on New Year's Day plus one. My eyes are now set on the Saturday matineé.

Talked to Billy Bischoff (doctor), who took a blood test before Christmas and reports my testosterone level is nine – normal is between 11 and 30. I am to have a jab tomorrow. What monster is he about to unleash? Is it the same one from which Socrates was so glad to be detached?

Larry Adler called out of the blue to tell me Shura Cherkassky had died. (He appeared amusingly on *Loose Ends* way back.) Also to tell me a jazz story prompted by last night's late-night jazz film. It appears that Willie 'the Lion' Smith (was he in it?) met Charlie Mingus just after his (Smith's) conversion to Judaism. Mingus said, 'Come for a drink.' Smith said, 'I can't. I have to go to Pesach.' 'What's that?' said Mingus. 'Pesach,' said Willie. 'What sort of a word is that?' said Mingus. 'You've heard of Shabbas?' asked Smith. 'Sure,' said Mingus. 'Well, Shabbas is shit to Pesach!' said Willie 'the Lion' Smith.

'It's a great story,' Larry told me, 'but, of course, you won't be able to use it.'

Wanna bet?

Friday 29ᵗʰ December

Worked on the novel. These clear days are magic. I have to finish this diary and take it away for a week in mid-January to tidy it up, so I must get the novel off on Tuesday to Reed. Then there is the introduction to the charity book about memorial services. I also got that off to Christine Motley (wonder typer) before Xmas, so maybe I can take that to Devon with me. I'm wondering about Cornwall. I love Salcombe, but the idea of Padstow, Atlantic gales and Rick Stein's cooking is very tempting.

Extravagantly, I ordered a cab to go to Dr Billy for my jab because I'd decided to do the entire New Year weekend shopping in one go. I was going to swoop on Waitrose but decided to raid Curnock's, the Fulham Road butchers, first. No trotters but I came away with enough veal knuckle for an *osso buco* for one, a beefburger, dividable into two meals, and an expanse of well-sealed duck breast. That is in reserve for New Year's Eve. I know Barry and Gary can't come this year. Gary is very ill in hospital and Barry will be with him. After I'd picked up the Waitrose vegetable extras – I've got enough meat for a week – I phoned Bruce Hyman at whose home Desmond (see 1 Jan) was staying when last heard of. Now *he's* in hospital too. I shall have to devise the perfect dinner for one for New Year's. We never celebrated at home on the farm in Somerset – early morning milking preempted that – so it has no deep-down emotional significance for me. As I rarely go to bed before midnight I might as well make myself a party. I also have to fight through a lot of 'Yip' Harburg material for the radio show for Carole Allen. Half a dozen tapes and the son's biography to read. After *Side By Side By Sondheim*, the only other lyricist I wanted to sit on a stage and talk about, was 'Yip'. After he'd seen the *Song By Song By Harburg* for YTV and PBS in America I promised him I would. It will be good to have a chance to pay another tribute to the fertile old champagne socialist, caviar communist.

Saturday 30ᵗʰ December

I awoke with a pre-New Year Resolution. I have two wardrobes of old clothes I never wear. I am resolved to clear them out to Oxfam on Tuesday. Kevin will have little housework to do and I shall need someone to help me and make sure I carry it through.

An interesting Honours List – the usual political, boring rubbish but Cameron Mackintosh deserves his. Without a proper nose for musical theatrical quality he has by extraordinary managerial skill and dedication become *the* Musical Producer of all time. Such energy, such enthusiasm and also such generosity with the fabled sums he has made.

Poor Geraldine Aron – an exceptionally good Irish playwright – had filled in forms recommending me for some honour. Very sweet and totally useless! A knighthood indeed! Her Christmas card said, 'If you get it you'll have to marry me!' A lucky escape for her.

Actually I think I'd prefer the Lords. Then I could be Lord Sherrin of High and Low Ham. I was born half-way between the two villages and it would be the perfect name for a raddled old showbiz luvvy peer.

Harold Macmillan declined the Garter joking privately that he did not want to have to meet Field-Marshal Montgomery socially. The 10th Duke of Devonshire (father of the present Duke, Andrew Cavendish) disliked the Garter too. When his friend (and fellow Lord Lieutenant) Lord Lansdowne arrived for dinner unexpectedly wearing the Garter sash over his evening dress the Duke peevishly came down wearing his Garter sash over an old cricket shirt.

The *Times* anniversaries jogged another memory out of my friend Michael Hill. It is the anniversary of the birth of Carol Reed (who directed *The Third Man*) in 1906. Orson Welles is always credited with the much-quoted line in the film about the only contribution to culture by the Swiss being the cuckoo clock. Michael says that in fact the joke was first made in 1890 by the American painter and wit James Whistler. I wish I'd known it when we were putting together the *Oxford Dictionary of Humorous Quotations*. I gave it to Welles.

À propos of nothing Michael told me another neat tale. Encountering Lord Derby, the corpulent ambassador in Paris in the 1900s, Baron Maurice de Rothschild tapped his tummy and asked, 'What are you going to call it?' Lord Derby replied, 'If it is a boy I shall call it George after the King. If it is a girl I shall call it Mary after our Queen. But if it is, as is more likely, a lump of shit, I shall call it Maurice.'

The compilation of *Loose Ends* was, I thought, beautifully edited by Jon Rowlands and colleagues. Emma and I had just recorded the links so I had little idea exactly what would be included. His device was to have Emma skim about on the Internet – or Inter Ned – Ho! Ho! It enabled him to summon up splendid single sentences from some celebs and solid interviews, significant in retrospect, from Stephen Fry, Tony Benn and Jarvis Cocker. All three were very entertaining.

Desmond rang to say he couldn't come on New Year's Eve after the programme. He sounded very low but did not want to be visited.

I reconsidered New Year's Eve as a solo occasion. I have often relished it this way. Remembering the Christmas Eve lobsters at Hickstead I decided one would make the perfect feast. I set out unaware how slippery the frozen shaky pavements were and went ass over tip on to the rubble. I collected myself and slumped, feet splayed wide to prevent a recurrence. 'Ray the Fish' in the King's Road had doubted there would be a lobster two days before – 'they're asking more than we could sell 'em for' – but he had plainly relented and I chose the apparently fattest and most tender. Extravagantly I augmented it with a pot of caviar, on which I propose to gorge myself throughout the weekend.

I have a lot of cans of soup, fruit, cheeses, wine and vodka. I'll put a bottle of champagne in the fridge and sip a glass at midnight tomorrow – the rest will survive for New Year's Day. The year is going out on a full fridge. Ian Gardhouse sent me some lovely smoked salmon. I have cooked the *osso buco*. The meat feels soft and the sauce tastes delicious. I don't think I shall get to it until New Year's Day. The pheasant I demolished over the last two days has yielded a wonderful consommé. The duck breast and the beefburger are unassailed.

Early bed. Dr Billy's injection has no obvious, electrifying immediate effect.

Sunday 31st December

I suppose I could have gone to church – Chelsea Old Church does a 12.15 communion, except on the first Sunday of the month. But I didn't. A long leisurely breakfast.

Wendy Toye called. She always has a New Year's poker party. Wendy, Irving Davies, the revue actor, Christopher Hewitt (who comes home from America for Xmas) and Lis Welch. We can't get through to Lis. Ken Partridge, who has a key, is away. Jane Buchanan Smith, a neighbour, can't get an answer at the outer door. Lis is downstairs from the Taylors (Lady Helen is the Duchess of Kent's daughter) but there is that outer door and Jane can't get past. A second call suggests that a neighbour (outside the stockade) has heard the radio on. Oh dear! Wendy agreed to reconsider the situation in the morning. I rang a few more times during the evening but no reply. I indulged myself in happy solitude and pampered myself relentlessly. A couple of phone calls were the only interruption – Marti Stevens from New York and Trevor Leech, an old friend who calls every New Year but whom I never seem to see in between – he used to come on New Year's with his friend Adrian; but Adrian died of AIDS three years ago and Trevor hasn't been since.

The pampering consisted of toast and caviar, generously scooped, then the lobster bathed in butter and some grapes. I'm not sure God approves this indulgence. I nicked my finger with the knife slicing a lemon. Could be a judgement. I watched some television with half an eye and read Ernie Harburg's rather technical book about his father until the BBC started its countdown to the New Year with an hour of Angus Deayton – efficient rather than sparkling – in the spot that was always Clive James's before he defected to ITV. The year is ending on a sour note politically with an obscure back bencher, Emma Nicholson, deserting the Tories for the ghastly Lib Dems. There are dire warnings of others to follow as the party goes further right. They should learn from the Famous Four, who departed Labour, and stay and fight from the inside. John Major should take heart from Iain Macleod's dictum: 'The Conservative party in time forgives those who are wrong. Indeed, often in time, they forgive those who were right.'

I opened a bottle of champagne as Big Ben struck and sipped one glass, channel-hopped for a bit, including David McAlmont on Jools Holland's show, singing radiantly. I retired when Barbara Windsor's bra finally flew into Kenneth Williams's face in *Carry On Camping*. I think I ended 1994 (I haven't checked) feeling sorry it was over; 1995 has been even kinder to me and I'm sad to see it go. I got some of Simon Hopkinson's chitterlings out of the deep freeze in order to start 1996 on a good note, washed down with the rest of the champagne for breakfast. I do hope Lis is OK.

Marine Hotel, Salcombe
January 1996

Afternotes

LIS WELCH IS well and happily installed at Denville Hall which
cares for actors.

Salad Days came successfully to the Vaudeville Theatre in London
where it opened 41 years ago.

Bing Bong looks on the cards for 1997.

Robin Hawdon's farce *Perfect Wedding* was due to try out in Bromley
in June – now postponed until January 1997.

Another tour of *A Passionate Woman* opened to full houses in York
in February.

Kavanagh QC went rather well. The *Mail* said I should have been
given more witty lines. The *Mirror* said I should have a series. The
Telegraph said that when I appeared in this serious role they didn't
stop laughing!

A week in Salcombe – in driving wind and rain – was time to check this
Diary and the foreword to *Remembrance*, the book about Memorial
Services, published by Michael Joseph in May.

Gary Pollard, who couldn't come on New Year's Eve, died on 11
January.

I became eligible for a pension on 18 February.

Keith Waterhouse adapted the Alan Clark *Diaries* for rehearsal in
September in Birmingham. Then Alan Clark withdrew his consent.

Catch an Actor comes out at about the same time as this book.

July 1996

Index